Justice, Power and Resistance: The Journal of the
European Group for the Study of Deviance and
Social Control

Foundation Issue: Non-Penal Real Utopias

Editors: Emma Bell and David Scott

September 2016

Published by the EG Press Limited,
London, England

www.egpress.org/

ISSN 2398-2764

ISBN 978-1-911439-02-8

Published on behalf of the European Group for the Study of Deviance and Social Control

The European Group for the Study of Deviance and Social Control held its first conference in Italy in 1973. Since then, annual conferences have been held at different venues throughout Europe with academics, researchers, activists and practitioners in criminology and related fields participating. While initially class and certain political hierarchies were the focus, the European Group gradually sought to address other national, linguistic, class, ethnic, sexual, and gender barriers in an effort to develop a critical, emancipatory, and innovative criminology. This was to be done through the topics of members' research and in the conduct of conferences, with the ultimate aim being to provide a forum for, and recognition of, emancipatory science and emancipatory politics as legitimate areas of study and activism. One goal of the group has been to highlight social problems in the field of deviance and social control which are under-exposed by criminologists in many other contexts; thus to create a forum not commonly provided at other conferences and international networks for academics, practitioners, and activists working towards the promotion of social justice, human rights and democratic accountability.

www.europeangroup.org/

Non-Penal Real Utopias

September 2016

Justice, Power and Resistance:
The Journal of the European Group for the Study of Deviance and Social Control

Editors:
Emma Bell and David Scott

Associate Editors:
Monish Bhatia and Joanna Gilmore

Associate Production Editors:
Kym Atkinson, Helena Gosling, Aki Kaur, Agnieszka Martynowicz, Maeve McMahon, Rimple Mehta, Steve Tombs, Azrini Wahidin, Lisa White and Richard Wild

Editorial Collective
Andrea Beckmann, Victoria Canning, Gilles Chantraine, Athanasios Chouliaras, Victoria Cooper, Bettina Cummerow, Caroline De Geest, Aleksandras Dobryninas, Slavka Dimitrova, Katja Eman, Christina Ericson, Alejandro Forero Cuellar, Rita Faria, Sam Fletcher, Stratos Georgoulas, Hasan Jashari, Andrew Jefferson, Anna Markina, Rimple Mehta, Maeve McMahon, J.M. Moore, Ida Nafstad (European Group Coordinator), Georgious Papanicolaou, Monika Platek, Léna Podoletz, Scott Poynting, Paddy Rawlinson, Miranda Rira, David Rodríguez Goyes, Kari Saari, Alvise Sbraccia, Phil Scraton, Ragnhild Sollund, Demetra Sorvatzioti, Ekaterina Tishchenko, Steve Tombs, Waqas Tufail, Meropi Tzanetakis, Aimilia Voulvoul, Tatjana Vukelic, Richard Wild and Per Jorgen Yestehde (European Group Secretary)

International Advisory Board
Anette Ballinger, Vanessa Barker, Michelle Brown, Mary Corcoran, Mauricio Dieter, Michael Dellwing, Giulia Fabini, Jehanne Hulsman, Maria Karam, Jude McCulloch, Margaret Malloch, Thomas Mathiesen, Linda Moore, Christina Pantazis, Simon Pemberton, Laura Piancentini, Rebecca Roberts, Vincenzo Ruggerio, Mick Ryan, Ann Singleton, Joe Sim, Holger Schmidt, Elizabeth Stanley, Rene Van Swaaningen, Tony Ward, Michael Welch and Dave Whyte,

Review Editor
J.M. Moore

JUSTICE, POWER AND RESISTANCE

Justice, Power and Resistance is a unique peer-reviewed international journal which publishes high-quality, original essays, book reviews, and scholarly and creative narratives alongside providing a platform for the voices of activists, individuals and groups confronted by state power. The editors welcome theoretical and ethnographic studies from interdisciplinary perspectives including sociology, zemiology, geography, law, history, criminology, penology, philosophy, social policy and socio-legal studies from scholars and activists. The journal is primarily a vehicle to make accessible and advance challenging research and scholarship that can be utilised to critically inform contemporary debates and policies. It is also committed to facilitating and enhancing communication and collaboration across critical and radical networks. Consequently, it welcomes short papers, campaign updates, poetry, personal reflections and (auto)biographical accounts from academics and non-academics alike. The scope of the journal includes a range of topics including the critical analysis of social harms; theories of state power; authority and legitimacy; gendered and racialised violence; the politics of social control; austerity, poverty and marginalisation; the legacies of colonialism, neo-colonialism and post colonialism; penal policies and penal practices; harms of the powerful; criminalisation; comparative studies and internationalist standpoints; abolitionist perspectives; social movements engaged in direct struggles of resistance and contestation; interventionist strategies and radical alternatives promoting human rights, social justice and democratic accountability.

Justice, Power and Resistance aims to reflect the key values of the European Group. These are namely:

- to foster mutual support and cooperation;
- to nurture comradeship, collegiality and solidarity;
- to emphasise political commitment and direct engagement;
- to promote craftsmanship, intellectual autonomy and integrity;
- to facilitate truly emancipatory knowledge.

Foundation Issue: Non-Penal Real Utopias

September 2016

1. Editorial: 'Justice, Power and Resistance'   **1**

2. *David Scott and Emma Bell*   **11**
   Reawakening our Radical Imaginations: Thinking
   realistically about dystopias, utopias and the non-penal

3. *Erik Olin Wright*   **33**
   Real Utopias and Dilemmas of Institutional Transformation

4. *Emma Bell and David Scott*   **53**
   Reimagining Citizenship: Justice, responsibility and
   non-penal real utopias

5. *Lynne Copson*   **73**
   Realistic Utopianism and Alternatives to Imprisonment:
   The ideology of crime and the utopia of harm

6. *William Munro*   **97**
   What is to be Done? A reconsideration of Stan Cohen's
   Pragmatic Utopianism

7. *J.M. Moore and Rebecca Roberts*   **115**
   What Lies Beyond Criminal Justice? Developing
   transformative solutions

8. *Thomas Mathiesen and Ole Kristian Hjemdal*   **137**
   A New Look at Victim and Offender: An abolitionist
   approach

9. *Margaret Malloch*   **151**
   Justice for Women: A penal utopia?

10. *David Scott and Helena Gosling*   **170**
    Otherwise than Prisons, not Prisons Otherwise:
    Therapeutic communities as a non-penal real utopia

11. *Steve Tombs*   **193**
    What to do with the Harmful Corporation?

12. *Thomas MacManus and Tony Ward*   **217**
    Utopia in the Midst of Dystopia? The peace community
    of *San José de Apartadó'*

13. *Nils Christie*   **235**
    Apartheid in Modernity

Justice, Power and Resistance
Editorial

The European Group and *Justice, Power and Resistance*

This journal has been 44 years in the making. The first meeting of the *European Group for the Study of Deviance and Social Control* [European Group] took place in September 1972 at Impruneta, Florence, Italy and it was agreed by those founding members present – who included Stan Cohen, Margherita Ciacci, Karl Schumann, Mario Simondi and Laurie Taylor – that the following year the European Group would host its first annual conference at the same location. Annual conferences of the European Group have been held each year since 1973 and this, the Group's first journal, is to be launched at the 44th Annual Conference at Braga, Portugal 1st-3rd September 2016 (see Gilmore et al, 2013, for further details on the Group's annual conferences). The first publication to come under the auspices of the Group was the 'European Group Manifesto', which was adopted by members at the 1974 Colchester conference and published in the American Journal *Crime and Social Justice* in 1975. Laying down the principles and organisational structure of the Group, the Manifesto noted that its early focus had been concerned with 'penal institutions and prisoner movements, psychiatric control, police practices and procedures, politics and deviancy and the changing nature of legal repression' (European Group, 1975: 57).

A more detailed publication of early European Group conference papers was also released in 1975. Edited by Herman Bianchi, Mario Simondi and Ian Taylor, *Deviancy and Control in Europe* brought together national reports on deviancy and social control in five countries (Britain, Italy, Netherlands, West Germany and Norway) and also provided a number of chapters exploring prisoner movements across Europe as well as a selection of conference papers. Many European Group conference papers have been published in journals, books and other publication formats over the last forty years but there have also been a number of other books published which have been specifically based on conference proceedings. From 1980 through to 1990 the European Group published ten volumes of its *Working Papers in European Criminology*. These were all published within a year of the conference at which they were delivered. Written by scholars from across the world, they were largely edited by Bill Rolston and Mike Tomlinson. Their task was by no means easy, especially given the technological challenges they faced at the time which required painstakingly typing all the edited papers onto a mainframe computer (a VAX 780), transferring them to floppy disc and word processing them onto a micro-computer (a Gemini Galaxy 1); all this before they could even begin the slow printing stage (see Bill Rolston, cited in Gilmore et al, 2013: 26). *Working Papers in European Criminology* represent an incredibly rich and innovative critical criminology resource and provide a fascinating insight into the early work of the Group. In total, they brought together 163 conference papers (see Gilmore et al, 2013: 370-381). The working papers explored issues around terrorism and state violence; state control and the security state; the experiences of young people; social movements and social conflicts; technologies and social control; expanding penal systems; civil rights; justice and ideology; and gender, sexuality and social control (ibid). Although there was to be one further volume in 1996 bringing together a further 14 papers (ibid: 382) exploring issues on citizenship, human rights and minorities, focus eventually shifted away from *Working Papers in European Criminology* and towards the idea of developing a 'European Group Journal'.

The initial proposal for a 'European Group Journal' reached its full development in the early years of this century. Paddy Hillyard, who had been one of the editors of the *Working Papers in European Criminology*, alongside other members of the Group such as Steve Tombs, Christina Pantazis and Simon Pemberton, compiled a detailed proposal identifying the core aims of the journal and also the constitution of its editorial board. Although this proposal was passed by the European Group steering committee and the Annual General Meetings in 2004 and 2005, problems subsequently arose with the proposed publisher. The development of this journal, *Justice, Power and Resistance,* has drawn upon both the *Working Papers in European Criminology* and the journal idea originally proposed by Hillyard and others.

Two important things happened which directly led to the 'European Group Journal' being established, both of which find their origins at the 2010 Annual Conference in Lesvos. The first development occurred when the conference convenor, Stratos Georgoulas (2012), edited a book bringing together a number of the papers delivered in Lesvos. This revived the tradition of bringing out an edited book of working papers after each conference. The papers from Chambéry, France in 2011 (Bell, 2012), Nicosia, Cyprus in 2012 (Sorvatzioni et al, 2014) and Oslo, Norway 2013 (Sollund, 2014) were all published, building momentum for a specific European Group outlet. An edited book to celebrate the 40th Conference of the European Group was also published in 2013 (Gilmore et al, 2013). The second development arose in the months leading up to the Lesvos conference when David Scott and John Moore started to work on reviving the 'European Group Journal'. This went as far as putting together a new journal proposal and editorial collective and international advisory board and tying this together with the 2004/2005 journal proposal. After discussions at the 2010 conference, it was agreed that the new journal would need to be developed over a number of years and that lessons should be learnt from the difficulties that had been encountered previously.

At the Annual General Meeting in Oslo in 2013, 40 years after the first conference, Emma Bell and David Scott began the process of working towards developing a proposal and timescale for a new 'European Group Journal'. At the same time, John Moore (later with Emma Bell and David Scott) revived the tradition of the European Group of publishing its own conference papers. The European Group had, for example, published the first 10 *Working Papers in European Criminology*. The first new publication was a selection of papers on penal abolitionism drawn from the now largely unavailable working papers (Moore et al, 2014) and this was followed shortly by a collection of papers from the first conference of the re-established 'Working Group on Prisons, Detention and Punishment' held in Liverpool in March 2013 (Canning, 2014). At the 42nd Annual Conference, Liverpool, England it was agreed that a new 'European Group Journal', to be edited by former co-ordinators of the European Group David Scott and Emma Bell, would be established. It was also agreed that EG Press, the European Group's publisher, be set up as a limited company to publish the new Journal and other group related publications. Finally, after much discussion the Steering Group recommended that the new journal be called – *Justice, Power and Resistance: The Journal of the European Group for the Study of Deviance and Social Control* – and this name was approved at the 43rd Annual Conference in Tallinn, Estonia.

The principal aim of the journal is to develop a new critical epistemology to promote critical criminology as a legitimate field of research and to provide a forum through which critical academics can connect with those outside the academy who are actively working for social justice. Although critical research does find a place in social science publications – for example in journals such as *Social Justice* or *Critical Social Policy* – it can be marginalised in favour of mainstream criminologies which largely fail to challenge dominant discourses about 'crime' and social problems. Whilst it is true that many journals are not exclusively focussed on the dissemination of critical scholarship and activism, this does not provide grounds to argue that critical criminological work should not been published in current leading international journals. On the contrary, critical scholarship should be disseminated in all possible forums inside and outside the academy. Indeed, this has often been the case. Yet, despite publishing opportunities in a broad range of journals, researchers who seek to examine the operation of the law in its social context are sometimes regarded as 'deviant' criminologists (Schumann, 2013) and their work may be seen to fall short of narrowly-defined 'scientific' standards. A concern often raised over the years is that mainstream criminology itself may be regarded as a 'pseudo-science' practised by 'charlatan-scientists' who limit their focus to 'crime' as defined only by the penal law and who search in vain to develop one all-encompassing theory to explain radically different kinds of deviant behaviour (ibid). It is because of these very limitations that such 'scientific knowledge' often appeals to the State. Whilst it is important not to over-play the case here, or indeed to have too firm a dividing line between what is considered 'critical' and 'mainstream' scholarship (there is clearly much overlap and continuities in analysis), writings of members of the European Group have often had the explicit goal of challenging state power. 'Scientific knowledges' which fail to challenge penal common sense (Sim, 2009) can undoubtedly perform a legitimating role (Behr et al, 2013), helping to reinforce and even to manufacture stereotypes that can lead directly to discriminatory state practices. Thus, as Behr et al, (2013) remind us, whilst individual researchers may have some control over the research process itself, the independence of government-sponsored researchers is fatally undermined as they operate within the definitions of the State. Accepting state definitions of a given set of social circumstances rules in and rules out certain realities, thus shaping legitimate knowledge. Discussions generated and/or explored at European Group conferences have kept academic independence at the forefront of their analysis, and emphasised the importance of hearing all voices, especially those marginalised in official discourse.

This emphasis of the Group on research independence and the fostering of a 'criminology from below' (Sim et al, 1987) is particularly important in the context of neoliberalism, a phenomenon which has created a veritable 'political economy of knowledge' (Wacquant, 2011: 441-444) whereby knowledge itself is commodified, transferred out of the public sphere and into the realm of the private, as academics find themselves under increasing pressure to sell their services to the highest bidder. A culture of managerialism means that research which is not easily quantifiable, producing results that are immediately clear and implementable, is simply not considered 'relevant'. Whilst those who legitimate state agendas make a great deal of 'noise', those who propose alternative narratives are 'silenced, inaudible above the consensus of the technicians and the suffocating policy demands of the state' (Hillyard et al, 2004: 372). Here, the definition of 'relevant' research is research that serves the interests of the State and the growing private security industry by legitimating existing policy initiatives, especially those that encourage privatisation and the growth of new security apparatuses (ibid: 374). To the extent that mainstream criminology strives always to be 'relevant', it has come to exercise a form of imperialism over the entire discipline (ibid). It is important then that such understandings of 'relevancy' are contested and alternative formulations – grounded in what is *relevant* for ordinary people and the harms, problems and difficulties they encounter on a day-to-day basis – are at the forefront of critical criminological interventions.

The concern is that this trend could in future be reinforced by mainstream academic social science journals which will themselves be driven by neoliberal imperatives to make maximum profit rather than to disseminate knowledge in the public interest. Neoliberal imperatives in the universities also place immense pressure on researchers to publish in 'high impact' journals if they hope to attract funding and climb the academic ladder. When submitting to such journals, academics may find that they will be expected to produce the kind of research which will be considered most 'marketable'. This would leave academics with a very constrained space in which to work. Hillyard et al, thus ask, 'where can academics find the space to conduct rigorous, challenging and socially relevant research that will alleviate rather than exacerbate the problems caused by conventional crime, while simultaneously confronting the social harms generated by the powerful? (ibid: 385) The European Group has always prided itself on providing such a space. For the past 44 years, it has served as a forum for reflection upon the 'big picture' and provided the opportunity for researchers and activists to create emancipatory knowledge that can be used to critique discriminatory and repressive policies and practices rather than servicing the state machine. It is hoped that the European Group Journal can help to expand this space, providing an outlet for critical researchers to challenge 'criminological imperialism' (ibid) and rupture the silence to which they are so often condemned.

The European Group Journal therefore values academic independence and seeks to preserve it by retaining its own independence from the huge multinational publishing groups that currently dominate the market. It is for this reason that the new journal is published by the European Group Press [EG Press], an independent publishing house run on a purely voluntary basis by and for European Group members. In the long term, this seems like one of the best ways to protect the values of the Group from the growing reach of neoliberalism within and outside the academy. We hope that this measure will ensure that it cannot be captured by either the State or private interests. If in so doing the journal, like the Group, finds itself somewhat marginalised from the priorities of government agencies, then this should be seen as a strength rather than a weakness. This reflects the Group's broader commitment to break away from dominant analytical frameworks for understanding deviancy and social control and offer a genuinely critical, emancipatory politics and praxis (Scott, 2016).

For the European Group, *critique* means more than being just 'critical'. Critical theory should be grounded within socio-economic and political contexts, linked with the work of grassroots social movements (or at least the interpretation of their interventions) and intended to facilitate emancipatory change. Making connections between everyday struggles and lived experiences and social structures, initially around class, but subsequently around 'race', sexuality, gender, age and disability, the European Group has helped produce a new critical discourse for understanding conflicts, harms and troubles as well as the violence and repression of state policies and practices. Constructions of 'crime', deviance and social control have been located within the power-knowledge axis and social structures pertaining in our given historical conjuncture. This has ultimately led to the centrality of questions concerning justice, power, and resistance that continue to be fundamental for the Group and its journal.

In examining these questions, researchers and activists in the European Group seek to uphold the highest of scholarly standards. These standards are not narrowly defined as in the case of 'administrative' criminology and 'crime science'. They are not limited to collating data or to providing policy recommendations that can be immediately implemented. They do not seek to subject social phenomena to empirical verification but to understand these in their broader social context and thus to facilitate their understanding. The aim is to reveal the truth by deconstructing common sense knowledges while separating truth from power. This does not mean simply substituting populist appeals for power with a scholarly common sense 'which parrots, in technical jargon and under the official trappings of scientific discourse, the discourse of common sense' (Bourdieu, 1992: 248). It means challenging power and questioning the social world, engaging with issues that are genuinely 'relevant'. The tools that allow us to do this are not predefined. We cannot ply our craft by adopting strict methodological rules. It is necessary to constantly question ourselves and to apply our lived experience to intellectual practice. We should above all think of the intellectual craft as a creative task that allows each of us to develop our own methodology and our own theory, allowing us to release our creative spirit rather than imprisoning us in an intellectual straightjacket (Mills, 1959; Barton et al, 2006).

Respecting these high standards of intellectual craftsmanship will, we hope, ensure that *Justice, Power and Resistance* produces work that is engaging, relevant and hard to ignore. Our policy of ensuring open access to all articles six months after publication (i.e. being freely available on the *EG Press* website) prevents the critical research published in it from being marginal and 'ghettoised' (Hillyard et al, 2004). Its engagement with contemporary social problems and social injustice ensures that it has much broader relevance than those criminology journals that restrict their focus to crime alone. It therefore also has relevance beyond academia, with its focus on all those affected by social harm and injustice. This is reflected in the fact that it seeks to give voice not just to academics but to those directly affected by the repressive practices of the State. *Justice, Power and Resistance* also has relevance beyond a narrow geographical sphere. Although the European Group has retained the term 'European' in its title, this largely reflects the Group's historical origins. The Group is now truly international, comprising members from across the global north and south. Not only does this help to foster solidarity when it comes to challenging commonsense constructions of 'crime' and social harm but a 'more explicit international orientation' can also help a genuinely comparative critical criminology to emerge which is able 'to do justice to (the) diversities' of different countries' political, economic and legal structures (van Swaaningen, 2013). Only such a broad understanding of the challenges facing us can allow us to develop emancipatory alternatives that draw explicitly upon a 'criminology from below' (Sim et al, 1987). We hope that you will support this endeavour to expand the work of the European Group and that you contribute by subscribing and writing for us.

References

Barton, A., Corteen, K., Scott, D. and Whyte, D. (eds) (2006) *Expanding the Criminological Imagination* Abingdon: Routledge

Behr, C-P., Gipsen, D., Klien-Sconnfeld, S., Naffin, K. and Zilmer, H. (2013) 'State Control: The Use of Scientific Discoveries' in Gilmore, J, Moore, JM and Scott, D. (eds) (2013) *Critique and Dissent* Ottawa: Red Quill Books

Bell, E. (ed) (2012) *No Borders* Chambery: University of Savoie Press

Bianchi, H., Simondi, M. and Taylor, I. (eds) (1975) *Deviancy and Control in Europe: Papers from the European Group for the Study of Deviance and Social Control* London: John Wiley and Sons

Bourdieu, P. (1992) 'The Practice of Reflexive Sociology (The Paris Workshop)' in Wacquant, L. and Bourdieu, P. *An Introduction to Reflexive Sociology* Cambridge: Polity Press

Canning, V. (ed) (2014) *Sites of Confinement* Bristol: EG Press

European Group for the Study of Deviance and Social Control (1975) 'Manifesto' in Gilmore, J, Moore, JM and Scott, D. (eds) (2013) *Critique and Dissent* Ottawa: Red Quill Books

Georgoulas, S. (2012) *The Politics of Criminology: Critical Studies on Deviance and Social Control* Berlin: Lit Verlag

Gilmore, J, Moore, JM and Scott, D. (eds) (2013) *Critique and Dissent* Ottawa: Red Quill Books

Hillyard, P., Sim, J., Tombs, S. and Whyte, D. (2004) 'Leaving a "stain upon the silence": contemporary criminology and the politics of dissent', *British Journal of Criminology* 44(3) 369-90

Mills, C.W. (1959) *The Sociological Imagination* Oxford: Oxford University Press

Moore, J.M., Rolston, W., Scott, D. and Tomlinson, M. (eds) *Beyond Criminal Justice* Bristol: EG Press

Schumann, K. (2013) 'On Proper and Deviant Criminology – Varieties in the Production of Legitimation for Penal Law' in Gilmore, J, Moore, JM and Scott, D. (eds) *Critique and Dissent* Ottawa: Red Quill Books

Scott, D. (2016) *Emancipatory Politics and Praxis* Bristol: EG Press

Sim, J. (2009) *Punishment and Prisons* London: Sage

Sim, J., Scraton, P. and Gordon, P. (1987) 'Introduction' in Scraton, P. (ed) *Law, Order and the Authoritarian State* Milton Keynes: Open University Press

Sollund, R. A. (2014) *Green harms and crimes: Critical Criminology in a Changing World* Basingstoke: Palgrave

Sorvatzioti, D., Antonopolous, G., Papanicolaou, G. and Sollund, R. (eds) (2014) *Critical Views on Crime, Policy and Social Control* Nicosia: University of Nicosia Press

Swaaningen, R. van (2013) 'The European Group for the Study of Deviance and Social control: Inspirations and Aspirations of a Critical criminology' in Gilmore, J., Moore, J.M. and Scott, D. (eds) (2013) *Critique and Dissent* Red Quill Press

Wacquant, L. (2011) 'From "Public Criminology" to the Reflexive Sociology of Criminological Production and Consumption: A Review of *Public Criminology* by Ian Loader and Richard Sparks', *British Journal of Criminology*, volume 51 pp 438-448

Reawakening Our Radical Imaginations:
Thinking realistically about utopias, dystopias and the non-penal

Introduction

David Scott and Emma Bell[1]

Abstract

In this introduction we consider the relationship between the European Group *for the Study of Deviance and Social Control [European Group] and the promotion of non-penal real utopias. The article begins by considering the historical connections between the New Left, utopian ideas, abolitionism and critical criminology, highlighting the role played by the European Group in the development of utopian thought. It then considers the utopian imagination in critical criminology, paying particular attention to Penal Abolitionism and Zemiology as utopia. It briefly analyses the crisis of utopia undergone by critical criminology in the 1980s before moving on to discuss the recent reawakening of the utopian criminological imagination and discussing the normative framework on which it should be based. Finally, it highlights the importance of developing an emancipatory politics and praxis.*

Introduction: The utopian imagination

Since the publication of Thomas More's *Utopia* (1516) some 500 years ago, the concept of utopia has been applied in widely different ways. It has taken on both a negative and positive meaning (Malloch and Munro, 2013). When used negatively, it is so as an insult: it is a way of ridiculing an idea as unrealistic, impractical and hopelessly idealistic. This dismissive use of the term draws upon the original Latin meaning of utopia as 'nowhere'. It regards utopia as the impossible dream, something/ somewhere which does not exist. This view was

---

[1] David Scott is senior lecturer in criminology at the Open University and his most recent book is *Emancipatory Politics and Praxis* (EG Press, 2016). He was coordinator of the European Group for the Study of Deviance and Social Control from 2009-2012. Contact: D.G.Scott@open.ac.uk. Emma Bell is Professor of Contemporary British Politics at the Université Savoie Mont Blanc and author of *Criminal Justice and Neoliberalism* (Palgrave Macmillan, 2011) and *Soft Power and Freedom under the Coalition* (Palgrave Macmillan, 2015). She was coordinator of the European Group for the Study of Deviance and Social Control from 2012-2015. Contact: bell.emma@neuf.fr.

particularly marked with the advent of neoliberal consensus politics following the failure of utopian experiments across the world in the post-war period. This led to a 'crisis of utopias' (Duménil, 2016) and the assertion of TINA politics[2] advancing neoliberalism as the only possible programme adapted to the new realities of globalised capitalism.

However, there is an equally strong tradition using the term utopia in a positive sense. In this tradition, which unites thinkers from a broad range of perspectives such as feminism, anarchism, socialism and religious beliefs such as Christianity, the word 'utopia' is defined as 'a good place', as an ideal and desirable potential alternative to the present. The French economist, Gérard Duménil, describes utopias as follows:

> Highly optimistic projections towards a future of emancipation and humanity. Only utopias are capable of mobilising activist energies beyond societies based on class distinctions and neoliberal desperation, whilst recognising that the process will be long and that perfection does not exist. From the Enlightenment and the French revolution through to the formation of the workers' movement, a tremendous wave of hope rose up – only to turn to tragedy in countries which called themselves socialist. We need to start from scratch after having understood the reasons for this failure. (Duménil, 2014)[3]

So, although utopia is seen as a positive, emancipatory alternative to current injustices, it must be realistic. Those proposing utopian visions must be aware of their potential pitfalls and capable of critique, not just of the present, but also of past utopian experiments, in order to provide concrete, realistic utopian futures. We therefore strongly adhere to Wright's idea of 'real utopias':

---

[2] The term 'TINA' is a commonly-used acronym for the idea that 'There Is No Alternative'. It was first used by the leader of the UK's House of Commons, Norman St John Stevas (1979–1981), to refer to Margaret Thatcher and her dogmatism.

[3] Translated from French by the authors; 'Par 'utopies', j'entends des projections très optimistes vers un futur d'émancipation de l'humanité. Elles sont seules capables de mobiliser les énergies militantes au-delà de l'horizon des sociétés de classe et de la désespérance néolibérale, sachant que ce sera long et que la perfection n'est pas de ce monde. Des lumières et de la révolution française jusqu'à la formation du mouvement ouvrier, une vague prodigieuse d'espoir s'était levée - qui a tourné à la tragédie dans les pays qui se réclamèrent du socialisme. Tout est à refaire, en prenant d'abord conscience des causes de cet échec.'

utopian ideals that are grounded in the real potentials of humanity, utopian destinations that have accessible waystations, utopian designs of institutions that can inform our practical tasks of navigating a world of imperfect conditions for social change. (Wright, 2009: 4)

A real utopia is something which already exists. Yet, whilst it is part of the present landscape, it is grounded in principles and values that can be considered as going against the countervailing norms of our advanced capitalist, neo-colonial and patriarchal society. We argue that this concrete and already existing real utopia can help feed our imagination and help inspire us to formulate radical alternatives to society and its institutions. In this sense the real utopia can help us 'visualise' new possibilities and foster a dramatic break with the present. It can provide a conduit in which we can transform everyday life and promote emancipatory change (Levitas, 1990). Like the 'good place' of the utopian imaginary, a real utopia provides us with a vision of an alternative, but this alternative is not simply in the mind – it is one which is rooted in concrete realities. The realism of this utopian vision adds plausibility and feasibility to its promotion. It indicates that the proposed alternative is possible within our given historical conjuncture: the alternative is historically immanent and potentially ripe for further development or expansion. For Erik Olin Wright (2009/2010 and this volume) the idea of 'real utopias' embraces this tension between dreams and practice. It is grounded in the belief that what is pragmatically possible is not fixed independently of our imaginations, but is itself shaped by our visions.

Thus, and hugely significantly, the real existence of the utopian practice can disrupt the ideological closure of the dominant institutions and practices of the present. It highlights how we can influence the present and realise a new 'good place' (Levitas, 1990). A currently existing utopian practice can provide a firm basis for critique and illuminate a pathway to radical change. Significantly, focusing on such a 'good place' – a real utopia – also provides an opportunity for critics of the existing society to define themselves positively, to express themselves in terms of what they are for, rather than just what they are against – the bad place. This has underscored what David Scott (2013) has called an 'abolitionist real utopia' which envisages non-penal alternatives that are present in the here and now that can be drawn upon as a means of facilitating radical transformations of handling conflicts and responding to problematic and troublesome behaviours. Such as position is abolitionist because it is based upon a clear set of normative principles and values; it uses this normative framework to assess, evaluate and critique the legitimacy of existing institutional practices and social structures, and, where appropriate, call for change. It has a strategy for transformation grounded in emancipatory politics and praxis; and, finally, has a vision of non-penal 'real utopian' alternatives that are consistent with its normative framework (Scott, 2013).

The word 'dystopia' – which literally means 'bad place' – was introduced into the modern lexicon in 1747 by Henry Lewis Younge. Dystopia is often presented as a vision that is in direct opposition to 'utopia'. However, there is no neat separation between utopias and dystopias. For Terry Eagleton (1999:31) 'all utopia is thus at the same time dystopia' because both the positive and negative possibilities stretching into possible futures inevitably remind us that our current 'bondage' is historically contingent and that we must somehow break from the constraints of our historic conjuncture. Dystopias can also of course justify the present penal state by conjuring an image of an even worse future. They can frighten us into 'no change' and make people look backwards rather than forwards for visions of human communities. But the critical use of dystopia may also facilitate radical change for it can also be seen as a warning of what will happen if we continue to follow current trends and practices. In pointing us towards the worst possible scenario, dystopias provide a warning from the future in our present. They give us new eyes to look at how current developments may evolve. Dystopias then also give us new ways of seeing and critiquing power, domination and exploitation:

> Whereas utopia takes us into a future and serves to indict the present, dystopia places us directly in the dark and depressing reality, conjuring up a terrifying future if we do not recognise and treat its symptoms here and now. Thus the dialectic between the two imaginaries, the dream and the nightmare, also beg for inclusion *together*. (Gordon et al 2010:2)

Dystopic analysis then damns contemporary penal realities by projecting the critics' worst fears onto current penal realities – something which has in recent times been especially associated with the work of Loic Wacquant (2013) and his critique of the penal state, which provides a nightmare vision of a future of less freedom and more penalisation and social control unless we act urgently to stop current punitive developments. In other words, whereas 'utopias seek to emancipate by envisioning a world based on new, neglected, or spurned ideas; dystopias seek to frighten by accentuating contemporary trends that threaten freedom' (Jacoby, 2005: 12).

As Stan Cohen (1988) has highlighted, both dystopia and utopia are part of the tradition of critical criminology with its focus on both the 'dark side' of human interactions – such as social controls, state repression, dehumanising institutional practices – and on the 'light side' of these same interactions – such as the principles of libertarian socialism and visions of a more free society grounded in our cherished 'values and preferences' (Cohen, 1985: 248). The utopia/ dystopia coupling is evident in the work of Cohen, and especially in his magnum opus *Visions of Social Control*. In this text Cohen (1985) drew extensively upon the dystopian vision of George Orwell's *1984* to provide a vocabulary and imagery of contemporary 'social control talk' in the 'punitive city'. Whilst dystopias such as Orwell's may well breed feelings of despair and sadness, they have also brought with them an imagery and vocabulary that can help us understand the present – Orwell's (1949) descriptions of 'big brother', 'Room 101', as well as many of the other euphemisms that permeate his classic text, are now all part of modern-day understandings of state repression and a short-hand way of critiquing current policies and practices. Yet, in *Visions of Social Control*, Cohen takes care to remind us of the importance of utopian visions. Though highlighting his concerns about 'sentimental anarchism' (Cohen, 1985: 35) and the 'flaws in beautiful theory' (ibid: 268), he tells us that much can still be done. Indeed, his 'preference is to be pragmatic about short term possibilities but to be genuinely utopian about constructing long-term alternatives' (ibid: 252). In fact, despite his often dystopian tone, Cohen never loses his desire for building a new more 'utopian' society on the principles of mutual aid, fraternity and good-neighbourliness (ibid: 267).

The task that all the contributors to the current volume have set themselves is to develop practical alternatives to dystopian penal futures. This entails imagining non-penal alternatives to current repressive policies which fail to address the underlying inequalities leading to social harm. In an attempt to better understand these visions, we situate them in their recent history, that is the development of critical criminology (also referred to as the 'new criminology'),[4] notably within the European Group, from the 1960s onwards.

---

[4] The 'New Criminology' was a title coined by Ian Taylor, Paul Walton and Jock Young in 1973 for their book-length critical review of the development of criminological thought. This distinguished the text from the 'new deviancy' approach which had been adopted by Jock Young and Stan Cohen a couple of years previously when adapting labelling theory from the USA to the British context. In 1975 the same three authors (Taylor et al, 1975) edited a collection of critical readings in a book entitled *Critical Criminology* which made the

The 'New Criminology' and the 'New Left'

The 'critical' criminology that emerged from the 1960s onwards was very much a product of its time. Like the new social movements that were developing, it set itself against the prevailing norms of patriarchal, authoritarian, capitalist society, questioning the status quo and promoting radical democratic alternatives to existing repressive practices. It was highly critical of institutionalised criminological endeavours which reinforced existing power structures by accepting state-defined definitions of 'crime' and deviance. Rather than seeing 'crime' as a phenomenon just waiting to be discovered, it argued that it is political in nature, defined and responded to by those in power. As such, it has no ontological reality – like deviance, it is a social construction reflecting the interests of the powerful, especially by deflecting attention from the social harms produced both directly and indirectly by the political and economic elites.

The new criminologists thus sought to develop their own understanding of 'crime', 'deviancy' and social harm, independently from those promoted by individuals in positions of power. Feeding off the new sociological studies of the 1960s, notably in America, which aimed to understand deviancy from below by working closely with the so-called deviants in an attempt to understand their behaviour from within, they followed Howard Becker (1967) in deliberately 'choosing sides'. Rather than lining up with the rule-enforcers, whose viewpoint tends to be disproportionately represented on account of the fact that they sit at the apex of what Becker described as the 'hierarchy of credibility', the new criminologists attempted to give a voice to the subjects of the rule-enforcers in order to discover new social worlds or at least develop a new understanding of those we previously thought we were familiar with (Becker, 1967: 105). The new criminologists explored lived realities and experiences, engaging directly with people to understand their world view, thus contributing to an entirely novel conception of deviancy. Their new studies of deviancy adopted an interactionist approach to the analysis of deviant behaviour, displacing the emphasis on individual pathologies towards the wider social and structural contexts in which the 'deviant' acts.

The critical approach adopted by new deviancy criminology was largely a reaction against positivism, notably its claims to scientific neutrality or what Bourdieu described as 'the falsely rigorous observations of positivism' (Bourdieu and de Saint Martin, cited in Bourdieu and Wacquant, 1992: 27-8).

---

connections to Marxist political economy much more explicit.

Taylor, Walton and Young, the radical proponents of what they called the 'new criminology' explained:

> The evocation of natural science presents the positivist with a powerful mode of argument. For the system of thought which produces miracles of technology and medicine is a prestigious banner under which to fight. It grants the positivist the gift of 'objectivity'; it bestows on his pronouncements the mantle of 'truth'; it endows his suggestions of therapy, however threatening, to individual rights and dignity, with the air of the inevitable. (Taylor, Walton and Young, 2003 [1973]: 32)

The positivist approach which had dominated criminology since at least the end of the 19th century was in many ways more akin to a religion than a science (Gouldner, 1968: 116) to the extent that it tended to reify empirical data thought capable of revealing the truth. It overlooked the fact that data is often detached from reality since it ignores the cultural and ideological contexts in which it is collected, leading to 'abstracted empiricism' (Mills, 2000 [1959]).

The new criminology specifically reacted against abstracted empiricism, attempting to place social problems in their political context. For David Matza, the study of 'crime' and 'deviance' necessarily had to be linked to the study of the State given that it is the State alone that has the power to criminalise and construct 'deviance' (1964; 1969). It was necessary to situate individual acts in their historical and structural context in order to develop a political economy of 'crime' (Taylor et al, 1973) capable of recognising that criminalisation is not a simple response to 'crime' but rather a means of exercising social control and neutralising resistance. For Taylor et al, 'the wider origins of the deviant act could only be understood... in terms of the rapidly changing economic and political contingencies of advanced industrial society' (ibid: 270).

Consequently, the new criminology did not limit its focus to the marginalised and 'deviant'. It also directed its critical gaze upwards in an attempt to understand the *political* need to control 'deviance'. In *Policing the Crisis*, Stuart Hall et al (1978/2013) argued that state reactions to 'crime' could only be understood in the context of the social and political crisis of the 1970s, namely the 'crisis of hegemony' that was in the process of undermining the political legitimacy of the State and its agents. 'Policing the crisis' meant attempting to stem the tide of unrest and to seek political legitimacy by scapegoating 'deviants' – often young black men – for contemporary social problems. Such work, often considered prophetic in its dystopian vision of the rise of 'iron times' and authoritarian populist policies retrenching the welfare state, was taken forward by long-time European Group member Phil Scraton in the important edited text *Law, Order and the Authoritarian State* (1987) which furthered understanding of the discriminatory and often brutal practices of the criminal justice system by placing them in the context of the Thatcher governments' need to strengthen the power of the State as a means of containing the unrest resulting from their social and economic policies. This entailed a significant reframing of the terms of the debate about 'crime' by situating 'crime' control in the wider context of political crisis and social divisions (Sim et al, 1987).

Crucially, the study of 'crime' and 'deviancy' entailed the study of power relations. As such, criminology became political. The criminologists seeking to understand the power relations which underpinned social control practices could not be 'bureaucratic intellectuals' (Merton, 1945), 'servants to power' (Christie, this volume) or 'social engineers' (Bourdieu, 2000) working to please state institutions and serving simply to 'rationalise the practical or pseudo-scientific knowledge that the powerful have of the social world' (ibid)[5], providing ideological programmes with scientific legitimacy (Chomsky, 2008 [1966]: 55) and masking state repression. The new criminologists were politically engaged and their studies inextricably linked to the politics of the new left and its project to link the personal and the political and to and formulate a political programme capable of challenging existing power structures. They did not just promote radical social change in the criminal justice system but also in broader power relations, engaging in a socialist critique of harms, power and repression that demands the organisation of society along the lines of solidarity, equality and mutuality (Tifft and Sullivan, 1980). The new criminologists adopted an explicitly normative position entailing the abolition of inequalities of wealth and power in order 'to create the kind of society in which the facts of human diversity...are not subject to the power to criminalise' (Taylor, Walton and Young, 1973: 282). This entailed joining with other social movements in order to bring the 'outsiders' in, thus promoting social, racial and gender justice.

---

[5] Translated from the French by the authors: '*une rationalisation de la connaissance pratique ou demi-savante que les membres de la classe dominante ont du monde social*'.

Bringing the 'outsiders' in

Feeding off the civil rights movement of the 1960s, the new criminology was especially concerned with 'race' issues. Stuart Hall and his colleagues highlighted the racialisation of street 'crime', notably mugging, demonstrating how the demonisation of black youths by the institutions of the State and the media created an authoritarian consensus around repressive state power (1978). *Policing the Crisis* effectively demonstrated how 'race' issues were tightly bound together with questions of power and legitimacy. Along with other seminal texts, such as Paul Gordon's *White Law* (1983), the book helped to highlight the institutionalised racism endemic to the post-colonial British state long before the publication of the Macpherson Report (Macpherson, 1999).[6] Hall et al's work helped to spark a whole range of studies into the disproportionate criminalisation of people of colour which highlighted the racialised bias inherent in official state definitions of 'crime'. Paul Gilroy (1987), in particular, investigated the myth of Black criminality which has been used to justify the over-representation of Black and Minority Ethnic (BME) communities in detention and in police stop and search statistics (see, for example, Equality and Human Rights Commission, 2015). Picking up on the earlier work of Paddy Hillyard on the Irish (1993), Pantazis and Pemberton (2009) have drawn attention to the construction of Muslims as new 'suspect communities' in the UK, considered as an 'enemy within' and specifically targeted by state surveillance on account of their ethnic appearance rather than on the grounds of their behaviour.

Carol Smart's ground-breaking *Women, crime and criminology* (1976) helped to bring feminist issues to the forefront of critical criminology. The text highlighted the limitations of 'malestream' criminological and penological thought and noted that criminological analysis had been in the main 'written for men, by men and about men'. The ontological and epistemological assumptions of 'malestream criminology' could not just 'add in women' to address its defects. Rather, there needed to be a new feminist epistemology, asking very different questions and grounded in sometimes very different values and principles. Feminist thought opened the pathway for thinking more critically about 'gender' and 'sexuality' – it opened up neglected dimensions

---

[6] The Macpherson Report published the findings of an official inquiry into the police investigation of the racist murder of black London teenager Stephen Lawrence in 1993. It noted that racism was 'institutionalised', pervading 'processes, attitudes and behaviour' throughout the English police service.

not only about the experience of women but also started to ask questions about what it meant to be a man (Heidensohn, 1985; Collier 1998). By placing new emphasis on both concerns about the role of law, societal expectations and power relations regarding both masculinities and femininities, the feminist critique led to a new openness and creativity when thinking about knowledge production and mechanisms of social control.

Critical criminology has continued its connection with feminisms and broader social movements fighting against various forms of injustice and discrimination. Most recently, for example, the specific issues affecting LGBTIQ[7] groups, notably the use of the law to reinforce normative gender roles, have been highlighted by queer criminology (Dwyer, Ball and Crofts, 2015). Following on from the National Deviancy Conferences[8] of the late 1960s and early 1970s, the European Group has been particularly concerned to connect to contemporary social movements, linking concerns about the repressive apparatuses of the State with wider issues of social justice and equality.

The European Group, critical criminology and social justice

The European Group was the brainchild of three well-known radical social theorists: Stan Cohen, then at Durham University, England; Mario Simondi, from the University of Florence, Italy; and Karl Schuman from Bielefeld University in Germany (Gilmore et al, 2013). They proposed the formation of an alternative critical criminology forum which would not just cover topics and hold debates marginalised or ignored by mainstream, administrative criminology but also establish a new network that could support, and provide solidarity with, emerging social movements (Swaaningen, 1997). Recognising the dominant influence of Anglo-American criminology, this new forum was to be characterised by a distinct European focus. The sense of place was to be significant on a further level, linking the conference theme with the conference location and offering support to local political activists, for example through press releases and resolutions and sometimes even joining them on demonstrations. Part of the very first conference held in Florence in 1973 (on the theme of *Deviance and Social Control in Europe: Scope and Prospects for a*

---

[7] Lesbian, gay, bisexual, transgender, intersex and queer.

[8] The first National Deviancy Conference was first held in York, England, as a dissident group in opposition to the mainstream criminology promoted by the Institute of Criminology at the University of Cambridge. For discussion of the conference's connections to radical social movements see Sim et al (1987); Cohen (1988) and Gilmore et al (2013).

Radical Criminology) was suspended so that participants could join a demonstration of 15,000 people against the overthrow of the democratic Chilean government of Salvador Allende. The conferences have thus always sought to move beyond the purely theoretical and outside the fixed boundaries of academia, joining together with activists to seek to bring about concrete political and social change. The Group was significantly inspired by, and in regular contact with, other radical activist groups such as: the *Groupe d'Information sur les Prisons (GIP)* founded by Michel Foucault in 1971 in order to give a voice to prisoners and inform the public about their daily lived experience; the German radical lawyers' group; and the abolitionist movement led by the Norwegian criminologists Nils Christie and Thomas Mathiesen which aimed to bring together activists, academics and prisoners to explore means of conflict resolution outside the logic of the formal criminal justice system (Christie, 1981; Mathiesen, 1974). In common with all these movements, the European Group was shaped by an unequivocal commitment to social justice (Scott, 2012).

By emphasising the study of *deviancy* and *social control*, the founders fashioned the political and theoretical priorities of the European Group (Scott, 2012). Through the notion of deviancy, they highlighted, among other things, the importance of understanding the essentially contested notions of 'crime' and disorder. Stan Cohen and colleagues pointed to the political nature of the construction of 'legitimate' protest and the intricate relationship between private troubles and public issues. In other words, the European Group set out to critically explore how understandings of human biography are fundamentally located within the historical and structural contexts of a given society (Mills, 1959). Further, by scrutinising the 'organised ways in which society responds to behaviour and people it regards as deviant, problematic, worrying, threatening, troublesome or undesirable in some way or another' (Cohen, 1985: 1), manifestations of social control such as migration and border controls, policing, the judiciary, detention and authoritarian statism, were placed firmly in the spotlight (Swaaningen, 1997). This focus on deviancy and social control has continued, albeit in modified form, for over 40 years and is clearly reflected in the contributions to the present journal.

In September 2010 Stan Cohen indicated that in the early days of the European Group, there was 'a strong anarchistic and libertarian ethos' (personal correspondence with David Scott). As time has passed, the philosophies of Marxism, phenomenology, penal abolitionism, feminism, anti-racism and the insights of Michel Foucault, among others, have also proved influential. What unites such diverse and potentially contradictory philosophies are their *critique of hierarchies of power* and the call for *progressive and emancipatory change* rooted in *alternative critical normative values* (Swaaningen, 1997). Whilst the critique and transformation of class hierarchies remains important, the focus has gradually expanded to address much wider concerns around nationalism, heterophobia, racism, ableism, ageism, sexism, homophobia, hetero-normativity and sexual orientation discrimination. The European Group therefore aims to foster 'emancipatory knowledge' (Wright, 2010) which has the explicit political and theoretical intention of not just understanding individual and social problems, but also challenging and transforming existing power relations (Gilmore et al, 2013). It has thus consistently sought to feed a radical and utopian imagination.

The radical imagination in critical criminology

Although critical criminology, as it emerged in opposition to mainstream criminology and the broader injustices it helped perpetuate, initially focused on critique of existing institutions and power structures, it soon began to propose radical and utopian alternatives to hegemonic visions of justice. This became increasingly necessary as dystopian visions of justice began to gain ground as the post-war welfarist consensus collapsed, only to be replaced a neoliberal consensus predicated on the logic of exclusion and rising social inequalities. Central to such a radical and utopian imagination in critical criminology has been a desire to promote justice, human flourishing and dignity, ethical responsibilities and reciprocal awareness, sympathy, mutuality and community (Tifft and Sullivan, 1980). Importantly, this entails finding new ways of framing issues and expanding our imagination regarding what is possible in the here and now. Below, we discuss two examples of what we mean by the radical and utopian imagination in critical criminology: Penal Abolitionism and Zemiology.

Penal Abolitionism and the radical imagination
Abolitionists recognise that prisons are inherently problematic institutions – they are places of interpersonal and institutional violence and legal, social and corporeal death – and these terrible outcomes are structured within the very fabric of penal institutions (Scott and Codd, 2010; Scott, 2013, 2015). It is possible that prisons can offer a place of reflection and refuge for a few people when all other options have failed but, given the deprivations, pains and

iatrogenic harms that underscore daily prison regimes, these cases are the exceptions that prove the rule. Abolitionists, in common with anarchist thinkers such as Kropotkin (1976) and Tifft and Sullivan (1980), highlight the impossibility of reforming such dehumanising institutions: 'A prison cannot be improved... there is absolutely nothing to do but demolish it' (Kropotkin, 1976:45). It is indeed entirely illogical to hope to be able to respond to harms by coercion and violence which do nothing to address the problems that may have led to such harms in the first place, merely exacerbating them. As Rene van Swaaningen has argued:

> At its core, criminal law ... is based on ... repressive assumptions ... From the beginning it has been seen to create problems instead of solving them. A penal reaction after the fact is not preventive but de-socialises an ever-increasing number of people. Therefore it would be better to abolish penal means of coercion, and to replace them by more reparative means. This briefly is the abolitionist message. (1986: 9)

Similarly, Hulsman argues that the criminal justice system has an extraordinarily narrow focus, based as it is on limited state-defined notions of 'crime', that ignore the broader reality in which harmful behaviour may occur (Hulsman, 1986). He thus recommends studying strategies for abolishing criminal justice, namely 'how to liberate organizations like the police and the courts [from] a system of reference that turns them away [from] the variety of life and the needs of those directly involved' (1986: 80) This 'liberation' may only occur, however, once we move outside that frame of reference. It is therefore necessary to empower ordinary people – be they victims or offenders – involved in conflict to ensure that they may help to construct new frames of reference, ensuring that the authorities do not 'have a monopoly on how to define what goes on in the relevant life world' (Mathiesen, 2008: 61). It is thus imperative to challenge the very definition of 'crime'.

Zemiology and the radical imagination
Critical criminology has indeed constantly challenged traditional state-defined notions of 'crime' and criminology which tend to ignore the existence of a considerable number of harms such as those perpetrated by the State itself, notably environmental, economic and social harms. The European Group, from its inception, has been involved in this task. Following on from the work of Tifft and Sullivan in the USA (1980), who sensitised us to the importance of thinking

about how *harms* (not just formally-defined *crimes*) prevent people from being fully human, researchers closely involved with the European Group, namely Paddy Hillyard, Steve Tombs, Christina Pantazis and Simon Pemberton, explored the alternative conception of 'social harm' (Hillyard et al, 2004). After discussions at a European Group Conference in Greece, Paddy Hillyard later adopted the term 'Zemiology' (drawing on the Greek word for harm), as an exhortation to academics and others to move beyond criminology which focuses on harm as defined by the criminal law towards a study of all forms of social harm, including those caused by the State.

   Neither of these examples of the radical imagination offer concrete alternatives to existing penal solutions but they do contribute to opening up utopian spaces in which new visions may be presented and enacted. They follow Mathiesen's exhortation to sketch out alternative visions rather than providing elaborate blueprints for change (Mathiesen, 1974). They may both be considered 'utopian' in the sense that they provide visions of a 'better place' (Malloch and Munro, 2013): for Penal Abolitionism, this good place is where there is an end to penal harms; for Zemiology it is when harms – whether they be harms of (state or corporate) power directed against people, the ecological system, or non-sentient beings – have been curtailed (Walters et al, 2013). Yet, whilst utopianism and the radical imagination may be considered as one of the strengths of critical criminology, allowing it to go beyond the limited analyses of mainstream criminology, it has also been a source of tensions.

Critical criminology and the 'crisis of utopias': from left realism to real utopias

In the 1980s, critical criminology underwent its own 'crisis of utopias' as some of its more utopian aspects were criticised by the 'left realists' (Lea and Young, 1984; Young and Matthews, 1986; Matthews, 2014). In some critical criminological writings, there was a certain utopian idealisation of working class people who broke the law. In rejecting deterministic and pathological explanations for 'crime', Taylor et al regarded criminality as a form of resistance to the dominant capitalist order:

> So long as authority takes the form of domination, [...] authority will always be problematic, and [...] any acts of deviance or dissent must be taken to be acts of resistance (however

inarticulately expressed or formulated). (Taylor et al, 2003 [1973]: 252)

In this, there appeared to be a return to the classical criminological view of the criminal as a perfectly rational actor with the important distinction being that s/he does not choose 'crime' but resistance. S/he was even considered as a sort of working class hero or Robin Hood (Cohen, 1996: 4). The real problem was not considered to be that of 'crime' or the harm it caused, but of criminalisation.

The left realists argued that this focus on the social harm caused by criminalisation, whilst important, tended to deflect attention from the harm caused by criminal acts. Jock Young, one of the original authors of the *New Criminology* (1973), together with John Lea, argued that 'crime' must be taken seriously, especially by the Left since it is a problem that disproportionately affects poor communities. Instead of presenting the fear of 'crime' as an ideological construction without ontological reality, they aimed to measure the real extent of the problem through victims' surveys. This was thought to be a way of making critical criminology policy-relevant and ensuring that law enforcement attended to social inequalities and was democratically accountable.

The idea that the 'crime' problem should not 'belong' to the Right was taken up in Britain by Tony Blair in 1996 when he declared: 'Law and order is a Labour issue. We all suffer from "crime", the poorest and vulnerable most of all' (Blair, 1996: 68). Yet, New Labour appeared to be more influenced by 'right realism' when it came to discussing the causes of 'crime'. Following the conservative American sociologist Charles Murray (1996), it considered offenders as an 'underclass' that was culturally isolated from the mythological 'law-abiding' majority (Bell, 2011: 94-5). This image of the offender was radically opposed to that of the 'left idealists' (Young, 1979) but it was also very different from that originally proposed by the 'left realists'. Indeed, in focusing on pathological causes of 'crime', New Labour ignored one of the key principles of 'left realism', namely the idea that capitalism itself can be criminogenic on account of its tendency to engender economic inequalities which feed feelings of relative deprivation.

That the structural causes of 'crime' should be ignored by politicians claiming to be inspired by left realism was no surprise to those who criticised the theory. Hillyard et al (2004) argued that the left realists' disproportionate focus on street 'crime' meant that other forms of harm, were neglected. Indeed, Zemiology emerged as a reaction against this focus on the most visible forms of 'crime'. Contrary to what left realism seemed to suggest, Hillyard et al argue that critical criminologists did not want to play down the 'crime' problem, above all for the poor, but they aimed to show that white collar 'crime' and harms perpetrated by the State and private corporations could be just as harmful as street 'crime' (Hillyard et al, 2004). Zemiology and Penal Abolitionism do not ignore the victims of 'crime'. On the contrary, the proponents of both critical approaches argue that taking harm seriously means that the notion of 'victim' must be understood in a much broader sense to include victims of social injustice rather than just of 'crime'.

The turn towards realism was perhaps understandable in a dystopian political context, but it lost too much of its radical 'utopian' imagination and ended up being co-opted by mainstream politicians in the 1990s who used it to justify penal repression. Today the 'criminological imagination' is threatened by a revival of positivism and a 'realist' agenda promoting more evaluative research defined by the interests of policy makers and government (Young, 2011), thus placing a 'straightjacket' on critical and independent thought (Barton et al, 2006). The recent move towards taking *harm* seriously is not radically opposed to the left realists' exhortation to take *crime* seriously but by reframing the terms of the debate, it permits a much broader focus on all forms of injustice. It also allows us to go beyond the somewhat idealistic notion of criminals as political actors by showing that those who cause harm are as likely to be situated at the top or the bottom of the social hierarchy. It is the social harm approach that lays the groundwork for a reawakening of a critical criminological imagination (Barton et al, 2006; Copson, 2013) which may be capable of moving towards a new form of realism: *the real utopia*.

Reawakening our radical imagination

There is a pressing need to develop non-penal real utopias to provide a new cultural script and resources for a radical imagination to inspire transformative justice and emancipatory politics and praxis capable of moving beyond repressive penal dystopia. Inspired by abolitionism and the social harm approach, a non-penal real utopia should promote visions of radical alternatives. What is required is an alternative space designated to foster *self-empowerment* which utilises a holistic approach based upon principles of self-help and mutual aid. Non-penal interventions should help troubled individuals understand and, as far as possible, lessen or overcome their psychological, social and/or emotional issues and difficulties. It requires a *democratic* impulse that aims to foster a balanced and *supportive dialogue* between clients and staff where agreement and consensus can be reached. Radical alternatives can aspire to engender respect for the self, the environment and other people and develop new skills for inter-personal communication and action.

By promoting values and principles, such as empowerment, participatory democracy and mutual aid, we can also point to the defects of the existing operation of the criminal law and to social injustice. Working backwards so to speak, the non-penal real utopia can be a way of proposing ideas and principles upon which the penal apparatus of the capitalist state can be judged. The daily workings of the intervention can help inform a normative framework challenging the pain, suffering, harm and death characterising the prison place. It thus gives us a solid and principled moral platform from which we can critique the failures of the penal law. Following Scott (2013), non-penal real utopia must be grounded in the following five normative principles that build upon continuities and possibilities in our historical conjuncture (see also Scott and Gosling, this volume).

- Non-penal real utopias must *not* be predicated upon the penal rationale – the intervention must *not* aim to penalise – it must therefore be non-punitive. Because a non-penal real utopia must stand outside the criminal process, it should also reflect the need for radical restructuring and transformation rather than merely tinkering.
- Non-penal real utopias must compete with, and contradict, current penal ideologies, discourses, policies and practices. Those in power must find it difficult to ignore or dismiss the proposed radical alternative but at the same it must be impossible for them to re-appropriate the alternative within the logic of the penal-rationale.
- Non-penal radical alternatives must be plausible and something that can be considered *in place of* a prison sentence.
- Non-penal radical alternatives must have a non-punitive ethos aiming to uphold, respect and protect the intrinsic worth and value of human beings. There must be no violations of human dignity, nor should the intervention create stigma, injury or harm. Care should therefore be taken to ensure that any proposed non-penal alternative intervention for handling conflicts does not become a form of punishment in disguise.
- Non-penal real utopia must be grounded in lived experience and deeply rooted in the practices of everyday life. They must be

examples that already exist and could be developed or expanded (Scott, 2013).

Furthermore, non-penal real utopias should not be considered in isolation. Since the social harm that they seek to address is bound up with a whole range of other contextual issues, they need to be thought of as just one part of a project helping to inform a broader vision of social justice. They may do this by giving people the opportunity to see the world differently and encouraging them to understand the Other. At a time when social and economic insecurities are encouraging scapegoating, it is ever more important to foster a more reflective understanding of the causes of social problems. Indeed, the darker the times, the greater the need for enlightened thinking. The reflection upon the principles and practices of non-penal real utopias present us with a clear ability to reflect upon social injustice in contemporary society. It offers us a template of the 'good life', a space in which we not only challenge but can imagine new radical alternatives. It therefore has *emancipatory* potential, encouraging us to think more broadly about how the principles and values of social justice can work in practice. A non-penal real utopia may help us to see beyond the constraints of the present neo-liberal society that privileges the market above everything else, especially human need.

Thinking about non-penal real utopias must also be a collective endeavour if we are to hope to develop alternatives to current top-down, state-controlled penal practices. It is hoped that this collective exercise in imagination may help foster visions of a society grounded in mutual aid and respect; democratic participation; communal living and equitable distribution of resources; and where people have a voice that is both heard and listened to. Thus, the radical alternative can provide us with a set of alternative values to neo-liberal capitalism and can inform constructive criticism of the present. The very act of awakening the utopian imagination may be constitutive of wide-ranging change.

Moving forward: utopias and the non-penal

The contributions to this special foundation issue of the journal *Justice, Power and Resistance* put forward some concrete examples of non-penal real utopian thinking and practice. They are all guided by a concern with justice, solidarity and emancipation, values which need to underpin any attempt to develop genuine alternatives to current penal practices. Following an abolitionist approach, they all adopt 'an attitude of saying "no"' (Mathiesen, 2008: 58), of critiquing existing dystopian institutions and practices and failed attempts at reform. Following a social harm approach, they focus their attention outside state-defined notions of 'crime' to explore all forms of harm, whether caused by individuals, corporations or state institutions. In doing so, they encourage us to think about these harms, and consequently about means of addressing them, in their wider social context.

It is to be hoped that the (re)awakening of the critical criminological imagination in a real utopian direction will provide the basis of an ongoing debate which may lead to transformative, emancipatory change, thus offering a way out of the 'crisis of utopias'. The task of critical criminology, together with progressive thinkers and activists, could not be more pressing.

References

Barton, A., Corteen, K., Scott, D., Whyte, D. (eds) (2006) *Expanding the Criminological Imagination* Abingdon: Routledge

Becker, H. (1967) 'Whose Side and We On?' in *Social Problems* Volume 14, No. 3 pp 239-247

Bell, E. (2011) *Criminal Justice and Neoliberalism* Basingstoke: Palgrave Macmillan

Blair, T. (1996) *New Britain: My Vision of a Young Country* London: Fourth Estate

Bourdieu, P. (2000 [1972]) *Esquisse d'une théorie de la pratique* Paris : Seuil

Bourdieu, P. and Wacquant, L. (1992) *An Introduction to Reflexive Sociology* Cambridge: Polity Press

Chomsky, N. (2008) [1966] 'The Responsibility of Intellectuals' in Arnove, A. (ed.), *The Essential Chomsky* London: The Bodley Head

Christie, N. (1981) *Limits to Pain* Oslo: Oslo University Press

Cohen, S. (1985) *Visions of Social Control* Cambridge: Polity Press

Cohen, S. (1988) *Against Criminology* Cambridge: Polity Press

Cohen, S. (1996) 'Crime and Politics: Spot the Difference' in *British Journal of Sociology* Volume 47, No. 1 pp 1-21

Cohen, S. (2010) (*personal correspondence* with David Scott, September, 20th)

Collier, R. (1998) *Masculinities, Crime and Criminology* London: Sage

Copson, L. (2013) 'Towards a utopian criminology' in Malloch, M. and Munro, B. (eds) (2013) *Crime, Critique and Utopia* London: Palgrave

Duménil, G. (2014) 'Les utopies peuvent mobiliser les énergies', *La Marseillaise*, 9 December.

Duménil, G. (2016), seminar delivered to 'Les amis de Veblen', Lyon, 2 March.

Dwyer, A., Ball, M. and Crofts, T. (2015) *Queering Criminology* Basingstoke: Palgrave Macmillan

Eagleton, T. (1999) 'Utopia and its Opposites' pp 31-41 in Panitch, L. and Leys, C. (eds) (1999) *Necessary and Unnecessary Utopias: Socialist Register 2000* Rendlesham: Merlin

Equality and Human Rights Commission (2015) *Stop and Think: A critical review of the use of stop and search powers in England and Wales*, http://www.equalityhumanrights.com/ sites/default/files/documents/raceinbritain/ehrc_stop_and_search_report. pdf (consulted 13 May 2016)

Gilmore, J., Moore, J.M and Scott, D. (eds) (2013) *Critique and Dissent* Ottawa: Red Quill Books

Gilroy, P. (1987) "The Myth of Black Criminality" in Scraton, P. (1987) *Law, Order and the Authoritarian State* Milton Keynes: Open University

Gordon, M.D., Tilley, H. and Prakash, G. (2010) 'Utopia and dystopia beyond space and time' pp 1-20 in Gordon, M.D., Tilley, H. and Prakash, G. (eds) (2010) *Utopia/Dystopia: Conditions of historical possibility* Oxford: Princeton University Press

Gordon, P. (1983) *White Law: Racism in the police, courts and prisons* London: Pluto Press

Gouldner, Alvin (1968) 'The Sociologist as Partisan: Sociology and the Welfare State' in *The American Sociologist* Volume 3, No. 2 pp 103-116

Hall, S., Critcher, C., Jefferson, T., Clarke, J., Roberts, B. (eds) (1978) *Policing the Crisis: Mugging, the State and Law and Order* London: Macmillan

Heidensohn, F. (1985) *Women and Crime* London: Macmillan

Hillyard, P. (1993) *Suspect Community* London: Pluto Press

Hillyard, P. Pantazis, C. Tombs, S. Gordon, D. (eds) (2004) *Beyond Criminology: Taking harm seriously* London: Pluto Press

Hulsman, L. (1986) 'Critical Criminology and the concept of "crime"' in *Contemporary Crises* Volume 10, No. 1 pp 63-80

Jacoby, R. (2005) *Picture Imperfect: Utopian Thought for an Anti-Utopian Age* New York: Columbia University Press

Kropotkin, P. (1976) *The Essential Kropotkin* London: Macmillan

Lea, J. and Young, J. (1984) *What is to be Done About Law and Order?* Harmondsworth: Penguin

Levitas, R. (1990) *The Concept of Utopia* Oxford: Peter Lang

Macpherson, W. (1999) *The Stephen Lawrence Inquiry*, Cm 4262-I London: Home Office

Malloch, M. and Munro, B. (eds) (2013) *Crime, Critique and Utopia* London: Palgrave

Matthews, R. (2014) *Realist Criminology* Basingstoke: Palgrave Macmillan

Mathiesen, T. (1974) *The Politics of Abolition* Oxford: Martin Robertson

Mathiesen T (2008) 'The Abolitionist Stance' in *Journal of Prisoners on Prisons* Volume 17, No. 2 pp 58-63

Matza, D. (1964) *Delinquency and Drift* New Brunswick: Transaction

Matza, D. (1969) *Becoming Deviant* New Jersey: Prentice Hall

Merton, R. (1945) 'The Role of the Intellectual in Public Bureaucracy' in *Social Forces* Volume 23, No. 4 pp 405-415

Mills, C.W. (1959) *The Sociological Imagination* Oxford: Oxford University Press

More, T. (1516) *Utopia* Harmondsworth: Penguin

Orwell, G. (1949) *1984* Harmondsworth: Penguin

Pantazis, C. and Pemberton, S. (2009) 'From the "Old" to the "New" Suspect Community' in *British Journal of Criminology* Volume 49, No. 5 pp 646-666

Scott, D. (2012) 'The European Group for the Study of Deviance and Social Control' in Bell, E. (ed) (2012) *No Borders* Chambery: University of Savoie Press

Scott, D. (2013) 'Visualising an Abolitionist Real Utopia: Principles, policy and praxis' in Malloch, M. and Munro, B. (eds) (2013) *Crime, Critique and Utopia* London: Palgrave

Scott, D. (2015) 'Eating your Insides Out: Interpersonal, cultural and institutionally-structured violence in the prison place' in *Prison Service Journal* September, 2015

Scott, D. and Codd, H. (2010) *Controversial Issues in Prison* Maidenhead: Open University Press

Scraton, P. (ed.) (1987) *Law, Order and the Authoritarian State* Milton Keynes: Open University

Sim. J., Scraton, P. and Gordon, P. (1987) 'Introduction' in Scraton, P. (ed.) (1987) *Law, Order and the Authoritarian State* Milton Keynes: Open University

Smart, C. (1976) *Women, Crime and Criminology* Abingdon: Routledge and Keegan Paul

Swaaningen, R. Van (1986) in Bianchi H. and Swaaningen R. Van (1986) *Abolitionism: Towards a non-repressive approach to 'crime'* Amsterdam: Free University Press

Swaaningen, R. Van (1997) *Critical Criminology: Visions from Europe* London: Sage

Taylor, I., Walton, P. and Young, J. (2003 [1973]) *The New Criminology: For a Social Theory of Deviance* Abingdon: Routledge and Kegan Paul

Tifft, L. and Sullivan, L. (1980) *The Struggle to be Human: Crime, criminology and anarchism* Orkney: Cienfuegos Press

Wacquant, L. (2013) 'Crafting the Neoliberal State: Workfare, prisonfare and social insecurity' in Scott, D. (ed) (2013) *Why Prison?* Cambridge: Cambridge University Press

Walters, R., Westerhuis, D.S. and Wyatt, T. (eds) (2013) *Emerging Issues in Green Criminology* London: Palgrave

Wright, E.O (2010) *Envisioning a Real Utopia* Cambridge: Polity Press

Wright, E.O. (2009) *Envisioning Real Utopias* Manuscript, http://citeseerx.ist.psu.edu/viewdoc/download?doi=10.1.1.152.6099andre p=rep1andtype=pdf (consulted 13 May 2016)

Young, J. (2011) *The Criminological Imagination* Cambridge: Polity Press

Young, J. and Matthews, R. (eds) (1986) *Realist Criminology* Sage: London

Young, J. (1979) 'Left idealism, Reformism and Beyond: From New Criminology to Marxism' in Fine, B. et al (eds) *Capitalism and the Rule of Law: From Deviancy Theory to Marxism* London: Hutchinson

Real Utopias and the Dilemmas of Institutional Transformation

Erik Olin Wright[1]

Abstract

The idea of 'real utopias' is a way of thinking about emancipatory alternatives to existing institutions of domination and inequality, about both the destinations to which we aspire and the strategies for getting there. This paper elaborates the values embodied in the idea of real utopias, explores the strategic problem of transforming society in ways that advance these values, and examines the dilemmas of creating real utopias in situations where the optimal design for ameliorating the harms of existing institutions is not the same as constructing real utopias.

Introduction

The idea of 'real utopias' is a way of thinking about emancipatory alternatives to existing institutions of domination and inequality, about both the destinations to which we aspire and the strategies for getting there. The term itself, of course, is an oxymoron, for utopia is a nowhere fantasy world of perfect harmony and social justice which could never actually exist in reality. A characteristic way of derisively dismissing a political proposal is to call it 'utopian'. Realists disdain such fantasies not just as distractions, but as

---

[1] Erik Olin Wright is Vilas Distinguished Research Professor at the University of Wisconsin, Madison. His academic work has been centrally concerned with reconstructing the Marxist tradition in ways that attempt to make it more relevant to contemporary concerns and more cogent as a scientific framework of analysis. His empirical work has focused especially on class analysis. Since 1992 he has directed *The Real Utopias Project* which explores a wide range of proposals for new institutional designs that embody emancipatory ideals and yet are attentive to issues of pragmatic feasibility. He was president of the American Sociological Association in 2011-12. His principal books include: *Class, Crisis and the State* (1978); *Classes* (1985); *Reconstructing Marxism* (1992); *Class Counts* (1997); *Deepening Democracy* (with Archon Fung, 2003); *Envisioning Real Utopias* (2010); *American Society: How it really works* (with Joel Rogers 2011 and 2015); *Understanding Class* (2015); and *Alternatives to Capitalism* (with Robin Hahnel, 2016). Contact: eowright@wisc.edu

dangers: 'the best is the enemy of the good'. This scepticism is well founded: utopian fantasies have sometimes lead political movements along extremely destructive paths. And yet, there is something crucial in the dream of utopia as an affirmation of our deepest aspirations for a just and humane world that does not exist. What we need to do is combine those utopian yearnings with the practical task of building real alternatives to the world as it is. The expression 'real utopia' is a way of capturing this tension between dreams and practice. It points to the possibility of building alternatives in the world as it is that prefigure an emancipatory world as it could be and help us to move in that direction.

In this article I want to link the idea of real utopia to the very difficult problem of emancipatory non-penal alternatives to existing social institutions of social control. I will begin by briefly discussing the values that underlie the idea of emancipatory alternatives. I will then give more theoretical precision to the idea of real utopias by locating real utopia within a conceptual space of alternative strategies for social emancipation. This will be followed by a few illustrative examples of real utopias. The paper will conclude with a discussion of the dilemmas of situations where the optimal design for ameliorating the harms of existing institutions is not the same as constructing real utopias.

Emancipatory Values[2]

The full agenda of an emancipatory social science – a social science that hopes to contribute to the collective project of challenging forms of human oppression – revolves around four interconnected components:

1. The *normative principles* of social emancipation.
2. The *diagnosis and critique* of existing institutions and social structures in terms of those principles.
3. A theoretical framework for analysing *alternatives to existing institutions* and structures that more fully embody the normative principles.
4. A *theory of transformation* that helps us understand how to get from here to there.

There was a time when many progressives, especially in the Marxist tradition, felt that it wasn't so important to develop explicit normative principles. The struggle against oppression should be waged under the banner of *interests*,

---

[2] A fuller exploration of these values can be found in Wright (2010), Chapter 2.

especially class interests, not *values*. While I think the problem of interests remain important, in the 21st century the cohesion of any plausible political movement for emancipatory social transformation will have to involve strong moral commitments, not just a clear understanding of self-interest. If this is correct, then it is important to clarify the core values of social emancipation.

Three clusters values have been especially important in progressive struggles for social change: equality/fairness, democracy/freedom, and community/solidarity. These have a long pedigree in social struggles going back at least to the ideals of *liberté, egalité, fraternité* proclaimed in the French Revolution. All of these values have hotly contested meanings. Few people say that they are against democracy or freedom or some interpretation of equality, but many people still disagree sharply over the real content packaged into these words. Debates of this sort keep political philosophers very busy. I will not attempt here to sort out these debates. What I will do is give an account of these values that can provide normative foundations for social emancipation.

Equality/fairness.

Some ideal of equality is held by most people in contemporary capitalist societies, whether it be equality of opportunity or equality of legal rights, or some notion of equality of wellbeing. The Marxian ideal is captured by the distributive principle, 'To each according to need, from each according to ability'. One way of generalizing the value of equality in the first part of this aphorism is this:

> *In a just society, all persons would have broadly equal access to*
> *the material and social means necessary to live a flourishing life.*

There is a lot packed into this statement. The most important element is the notion of *equal access* to the conditions needed for human flourishing. Equal access is a more generous and compassionate idea than 'equal opportunity', for it recognises that people screw up and squander their opportunities but that, in spite of this, they should still have access to what it takes to flourish. Unlike views that say that people should bear full responsibility for the bad choices they make and suffer the consequences, the equal access principle takes the sociologically and psychologically more realistic view that, to a substantial extent, both good and bad decisions are the result of social and psychological forces, not things for which a person has any meaningful responsibility.

The value of equality/fairness is also deeply connected to environmental concerns. On the one hand, *environmental justice* concerns the ways in which the burdens of environmental harms are distributed within a society. The value of equality/fairness implies that it is unjust for the burden of toxic waste, pollution and other environmental harms to be disproportionately borne by poor and minority communities. On the other hand, if we extend the value of equality/fairness to future generations, then they are also entitled to the same access to environmental conditions to live flourishing lives as the current generation. Issues like global warming can thus be seen as a problem of inter-generational justice: Future generations should have access to the social and material means to live flourishing lives at least at the same level as the present generation.[3]

Democracy/freedom

Democracy and freedom are closely linked ideas, connected through what can be called the value of self-determination:

> *In a fully democratic society, all people would have broadly equal access to the necessary means to participate meaningfully in decisions about things which affect their lives.*

If the decisions in question affect me and only me, then I should be able to make them without interference from anyone else. That is what we call freedom or liberty. But, if the decisions in question affect other people, then they should be parties to the decision as well or, at least, agree to let me make the decision without their participation. Of particular importance are decisions which impose binding, enforced rules on everyone. These are decisions made by states, and for those kinds of decisions all people affected by the rules should be able to meaningfully participate in making the rules. This is what we normally mean by democracy: control 'by the people' over the use of the power of the State to impose rules on the way we live. But a democratic *society* (rather than simply a democratic state) implies more than this; it requires that people should be able to meaningfully participate in all decisions which significantly affect their lives, whether those decisions are being made within the State or other kinds of institutions. A democratic workplace and a

---

[3] This is definitely an anthropocentric view of environmental ethics. There may well be other reasons to protect the environment aside from the harms – immediate and long-term – on human beings, but I regard these as of secondary importance.

democratic economy is as much a part of a democratic society as is a democratic state.

In this formulation the fundamental idea is that people should be able to determine the conditions of their own lives to the greatest extent possible. This is what self-determination means. The difference between freedom and democracy, then, concerns the contexts of actions that affect one's life, not the underlying value itself. Again, the context of freedom is decisions and actions that only affect the person making the decision; the context of democracy is decisions and actions which affect other people as well.

As in the case of fairness, the democratic ideal rests on the egalitarian principle of equal access. In the case of flourishing, the issue was equal access to the necessary means to live a flourishing life. Here the issue is equal access to the necessary means to participate meaningfully in decisions; in short, equal access to the exercise of power. This does not imply that all people actually do participate equally in collective decisions, but simply that there are no unequal social impediments to their participation.

Community/solidarity

The third long-standing value connected to emancipatory ideals is community and the closely related idea of solidarity:

> Community/solidarity expresses the principle that people ought to cooperate with each other not simply because of what they personally get out of it, but also out of a real commitment to the wellbeing of others and a sense of moral obligation that it is the right thing to.

When such cooperation occurs in the mundane activities of everyday life in which people help each other out, we use the word 'community'; when the cooperation occurs in the context of collective action to achieve a common goal, we use the term 'solidarity'. Solidarity typically also suggests the idea of collective power – 'united we stand, divided we fall' – but the unity being called for is still grounded in the principle it shares with community: that cooperation should be motivated not exclusively by an instrumental concern with narrow individual self-interest, but by a combination of moral obligations and concern for others.

The value of community applies to any social unit in which people interact and cooperate. The family, in this sense, is a particularly salient community, and in a healthy family one certainly expects cooperation to be rooted in both love and moral concern. A family in which parents made 'investments' in children not because of any concern for the wellbeing of their children but only because the parents felt they would get a good financial 'return on their investments' would seem to most people to violate important family values. Religiously-backed moral precepts often embody this value: 'Love thy neighbour as thyself' and 'Do unto others as you would have them do unto you'. The heartfelt chant of the labour movement, 'An injury to one is an injury to all', expresses this value. Neighbourhoods, cities, nations, organisations, clubs, and any other setting of social interaction and cooperation are also sites for the value of community.

These three normative principles provide crucial motivations for wanting a different social world from the one in which we live, but they do not in and of themselves tell us much about the institutional properties of desirable alternatives or how to get achieve them. This is what a theory of real utopias is meant to facilitate.

Strategic logics of social transformation

Much social change in human history operates behind the backs of people as the cumulative effect of the unintended consequences of human action. To be able to have a 'strategy', in contrast, it must be possible to produce desirable social transformation through deliberate, intentional action. Different strategies of social transformation are embedded in different understandings of what precisely a strategy is thought capable of achieving. More specifically, strategies vary in terms of how encompassing and ambitious the primary goal of a strategy is thought to be.

One way of thinking about the ambitiousness and scope of strategy is through the metaphor of society as a game. Strategies in response to the harms generated by social systems can be directed at what *kind of game should be played*, at what precisely should be *the rules of a given game*, or at the *moves within a fixed set of rules*.[4] Think about this in terms of a sport: different games give athletes with different physical characteristics different advantages and disadvantages, and thus they have interests in playing one kind of game over another. Consider two athletes, one 1.7 meters tall, with great strength weighing 150 kilos, the other 2.1 meters tall with great agility and stamina, weighing 80 kilos. They live in a world where only one sport is

---

[4] This three-level analysis of the game itself, the rules of the game and moves in the game comes from Alford and Friedland (1985).

allowed to be played: American football or basketball. Clearly, if basketball becomes hegemonic, the heavy athlete becomes marginalised. Once playing a particular game, occasionally the rules themselves are called into question, and changes in the rules can also favour athletes with different attributes. For example, the change in the rules of basketball that allowed players to touch the rim of the hoop, which in turn made dunking possible, added to the advantages of height. And finally, given a set of fixed rules, the players of the game then adopt specific training regimes and strategies in their plays within the game. Dynamically, what can then happen is that players invent all sorts of new strategies and ways of training designed to exploit specific opportunities within the existing rules of the game. In time, these altered moves in the game begin to change the feel of the game in various ways. Sometimes these changes are seen as eroding the spirit or integrity of the game by spectators, players, or 'the powers that be' that govern the rules of the game. This can trigger changes in the rules which are then imposed as constraints on all players. Changes in the height of the pitching mound or strike zone in baseball to alter the balance of power between pitcher and batter, or changes in the rules about defences against the pass in American Football are familiar examples. Rules are altered to address what are seen as problems in the balance of power among players in the moves of the game.

Strategies of social emancipation can also be understood as operating at the level of the game itself, the rules of the game, or moves in the game. Let's call these the strategic logics of *Rupture*, *Reform*, and *Alleviation*:

> *Rupture:* This is the classic strategic logic of revolutionaries. The rationale goes something like this: 'The game' is so deeply oppressive and unjust and the ruling class and elites so powerful and entrenched that it is impossible to make life significantly better for ordinary people in the existing system. From time to time small reforms that improve things may be possible when popular forces are strong, but such improvements will always be fragile, vulnerable to attack and reversible. Ultimately it is an illusion that the existing system of domination and exploitation can be rendered a benign social order in which ordinary people can live flourishing, meaningful lives; at its core, the system is unreformable. The only hope is to destroy it, sweep away the rubble and then build an alternative. As the closing words of the early twentieth century labour song *Solidarity Forever* proclaim, 'We can bring to birth a new world from the ashes of the old'.

Reform: Social democracy in Europe and more generally the welfare state embody this strategy. The existing social system creates great harms. It generates levels of inequality that are unjust and destructive to social cohesion; it destroys traditional jobs and leaves people to fend for themselves; it creates uncertainty and risk in the lives of individuals and whole communities; it is organised through despotic workplaces; it harms the environment; it perpetuates deep social injustices based on race, gender, and other ascriptive attributes of people. Nevertheless, it is possible to modify the rules of the game by building counteracting institutions capable of significantly neutralising these harms. To be sure, creating and sustaining such institutions may require sharp struggles since they impinge on the autonomy and power of the capitalist class and other elites, and there are no guarantees of success in such struggles. To accomplish serious reform requires popular mobilisation and political will; one can never rely on the enlightened benevolence of elites. But in the right circumstances, it is possible to win these battles and impose the constraints needed for a more benign form of capitalism and other social institutions.

Alleviation: The existing social order is too powerful a system to destroy or even really tame. Truly taming capitalism would require a level of sustained popular mobilisation that is unrealistic, and anyway, the system as a whole is too large and complex to control effectively. The powers-that-be are too strong to dislodge and they will always co-opt opposition and defend their privileges. The best we can do is to try to alleviate the harms of the system at the micro-level of everyday life and individual suffering. This is the strategy of many grass-roots activists of various sorts: activist lawyers who defend the rights of immigrants, the poor, sexual minorities, and others; feminists who volunteer in half-way houses for battered women; environmentalists who protest against a toxic dump. It is also, in a different way, the strategy of much charity work that responds to the needs of oppressed communities through things like soup kitchens and homeless shelters. The rules of the game allow for moves that can help people; that is the best we can do.

These three strategic logics have defined the main responses to injustice and oppression in capitalist societies. There is, however, a fourth, less familiar strategy: *erosion.* While this logic is sometimes implicit in political strategies, it is not generally foregrounded as the central organising principle of a response to social injustice:

Erosion: The strategy of erosion is grounded in a particular understanding of the concept of 'social system'. Consider capitalism as an economic system. No economy has ever been – or ever could be – purely capitalist. Capitalism is defined by the combination of market exchange with private ownership of the means of production and the employment of wage-earners recruited through a labour market. Existing economic systems combine capitalism with a whole host of other ways of organising the production and distribution of goods and services: directly by states; within the intimate relations of families to meet the needs of its members; through community-based networks and organisations; by cooperatives owned and governed democratically by their members; though nonprofit market-oriented organisations; through peer-to-peer networks engaged in collaborative production processes; and many other possibilities. Some of these ways of organising economic activities can be thought of as hybrids, combining capitalist and non-capitalist elements; some are entirely non-capitalist; and some are anti-capitalist. Some are highly functional for capitalism itself; others are irrelevant to capitalism; and some are in real tension with capitalist relations. We call such a complex economic system 'capitalist' when it is the case that capitalism is dominant in determining the economic conditions of life and access to livelihood for most people. That dominance is immensely destructive. One way to challenge capitalism is to build more democratic, egalitarian, participatory economic relations in the spaces and cracks within this complex system where this is possible, and to struggle to expand and defend those spaces by changing the rules of the game within capitalist society. The idea of eroding capitalism imagines that these alternatives have the potential, in the long run, of expanding to the point where capitalism is displaced from this dominant role. Erosion thus operates at all three levels of the game: it envisions a fundamental transformation of the game itself – the long-term objective is an alternative game embodying the values of equality, democracy and solidarity; it recognises both the necessity and possibility of changes in the rules of the existing game in order to expand the prospects for counter-system alternatives; and it engages in moves within the existing rules of the game to build emancipatory alternatives in the spaces where this is possible.

The relationship of these four strategies to the metaphor of society as a game is illustrated in the figure below:

Strategic Logic	Target of strategy: *The Game Itself*	Target of strategy: *Rules of the game*	Target of strategy: *Moves in the game*
Rupture	X		
Reform		X	
Alleviation			X
Erosion	X	X	X

Four Strategic Logics of Social Emancipation

As a guide to practical action, the strategy of erosion embodies a distinction between what can be called *ameliorative reforms* and *emancipatory* reforms. Ameliorative reform looks at the problems and injustices in the world and seeks ways to make things better. Emancipatory reform also looks at the problems and injustices in the world, but then envisions a world in which emancipatory values are realised – an alternative game – and seeks ways to solve present problems by building constituent elements of that alternative world. This contrast is similar to what Andre Gorz called 'nonreformist reforms' in his book, *Strategy for Labor*. Gorz (1967) writes:

> A reformist reform is one which subordinates its objectives to the criteria of rationality and practicability of a given system and policy. Reformism rejects those objectives and demands—however deep the need for them—which are incompatible with the preservation of the system.
>
> On the other hand, a not necessarily reformist reform is one which is conceived not in terms of what is possible within the framework of a given system and administration, but in view of what should be made possible in terms of human needs and demands.
>
> In other words, a struggle for non-reformist reforms—for anti-capitalist reforms—is one which does not base its validity and its right to exist on capitalist needs, criteria, and rationales. A non-reformist reform is determined not in terms of what can be, but what should be.

An example of the contrast between simple ameliorative reforms and emancipatory reforms is the difference between two public policy responses to poverty: food stamps and unconditional basic income (UBI). Food stamps for the poor relieve hunger, and they are certainly a vital ameliorative policy in the context of poverty and hunger in the United States. But food stamps are not building blocks for an emancipatory alternative: the ideal world is not one in which food stamps would play a role. Unconditional basic income, on the other hand, also relieves hunger. Like food stamps, it helps neutralise harm in the world as it is, but it is also a critical element of a more egalitarian, solidaristic alternative. An unconditional basic income introduced within capitalism is a change in the rules of the game in a capitalist economy (i.e. an economy in which capitalism is dominant), but it also introduces one element of the rules of the game of an alternative to capitalism.

Real Utopias

Real utopias are the institutions and proposals that contribute to this long-term strategy of erosion of the dominant structures of domination, inequality and oppression through emancipatory reforms from above and activist practices from below. Real utopias can be found wherever emancipatory ideals are embodied in existing institutions, practices, and proposals.

Existing Institutions

There are many examples of actually existing institutions that embody to a greater or lesser extent emancipatory ideals in spite of their existing within capitalist societies. Two prominent examples are public libraries and worker cooperatives.

Public libraries might at first glance seem like an odd example. They are, after all, a durable institution found in all capitalist societies. Nevertheless, they embody principles of access and distribution which are profoundly anti-capitalist. Consider the sharp difference between the ways a person acquires access to a book in a bookstore and in a library. In a bookstore you look for the book you want on a shelf, check the price, and if you can afford it and you want it sufficiently, you go to the cashier, hand over the required amount of money and then leave with the book. In a library you go to the shelf (or more likely these days, to a terminal to see if the book is available), find your book, go to the check-out counter, show your library card, and leave with the book. If the book is already checked out, you get put on a waiting list. In a bookstore the distribution principle is 'to each according to ability to pay'; in a public library the principle of distribution is 'to each according to need'. What is more, in the library, if there is an imbalance between supply and demand, the amount of time one has to wait for the book increases; books in scarce supply are rationed by time, not by price. A waiting list is a profoundly egalitarian device: a day in everyone's life is treated as morally equivalent. A well-resourced library will treat the length of the waiting list as a good signal that more copies of a particular book need to be ordered. Libraries can also become multipurpose public amenities, not simply repositories of books. Good libraries provide public space for meetings, sometimes venues for concerts and other performances, and a congenial gathering place for people. Of course, libraries can also be exclusionary zones that are made inhospitable to certain kinds of people. They can be elitist in their budget priorities and their rules. Actual libraries may thus reflect quite contradictory values. But, insofar as they embody emancipatory ideals of equality, democracy and community, libraries are a real utopia.

Worker cooperatives are a different kind of example of a real utopia. Two important emancipatory ideals are equality and democracy. Both of these are obstructed in capitalist firms, where power is concentrated in the hands of owners and their surrogates, and internal resources and opportunities are distributed in a grossly unequal manner. In a worker-owned cooperative, all of the assets of the firms are jointly owned by the employees themselves who also govern the firm in a one-person-one-vote democratic manner. In a small cooperative this democratic governance can be organised in the form of general assemblies of all members; in larger cooperatives the workers elect boards of directors to oversee the firm. Worker cooperatives may also embody more capitalistic features: they may, for example, hire temporary workers or be inhospitable to potential members of particular ethnic or racial groups. Like libraries, they often embody contradictory values. But again, they are a real utopia to the extent that they embody anti-capitalist emancipatory ideals.

Practices

Another place we can find real utopias is the concrete activities of people living and working together. This is the real utopia of lived experience. It is found in natural disasters where people in a community come together in mutual aid. It is found in the joy of collaborative creativity in artist performances in music, theatre, and dance. It is found in the exhilaration of solidarity and connection experienced in social movements and struggles. The feminist cry 'sisterhood is powerful' is a claim about the collective capacity to change the world, but also about the real utopian realisation of the value of community in the form of sisterhood-in-struggle. Comradeship, sisterhood, brotherhood – these are powerful expressions of emancipatory struggles. They all express both the longing for a world where people feel deeply connected working together for common purposes, and the actual experience of such connection in the process of struggling for that world. When such lived experience is shared among participants in a social movement and becomes expressed in music, art, stories, and other cultural forms, we can talk about the real utopian dimension of culture.

Proposals
Real utopias can also be found in proposals for social change and state policies, not just in actually existing institutions and practices. This is the critical role of real utopias in long-term political strategies for social justice and human emancipation. Two examples are unconditional basic income and tax-funded journalism vouchers for a democratic media system.

We have already introduced the idea of unconditional basic income. Unconditional basic income gives everyone, without conditions, a flow of income sufficient to cover basic needs. It provides for a modest, but culturally respectable, no-frills standard of living. Unconditional basic income directly tames one of the harms of capitalism – poverty in the midst of plenty. But it also expands the potential for a long term erosion of the dominance of capitalism by channelling resources towards non-capitalist forms of economic activity. Consider the effects of basic income on worker cooperatives. One of the reasons worker cooperatives are often fragile is that they have to generate sufficient income not merely to cover the material costs of production but also to provide a basic income for their members. If a basic income were guaranteed independently of the market success of the cooperative, worker cooperatives would become much more robust. This would also mean that they would be less risky for loans from banks. Thus, somewhat ironically, an unconditional basic income would help solve a credit market problem for cooperatives. It would also underwrite a massive increase of participation in p2p collaborative production and many other socially productive and useful activities that do not themselves generate market income for participants.[5] This would include the arts as well as political activism.

---

[5] 'p2p' refers to peer-to-peer forms of networked cooperation that have emerged in the internet age.

Tax-funded journalism vouchers are one way of solving a problem faced by democracies within capitalist systems: the domination of news media by large capitalist corporations. Democracy requires vibrant, high-quality news media that is autonomous from centres of power. A media system dominated by capitalist corporations violates this requirement. Robert McChesney has proposed the idea of giving every tax-payer an annual tax-financed voucher that can only be used to support non-profit news journalism organisations.[6] Various criteria would need to be established to certify that a news organisation was in fact a legitimate candidate for these vouchers. The critical issue is that the organisation should be non-profit and that it actually produces news, but other criteria could be added. Such a system has the advantage over directly funded public sector news because it would have autonomy from the State and create much more diversity in the publicly-supported news sector The proposal harnesses the power of the State to extract the resources for a democratic media, but it assigns to citizens, on an equal basis, the responsibility for allocating the resources to specific organisations. It would create a democratically-grounded media system capable of effectively competing with corporate media.

The idea of real utopias is thus a way of evaluating institutions that exist, our experiences of future possibilities in our present activities, and proposals for new initiatives. It defines a destination, a process and a strategy.

Dilemmas of Optimal Design

A real utopia is an institution, practice or proposal which satisfies two conditions: first, it embodies at least some of the normative principles of a utopian aspiration, and second, it constitutes a possible building block of a future, emancipatory alternative to the present world. In this sense it is not simply a bridge between the present and an imagined future; it is importing into the present pieces of a possible emancipatory future. In the examples of real utopias above, the particular institutions and proposals we discussed satisfy both conditions. Publicly-funded libraries which make various kinds of materials available to people free of charge and which involve, where needed, some kind of rationing on a waiting list, would be a desirable element of a society that fully realises the values of equality, democracy and community. Worker cooperatives would almost certainly play some role in a democratic economy, at least if an emancipatory alternative to capitalism still had a role

---

[6] McChesney (2014), chapter 12.

for markets[7]. Similarly, unconditional basic income is a plausible mechanism for distributing part of the income people receive in such a society, and citizen vouchers for journalism organisations is plausible mechanism for allocating resources to news media. In each case, the real utopia both embodies emancipatory values and constitutes a component of the institutional configuration of the destination.[8]

There are situations, however, in which it is much more problematic to try to build the future we want inside of the world as it is. This occurs when, for some specific institution, the optimal design in terms of promoting human flourishing depends on the surrounding social conditions. The optimal institutional design in a context of high social inequality, thin democracy, and weak community can be quite different from the optimal design in a social context of low inequality, deep democracy, and robust community. In such a situation it may be very difficult to build real utopias within existing social contexts, not just because of the political obstacles to emancipatory reforms but because of the contradictions between the intended and unintended consequences of such reforms.

An example: real utopian schools
A good example of the difficulties posed by the context-dependency of real utopian institutional designs is education. It is one thing to think about what sorts of schools would best meet the needs of children in a world with a strong sense of community and civic engagement, robust democracy, and broad economic and social equality, and quite another in a society with weak communities, thin democracy, high inequality and significant poverty. Consider the proposal for the conventional public school run by the State to be replaced by charter schools, organised by groups in civil society and financed by publicly funded vouchers.[9] The idea is that groups of people in civil society can get

---

[7] Some anti-capitalists argue that a democratic economy is inconsistent with any role for markets. This is most notably the position of Albert (2003) and Hahnel (2012). For a debate between my views and those of Robin Hahnel, see Hahnel and Wright (2016).

[8] The claims that these examples are indeed real utopias should, of course, be treated as conjectures. There will be people who for one reason or another will object to the claim that these examples are constitutive elements of an emancipatory alternative. Nevertheless, they do embody in significant ways emancipatory values that are in tension with capitalism, and at least they constitute institutional bridges to a possible future that can be built in the present.

[9] For a discussion of the difficulty of specifying a real utopian design for education, see Jaime Ahlberg and Harry Brighouse (2004) 'Education Not a Real Utopian Design' in *Politics and Society*, Volume 42, No. 1 pp 51-72.

together to form a school, govern it as they choose, and have it funded by vouchers that come with the students they attract. In some versions of this kind of proposal the physical space for the school would still be provided as a public amenity, but the board of directors of the charter school would hire staff, decide on the curriculum, and so on. In a way, this proposal is to schools what the citizen news voucher is to journalism: a way of combining the State's capacity to mobilise resources for some socially important good while letting citizens directly decide on the allocation to specific projects. It would seem to advance the values of democracy and self-determination, and perhaps the value of community and equality depending on the details of the design of the system.

This kind of funding and governance model could be a normatively attractive way of organising schools *in a world in which the values of equality, democracy and community were already broadly in place*. Certainly, schooling, like other institutions in such a world would involve much more democratic practices in their governance and be more deeply connected to the communities in which people lived. Charter schools organised by parents and others in a community could be a way of advancing the value of self-determination, and the funding for any particular school could then be determined by the number of students enrolled. But in a society like the United States, it is far less obvious that this kind of voucher and charter school system would be desirable. A universalised voucher system could easily end up being a substantial subsidy for expensive private schools, if schools were allowed to receive funds from other sources. If charter schools were free to set their own curriculum and admissions criteria, they could intensify the tendencies towards self-segregation on cultural, ethnic, ideological and religious grounds. Self-governing charter schools could become institutions of social exclusion regardless of how internally democratic and egalitarian were their practices. The result could easily become an educational landscape in which the real access to the educational conditions to live a flourishing life became even more unequal. An institutional design that would embody emancipatory values in a just world could thus potentially undermine those values in the present world. The negative unintended consequences could overwhelm the intended consequences.

Now, there certainly could be ways of imposing constraints on charter schools and the use of vouchers that could significantly reduce these risks. A public authority could impose curriculum constraints on charter schools, forcing them all, for example, to teach scientific evolution. Schools could be prevented from receiving extra funds from parents, thus reducing the risks of schools having grossly unequal resources. Furthermore, one can imagine all sorts of devices being instituted to reduce the ability of charter schools to self-segregate. So it is possible, perhaps, to design a voucher and charter school system that would promote values of equality, democracy and inclusive community even in an adverse social context if the right sorts of state-enforced regulations were in place. My point here is not to pass definitive judgment on charter schools and vouchers, but merely to show that their real utopian potential may be highly contingent on the nature of the social context in which they occur and the fine-grained details of the design of the rules of the game under which they operate.[10]

Another way of framing this issue of the problematic context-dependent effects of a real utopia is to return to our initial discussion of society as a game with rules and moves. The central strategic idea of real utopias is that it is possible to modify existing rules of the game in ways that have two kinds of consequences. First, the altered rules could potentially be part of an alternative game. And second the altered rules set in motion new sorts of things that people can do by virtue of the new rules. The cumulative effect of these new moves in the game is to potentially expand the social density of people actually engaging in more emancipatory social realities. This is the reasoning in the idea, for example, that an unconditional basic income – a change in the rules of the game of distribution in a capitalist economy – enables people to engage much more easily in the moves-in-the-game of building worker-owned cooperatives, and thus expand the scope of a cooperative market economy within capitalism.

The claim that there are contexts in which there are serious contradictions between the intended and unintended consequences of a real utopian institutional design means that the new rules of the game unleash moves in the game that subvert the emancipatory purposes of the altered rules. A school system reform that makes it easy to create and fund charter schools could be motivated by the desire to replace bureaucratic, hierarchical governance of schools with more participatory forms of civic engagement, and nevertheless make it easier for people to organise schools on the basis of exclusionary, sectarian principles.

---

[10] For a discussion of a real utopian proposal that includes charter schools funded by vouchers, see Samuel Bowles and Herbert Gintis, *Recasting Egalitarianism: New rules for communities, states and markets*, volume III, The Real Utopias Project (1998) London and New York: Verso.

Real utopian social control in a world of poverty, inequality and anomie[11]

The issue of deviance and social control poses deep (and interesting) challenges to the idea of real utopias. It is easy enough to formulate a substantial agenda of important ameliorative reforms of the criminal justice system and other institutional contexts that bear on deviance and social control. Many current practices violate conventional liberal norms and clearly generate great harms. To list only a few familiar examples: drug abuse should be decriminalised and regarded as a public health issue requiring good quality treatment available for addicts; mass incarceration in the United States should be ended for nonviolent crimes; police should be prevented from using racial and ethnic profiling; solitary confinement should never be used as a punishment, and the physical isolation of someone in detention from others should only be occur when there is a danger to others[12]; torture should be prohibited in all cases. There is no need to invoke emancipatory ideals to argue for these kinds of reforms. The difficulty is in formulating in a coherent and rigorous way an agenda of emancipatory reforms that would create real utopian institutions of social control.

In the case of education, as argued above, while we can, with some confidence, formulate many emancipatory design features that would work well within a just and democratic society, it can sometimes be much more difficult to figure out how those emancipatory features would actually work in a deeply unjust social environment. In the case of deviance and social control, it is much less obvious for some issues how to even specify the relevant institutional designs in a just society.

Consider the problem of how to deal with people who behave in ways that harm others, particularly when the harms involve physical violence. It is certainly the case that in any future real society, no matter how fully it embodied the values of equality, democracy and community, there will be people who pose a serious threat to others, and some of these situations would be impossible to handle simply through the informal enforcement of social norms. What is the emancipatory institutional design for such

---

[11] I am not an academic expert on the subject of deviance and social control. My comments here are therefore intended to frame an agenda of problems rather than provide even a provisional sketch of answers.

[12] 'Solitary confinement', as practiced in penal systems, involves many forms of deprivation other than simply being physically separated from other people. While it might still be sometimes necessary for a person to be physically separated from others because they are dangerous to others, the conditions of that separation should minimise the sense of social isolation and should not involve other deprivations.

circumstances of social control? Should such situations be dealt with by specialised personnel with special training? Or can the 'police' function be carried out by ordinary members of communities as part of their civic responsibilities? If a person commits harms and poses a threat, should they be confined within specialised institutions analogous to what we now call 'prisons'? What exactly would be the design of an 'emancipatory prison'? These are certainly difficult questions to answer with any degree of confidence.

What is more, as in the case of education, even if we can find solid answers to some of these design questions for a just world, it will not always be the case that attempting to put in place those design features in the existing world would have desirable consequences. It might be the case, for example, that if a society were characterised by a strong realisation of the values of equality, democracy and community, then a deprofessionalised, community-based police force would be desirable, while in the world as it is, this would set in motion destructive forms of vigilantism. In a just world, arbitration and mediation processes of various sorts could be the primary basis for resolving most disputes, without the encumbrance of complex procedural due process with lawyers and professional judges. But in our world, unless very carefully designed, such processes could easily become a way of denying people without power the possibility of redress of grievances. Or consider the problem of prisons. In a truly just world, the idea of using incarceration as deterrence for harmful deviance would probably be rejected.[13] If it were necessary to detain someone for reasons of public safety, the form of detention should be designed to still provide as full access as possible to the conditions for a flourishing life, given the physical constraint of detention. Since the point of detention would not be retribution but simply preventing the person from creating more harms to others, there would be no justification for material deprivations. In a world of high levels of inequality, poverty and oppression, such a design of non-punitive institutions of detention could create perverse incentives for some people to seek detention.

None of this means that it is impossible to bring the values of human emancipation to bear on the problem of deviance and social control, as

---

[13] I say 'probably' here because one of the pivotal components of a just world is deep democracy, and this means that in a just world people will have to figure out the trade-offs they face in more fully realising the values of equality/fairness, democracy/freedom and community/solidarity. Since there certainly will be trade-offs, people might still decide that the deterrence function of punishment is worth retaining, even though this might violate some standards of fairness or freedom.

illustrated in a number of the articles in this volume on the idea of non-penal real utopias. The core values of equality/ fairness, democracy/ freedom, and community/ solidarity remain vital standards for the diagnosis and critique of the world as it exists. And they remain essential for any assessment of ultimate goals for social transformation. The idea of real utopias is a useful way of linking a conception of emancipatory alternatives in an imagined future to strategies of transforming institutions in the present. But, in seeking to bring forth a new game of human flourishing, we must always be attentive to the complex interplay between our desired changes in the existing rules of the game and the array of positive and negative consequences of new moves of the game that those changes may set in motion.

References

Ahlberg, J. and Brighouse, H. (2014) 'Education Not a Real Utopian Design' in *Politics and Society* Volume 42, No. 1 pp 51-72

Albert, M. (2003) *Parecon* London: Verso

Alford, R. and Friedland, R. (1985) *Powers of Theory: Capitalism, the State and Democracy* Cambridge: Cambridge University Press

Gorz, A. (1967) *Strategy for Labor* Boston: Beacon Press

Hahnel, R. (2012) *Of the People, By the People: The case for a participatory economy* Oakland: AK Press

Hahnel, R. and Wright, E.O. (2016) *Alternatives to Capitalism: Proposals for a democratic economy* London York: Verso

McChesney, R. W (2014) *Blowing the Roof off the Twenty-First Century* New York: Monthly Review Press

Wright, E.O. (2010) *Envisioning Real Utopias* London: Verso)

Reimagining Citizenship: Justice, responsibility and non-penal real utopias

Emma Bell and David Scott[1]

Abstract

This article regards exclusive conceptions of citizenship as the principal stumbling block to developing alternatives to repressive penal policies. Indeed, exclusive communities foster mistrust and suspicion of the Other, leading to punitive responses to 'outsiders'. It is therefore argued that the very notion of citizenship needs to be 'reimagined' in such a way that it is genuinely inclusive and encourages shared responsibility, thus enabling us to go beyond exclusive communities and penal policies generative of irresponsibilities. The idea of an inclusive citizenship of the common, founded on justice and responsibility, is promoted as a real utopian vision. Transformative justice is put forward as one means of realising this vision by allowing citizens to collectively institute a genuinely new penal rationality.

Introduction

As has long been recognised, any attempts to develop alternatives to current penal practices are seriously hindered by the social distance created between offenders and a mythical law-abiding majority. The commonplace treatment of the majority of offenders as non-citizens precludes meaningful dialogue and debate with 'the citizenry'. In recent years, debate about penal issues amongst those who are seen to be worthy of citizenship has often been reduced to base populism (Pratt, 2007). Consequently, if we wish to move beyond exclusionary responses to 'crime' and social harm, the very notion of citizenship needs to be 'reimagined' in such a way that it is genuinely pluralist and inclusive, incorporating all those affected by harmful behaviour, whether they are

---

[1] Emma Bell is Professor of Contemporary British Politics at the Université de Savoie Mont Blanc and author of *Criminal Justice and Neoliberalism* (Basingstoke: Palgrave Macmillan, 2011) and *Soft Power and Freedom under the Coalition* (Basingstoke: Palgrave Macmillan, 2015). She was coordinator of the European Group for the Study of Deviance and Social Control from 2012-2015. Contact: bell.emma@neuf.fr. David Scott is senior lecturer in criminology at the Open University and his most recent book is *Emancipatory Politics and Praxis* (London: EG Press, 2016). He was coordinator of the European Group for the Study of Deviance and Social Control from 2009-2012. Contact: D.G.Scott@open.ac.uk

regarded as victims or offenders. This will entail rejecting all forms of penal fatalism in favour of a 'real utopian' approach (Wright, 2009) which seeks to recreate citizenship based on the principle of mutual responsibility and social action within institutions of 'the common'. Following Pierre Dardot and Christian Laval (2014), the 'common' is understood here as emancipatory praxis, as the shared activity through which people come together to develop alternatives to social problems, different from those proposed by either the State or private interests. It is a useful concept in that it is genuinely inclusive and encourages shared responsibility, thus enabling us to go beyond exclusive communities and penal policies generative of irresponsibilities. Rather than de-responsibilising citizens regarding their response to social harm, as occurs when criminal justice issues are captured by the State, a real utopian conception of citizenship, based on this idea of the common would allow individuals and communities to play an active role in finding solutions to shared problems.

This article begins by discussing how exclusive notions of citizenship are detrimental to the very existence of a moral community based on mutual responsibility. It then explores how citizenship may be reimagined following the logic of 'considered utopianism' (Bourdieu) to foster a genuinely 'common' approach to problems of social harm. Drawing on the work of radical social theorists such as Proudhon (2011) and Dardot and Laval (2014), it is argued that a 'reimagined citizenship of the common' should foster both justice and responsibility. It is a citizenship that goes beyond communitarianism which, while fostering responsibility, often fails to promote justice, focusing as it does on the level of community rather than of state institutions. It is recognised that practices of the common will not emerge naturally and spontaneously but must be instituted (Dardot and Laval, 227). The final part of the paper aims to demonstrate how constructing non-penal real utopias may both result from and help to institute a reimagined citizenship of the common. Picking up on Enrique Dussel's (2013), notion of 'liberation praxis', it suggests that citizenship must not be merely inclusive but also transformative if it is to be truly just. Transformative justice is thus promoted as a means of instituting a genuinely new non-penal rationality through emancipatory praxis.

Exclusive citizenship and irresponsibility

Conditional citizenship

As Reiner has pointed out, 'the term "citizenship" is now more often used in political discussion in exclusive, nationalistic, and particularistic terms, focusing on barriers to the status of citizen, with the stress on hurdles, testing, pedigree, and desert' (Reiner, 2010: 244). This trend has largely coincided with the rise of neoliberalism with its emphasis on the need for individual citizens to become more 'active' in dealing with their own problems, rather than relying on the State. Consequently, citizenship has become increasingly conditional upon behaviour (Dwyer, 1998), upon individuals' capacity to accept personal responsibility. Those who are seen to have flouted the rules of the game are excluded from the normal rights of citizenship, notably 'social citizenship' (Marshall, 1950), as they find their social security benefits withdrawn. Access to political citizenship is also increasingly restricted: for foreign nationals, it is increasingly subject to formal testing and economic status – for example, citizens or settled foreign nationals wishing to sponsor their partner or spouse to join them in the United Kingdom must prove that they have a minimum gross annual income of £18,600. The civil rights of citizenship are also hard to enforce as individual freedoms are threatened by new surveillance technologies and strengthened police powers.

Renewed focus on the responsibilities rather than the rights of citizens has been a useful way for neoliberal governments to scapegoat individuals for social problems whilst simultaneously justifying reductions in state spending. Yet, the focus on the individual over the State was much criticised, notably by New Labour seeking to build a 'third way' between the excessive individualism of the Thatcher years and the statism of the post-war period, and by Cameron seeking to 'detoxify' the Conservative Party of its 'nasty' (May, 2002), uncaring image. For both, the active citizen was not to be regarded solely as an individual but as a member of a wider community. What Jean and John Comaroff describe as the 'Second Coming of Civil Society' was to be 'the ultimate magic bullet in the Age of Millennial Capitalism' (2001: 44), capable of providing the necessary social glue to hold together societies fragmented by the ravages of neoliberalism, whilst enabling successive politicians to rebrand their politics. For New Labour, civil society was to be boosted by communitarianism which would ensure that individuals assumed responsibility, not for their own ends, but in the best interests of the community as a whole. For Cameron's conservatives, the 'Big Society' was to enable individuals to work together to create 'communities with oomph – neighbourhoods who are in charge of their own destiny, who feel if they club together and get involved they can shape the world around them' (Cameron, 2010a). In both cases, individuals and communities were to be liberated from the State and all of its coercive capacity. Yet, this vision ignored the coercive power of communities themselves.

Coercive communities and deresponsibilisation

For Barbara Hudson, communities can be extremely coercive, especially when they seek to enforce values, often imposing 'a constriction of freedom of choice about how one lives' and grouping together to exclude those who fail to conform (Hudson, 2003: 91). Erik Olin Wright has also drawn attention to the fact that communities can foster 'exclusionary solidarities' as well as 'universalistic ones' (Wright, 2009: 267). The problem is often one of responsibility as the onus tends to be placed on individuals to integrate into the community rather than on the community to integrate individuals: responsibility is often 'a one-way street' (Hudson, ibid: 107).

Even more problematic is the fact that communities habitually divest themselves of responsibility altogether for individuals who they deem to be unworthy of citizenship. Offenders in particular are often cast out of the community, both physically – in prison – and symbolically – by loss of the basic rights of citizenship. This is illustrated by the loss of the right to vote. As Duff has explained, the law can no longer bind us as citizens, as it is no longer 'the law of an "us" to which [offenders] unqualifiedly belong': it becomes the law of a 'we' that they no longer form a part of (Duff, 2005: 213). Yet, the current Prime Minister regards stripping offenders of such essential civil rights as entirely normal. David Cameron, commenting on the issue following the European Court of Human Rights' declaration that the UK's current blanket ban on voting is incompatible with article 3 of the European Convention on Human Rights, declared, 'when people commit a crime and go to prison, they should lose their rights, including the right to vote' (Cameron, 2010b). The exclusivity of communities is thus supported, and even encouraged, by the State, demonstrating the importance of moving beyond the State when developing real utopias, a point we shall return to below.

Once communities exclude 'undesirables' from their midst, they are effectively exempt from further responsibility for them, despite the government rhetoric of community responsibilisation. Such deresponsibilisation is regarded as legitimate once the community is accorded the status of victim. Indeed, as crime is always seen as being perpetrated *against* the community rather than being produced *in and by* the community, responsibility is seen to lie solely with offending individuals. This line of thinking helps to construct offenders as 'Other', as lying outside the moral community. As Zygmunt Bauman has so eloquently explained, once such social distance is created, undesirables can be dehumanised and 'moral inhibition' regarding their treatment suspended (1989: 25). Using the work of Helen Fein, he effectively demonstrates how they are placed outside the 'universe of obligation', cast into a world where moral precepts do not bind. Punitive rather than welfarist responses to social harm are thus favoured.

The failure of liberal penal policies

Liberal penal polices have attempted to foster the development of more inclusive communities underpinned by the notion of responsibility. Communities have been encouraged to take more responsibility for dealing with harmful behaviour and reintegrating offenders whilst wrongdoers themselves have been encouraged to take more responsibility for their own actions. One of the most influential liberal penological approaches in this mould is the 'responsibility and justice paradigm' (Scott, 2001). Primarily influential in the 1990s and 2000s, this approach accepts the legitimacy of state punishments but advocates a new, more inclusive relationship between the prison and community (King and Morgan, 1980; Woolf, 1991). Prisons should be more like the community with 'permeable walls' and stronger 'community ties' (Woolf, 1991, para 1.148). Prisons should also be normalised in the sense that basic living standards and legal protection ought to be the same for all citizens, whether they reside inside or outside prison. Yet even this liberal rhetoric can be misleading. The prisoner is to be treated with 'respect' only if they make responsible choices whilst inside (Woolf, 1991; Scott, 2001). Community responsibility to reintegrate offenders is only to be activated once offenders deem themselves worthy by demonstrating their own capacity to take responsibility. In recent times, the new conservative government has sought to get communities involved in the rehabilitation of prisoners. The Justice Secretary, Michael Gove, exhorted ordinary citizens to 'help the hungry, the sick and the imprisoned' by playing a role in prisoner rehabilitation (Gove, 2015) whilst the Prime Minister encouraged businesses to offer former prisoners a second chance by providing them with employment (Cameron, 2016). Prisoners themselves are to be responsibilised for their own rehabilitation, with privileges and earned release determined by participation in educational activity in particular (Gove, 2015). Yet, in continuity with other 'liberal' reforms, community responsibility is conditional and selective: only those wrongdoers who are considered responsible are deemed worthy of reintegration into the moral community. As Cameron put it, the aim is to find the 'diamonds in the rough and [help] them shine' (Cameron, 2016). The 'irredeemables' can presumably then legitimately be kept apart from society, preferably behind bars.

The possibility of the moral inclusion of wrongdoers is thus generally predicated on a logic of exclusion. The current focus on the normalisation of prisons through education, as promoted by Gove, can be understood as playing a role in shaping hegemonic understandings of the most appropriate responses to 'crime' and social harm. However, imprisonment is profoundly unnatural. Without doubt, prisons are cruel, lonely and destructive places. Confinement within such painful, isolating and brutal institutions is compounded by the constant menace of systematic abuse, maltreatment and ultimately dehumanisation. Threats to dignity, self respect, personal safety and other pre-requisites of humanity seem endemic to the largely hidden world of the prison. The problem is that current policies and initiatives aimed at reform and education are defined and defended on the terrain of the State. The prison aims to coerce offenders into being responsible citizens, ignoring the fact that prisons are hardly the appropriate environment for such purposes. There is an urgent requirement to develop non-penal real utopian interventions, grounded in non-state understandings and practices of responsibilities and justice, which may effectively responsibilise *all* citizens, whether they are offenders, victims or potential victims of crime. It is necessary to reimagine the very concept of citizenship on which inclusive communities may thrive. We propose a real utopian vision of citizenship based on responsibility and justice which we hope may invite non-penal real utopian interventions to deal with offending behaviour. Rather than embedding 'penal utopias', it is hoped that these visions may open up possibilities for real *non-penal* utopian alternatives to the penal rationale.

Towards a real utopian citizenship of the common

Citizenship as real utopia
Reimagining citizenship entails abandoning fatalism – the idea that only exclusionary responses are appropriate for problematic behaviour – in favour of a 'considered utopianism'. Following Ernst Bloch, Pierre Bourdieu described this strategy as one whereby we 'work *collectively* on analyses able to launch

realistic projects and actions closely matched to the objective processes of the order they are meant to transform' (Bourdieu, 1997: 128, authors' emphasis). This idea fits closely with Wright's notion of real utopia: 'utopian ideals that are grounded in the real potentials of humanity, utopian destinations that have accessible waystations, utopian designs of institutions that can inform our practical tasks of navigating a world of imperfect conditions for social change' (Wright, 2009: 4). With regard to developing a more inclusive notion of citizenship on which non-penal real utopian solutions might be based, this entails delineating the actually existing principles which would inform such a notion and exploring the real potentialities of collective action. Non-penal real utopias are about thinking differently, visualising new possibilities and realities and facilitating transformative change (Scott, 2013). They involve enhancing life and promoting human flourishing and showing that another world is possible (Wright, 2009; this volume). Yet, they must be feasible and desirable – they must be possible in our historical conjuncture and also meet the demands of justice – that is, be democratic, be rights-regarding and facilitate (or are at least be consistent with) an equitable distribution of the social product and the meeting of human need (Dussel, 1985).

Key principles for inclusive citizenship
The first key principle which should inform an inclusive notion of citizenship is that of horizontality. Citizenship is commonly understood as a vertical relationship with the State whereby the latter determines the terms of that relationship in a top-down manner. Indeed, citizenship has been historically tied to the nation-state under whose authority associated rights and obligations are determined (Isin and Turner, 2002: 3). Although the State claims to delegate greater power to communities, it is essentially the State which determines which citizens should have access to which rights. Following John Hoffman, it is necessary to go beyond the State when thinking about citizenship since its monopoly on the 'legitimate' use of force means that those subject to force are necessarily prevented from exercising the rights and duties of citizenship (Hoffman, 2004). Furthermore, and this point is particularly relevant with regard to penal policy, 'the use of force is inimical to conflict resolution: only negotiation and arbitration can resolve conflicts of interest, since force crushes agency, and the agency of all the parties is essential if a dispute is to be successfully tackled' (Hoffman, 2004: 173).

Agency is the second key principle which must underpin inclusive citizenship. As suggested above, agency is effectively denied in mainstream notions of citizenship as communities are divested of responsibility for 'undesirable' citizens. Those who are excluded from citizenship, whilst deemed responsible for their own exclusion, are also denied the opportunity to exercise agency in terms of determining how reparation can be made for harmful behaviour. As Hoffman underlines, the agency of *all* parties to a dispute is essential. This leads us to the third key principle supporting inclusive citizenship: the idea that citizenship should be plural, excluding no one. This means including those on the margins and periphery of society as well as those in the centre.

Fourthly, all should be included on equal terms. As Nancy Fraser has explained, there must be 'parity of participation' based on 'social arrangements that permit all (adult) members of society to interact with one another as peers'. The principle of equality is best upheld by affirming basic human rights, not limited to narrowly-defined, and often conditional, citizenship rights. We thus suggest that it is necessary to go beyond 'remarshalling citizenship', as Robert Reiner advises, calling for a restoration of the political, social and civil rights of citizenship (2010: 261). Whilst this would certainly lead to a more inclusive notion of citizenship than that which currently exists, it is a version of citizenship which is understood primarily vis-à-vis the State rather than as solidaristic interaction with other citizens.

A citizenship of the common

These key principles ought to underpin what we describe as 'an inclusive citizenship of the common', based on justice and responsibility. This idea finds its origins in commonism. Commonism is a form of socialism promoting communities of mutual care and support and the collective organisation of the relations of production so that it can meet human needs for all. The concept has a long tradition. It finds its origins in the ideas of early English socialists such as Gerrard Winstanley (1649/2010) whose writings and activism aimed to emancipate 'common land' for the people and liberate the 'spirit of community' and the French socialist tradition of 'mutualism' promoted by Pierre-Joseph Proudhon[2] (2011). Yet, it is as a contemporary social movement that it has recently attracted renewed attention (Dardot and Laval, 2014). It aims to build non-authoritarian partnerships and networks of cooperation and collaboration in everyday settings such as the workplace, family, and wider

---

[2] Whilst we give a positive appraisal of the writings of Proudhon on justice, responsibility and non-penal real utopias, we distance ourselves from his notoriously anti-emancipatory writings on women and gender issues.

community (Shantz, 2013). Symbolically, commonism is a means of identifying our 'common heritage', recognising each person's 'common humanity' and facilitating 'meaningful participation in decision-making processes around housing, work, education and food' (ibid: 11). Of central concern is the development of anti-capitalist real utopian practices in the here and now, but there is also interest in non-penal means of resolving conflicts and addressing social harms.

Commonism questions the legitimacy of authoritarian power, structural inequalities and institutionalised practices of domination, exploitation and dehumanisation. Commonism morally condemns coercion and violence in all their manifestations, promoting instead non-authoritarian ways of organising human life through free agreements, voluntary associations and mutual reciprocation. Rather than cajole, control and destroy, commonism is life-affirming and promotes what Jun (2010: 56) calls 'vitality': the point is to help people live. Commonism is radically egalitarian with a strong emphasis on ethical judgement, diversity, freedom, direct participation in decision-making and the democratisation of political representation. As a basic principle of human dignity, ordinary people should be able to speak for themselves and democratic procedures ensure that their voice is both heard and listened to (Scott, 2016a, 2016b).

For Dardot and Laval, 'the common' is not just about ideals or institutions, it is about social action and *praxis*. This is what gives the notion of 'an inclusive citizenship of the common' its real utopian dimension: it is utopian in the sense that it goes beyond what actually exists, beyond a mere reformist agenda, yet it is real to the extent that it can only exist as lived experience. Commonism must therefore emerge from the common actions of *all* citizens. Dardot and Laval (2014) imagine a 'federation of commons' that is not limited to the boundaries of a nation state but one which is plural and decentred, based not on formal rights granted by the State but instead on practice. It aims to be 'popular' without being 'populist', guided by commonly-held principles such as dignity, solidarity, equity and freedom. It is also emancipatory in the sense that it enables individuals to directly participate in bringing about social change. Indeed, emancipatory praxis occurs when an individual consistently acts directly in accordance with the normative values and principles of human liberation – that is integrating their broader ethical worldview within daily practice (Scott, 2016c). Fundamentally, this entails taking on responsibility to act in the common good.

Concretely, in terms of developing a citizenship of the common, commonism may encourage collective practices such as 'associational democracy' whereby collective organisations come together to take decisions and directly influence the political process (Wright, 2009). This would certainly encourage an active, emancipatory politics of the common, provided that these organisations remain as porous as possible, avoiding an exclusive membership ethos. In the current neoliberal context in which many different states are facing the same problems of inequality and injustice caused by transnational corporate power networks, it is also necessary that these groups do not confine themselves to the nation state but join together across borders to seek common solutions. Associational approaches are particularly attractive, addressing as they do the problems of irresponsibility highlighted above by allowing citizens to take joint responsibility for social problems and engage in a common endeavour to institute new practices.

Commonism thus directly challenges state power from below through everyday collective actions and praxis. *Contra* Proudhon, we cannot assume that these practices of the common will emerge naturally and spontaneously (Dardot and Laval, 227). It is necessary to think strategically about how to institute the common. In other words, the utopia of the common must be *real*. In the next section, we will attempt to show how constructing non-penal real utopias may be regarded as both emerging from and helping to construct a truly common notion of citizenship.

Non-penal real utopias of the common

Non-penal real utopianism should draw upon both a radical imagination that steps outside of the assumptions of the penal rationale and currently existing community-based interventions that engage with human troubles and problematic conduct. Exploring alternatives to exclusionary penal practices should be regarded as social action, as part of exercising citizenship as praxis. This entails reclaiming the issue from the State in order to develop alternative forms of justice firmly rooted in inclusive communities: from stateless citizenship it may perhaps be possible to imagine forms of stateless justice, a genuine 'justice of the common'.

The dangers of community responses to social harm
Moving beyond the State will entail citizens assuming real responsibility for the social problems that affect them, engaging in collaborative practices to

address these in a meaningful way. It is not about communities getting involved in the existing institutions of the State, such as assuming a sense of 'ownership' of the prison (Faulkner, 2003: 306), but about communities being genuinely 'active' in developing inclusive, non-penal solutions. So far, attempts to resolve issues arising from harmful behaviour in the community context, notably restorative justice initiatives, have frequently been captured by the State (see, for example, Convery et al, 2008; Copson, this volume). Restorative justice, in placing the victim at the centre of analysis; providing a voice to all parties, including the voice of the offender; downplaying or removing coercive solutions; placing relationships at the heart of the response to a given problematic or troublesome act; focusing on positive and constructive *outcomes* and emphasising fixing, compensating, repairing or restoring balance, can certainly be deployed as a non-penal intervention. Yet, in practice, restorative justice is often punishment under a different name. Whatever the definition or benevolent intentions of practitioners, the application of pain infliction continues, but disturbingly now its reality is disguised (Scott, 2009). Restorative justice remains a vague and illusive concept. On a practical level, the concern is that the capitalist state is still given penal power, but that legal rights, safeguards and protections of wrongdoers are in effect removed, resulting in potentially heavier pain infliction than through the penal law. Restorative and shaming interventions, whilst non-penal in nature, have been and are used in addition to existing penal responses. Non-custodial responses to wrongdoing *must never* follow the logic that there must be a strengthening of community punishments to appear politically plausible. Finally, they do nothing to address structural inequalities and imbalances in power. There is no consideration of the implications (or harms) of the inequitable distribution of social product or how life choices, including the perpetration of wrongs and harms, are shaped by structural contexts. This example of restorative justice demonstrates that there is no guarantee that the community response/ stateless justice will be free of domination and coercion, especially when applied in profoundly unjust contexts. Non-penal real utopian solutions to social harm must therefore seek above all to promote genuine justice and responsibility.

Justice, responsibility and non-penal utopias
In his work on mutualism, Proudhon addressed the issue of justice and social harm (1989). He grounded his notions of justice in respect, inherent dignity and guaranteed mutually reciprocating relations. Citizens had a duty to protect

the dignity of their neighbour and ensure that there was 'natural harmony'. However, Proudhon also recognised that conflict and troubles would be inevitable. Proudhon, himself imprisoned for three years where he experienced solitary confinement and 'forced relationality' and where his health was, in the long term, broken, was a penal abolitionist. For him, no authority had the right to punish: punishment has nothing to do with justice, only with 'iniquitous and atrocious vengeance'. He was against penal servitude and argued that punishment was symbolic of the moral problems regarding inequality and injustice. Justice required that conflicts be handled through non-violent methods, such as reparations. There was for Proudhon a need to replace penal discipline with the morality of justice (Hyman, 1979).

Yet, Proudhon's vision of justice is limited to the extent that it fails to focus on the wider context in which injustice may occur. Enrique Dussel (2013: 413), on the other hand, though his vision of 'liberation praxis', demonstrates how we might broaden this focus by showing us how exactly justice may replace penal discipline. Central to the liberation praxis of Dussel (2013) is the 'paradigm of life'. Without ensuring that there are appropriate material conditions, there can be no justice. Both his understanding of responsibilities and justice are predicated on 'an ethics of life' (Dussel, 2013: 108), a 'community of living beings' where the 'ethical duty [is] to reproduce and develop the life of the human subject' (ibid: 217). For Dussel, there is an ethical responsibility to ensure that those who are in an 'asymmetrical' position to us – that is they have less power and resources than we do – are treated with dignity and that their basic needs are met. Such a responsibility does not have to be demanded by another person, but rather arises automatically through appearance of 'the face'. Through an encounter with, or knowledge of, a weaker person we are compelled to abandon reciprocity and undertake non-reciprocal acts of hospitality. Praxis 'is this and nothing more' (Dussel, 1985: 170): praxis is to make the stranger, the lost, the outcast and begotten part of our moral universe and to actively respond in aid of their plight.

Dussel (2013: 207) refers to such people, who are excluded, marginalised denied dignity and 'affected by a situation akin to death' as 'victims'. Liberation praxis entails not only recognising that such victims of social injustice are ethical subjects who have legitimate demands upon us in terms of meeting their needs but also ensuring that their voice is heard (Scott, 2016b). Victims are often silenced or their voice cannot be heard and liberation praxis demands that we challenge the validity of such denials from the perspective of the victim themselves. This means listening and learning to learn from victims. Whilst there is 'no single voice of all human kind' and to be treated the same is not equivalent to being treated equally, we must recognise the fluidity and contingency of categorisations; demonstrate a willingness to pay attention to the voices of 'concrete others'; and acknowledge that each voice comes from a specifically situated position, standpoint or worldview rather than a generalised and abstract universalism (Hudson, 2003; Scott, 2016a). Equality will be 'complex' (i.e. equity) but we must somehow find a way in which it can encompass the diversity of human subjectivities. For real justice there is a need for reflexivity and the promotion of freedom and autonomy; to hear different voices; and reconstruct a notion of universality that is sensitive to social contexts (Hudson, 2003).

A crucial analytical and normative innovation of liberation praxis is to view the world from the 'exterior' – to look at the world from the outside through the eyes of the marginalised and excluded victim (Scott, 2106a). The engagement with community then is through an external lens. Liberation praxis looks at life from its negation (Dussel, 2008). Ethical responsibility and principles of justice are based on the experiences of those on the outside of the system: the Other. More than this, Dussel (2008) develops a clear set of normative political principles upon which community values and attitudes can be externally evaluated. The 'formal principle' allows procedural safeguards ensuring the promotion of the voice of all people (including 'victims') so that a community is genuinely based on participatory democracy. The 'material principle' notes that the social organisation of any society must be grounded in principles of distributive and social justice. Finally, the 'feasibility principle' looks to promote and foster the most appropriate ways of delivering justice in the here and now.

The key question is not simply 'is this just?' but also 'who is granted justice and to whom is justice denied' (Hudson, 2003)? Those who most lack justice (and indeed also security) are the poor, powerless and disadvantaged. Too often their sufferings are neglected or marginalised; too often their voice de-legitimated; and too often their claims to equal respect denied. For Dussel (1985: 65) liberation praxis should result in 'liberative justice':

> Liberative justice, which does not give to each what is due within the law and the prevailing order, but grants to all what they deserve in their dignity as others. Thus liberative justice is not legal justice, whether distributive or communicative, but real

justice – that is, subversive: subverting the established unjust
order. (ibid)

An ethics of justice requires acknowledgement and respect towards people not
like us. Hudson (2003) refers to this as 'justice as alterity' and it has significant
connections to Dussel's (1985) liberative justice:

> Justice involves recognition of the likeness in the sense of shared
> humanness, but not insistence on reduction or elimination of
> differences, rather the respecting of differences. (Hudson 2003:
> 190)

Justice as alterity demands that we meet the other without violence and this
approach in effect translates into *love of the other*. In terms of slogans, whilst
equality, liberty and fraternity still pertain we could perhaps articulate them
today in terms of recognition and respect for irreducible differences; freedom
from dominance and oppression of the majority; and solidarity with, and
responsibility for, sufferers. Like Dussel (2013), critical scholars such as Barbara
Hudson (2003) have also argued that our responsibilities to other humans
stretch way beyond our close family, friends and community to also include
the 'stranger', 'outcast' and others not known to us directly or sharing similar
characteristics or social backgrounds. We must learn to accept differences,
acknowledge the existence of the stranger/ 'victim', but also to recognise what
we share – *common humanity*. It is important that rather than focusing on the
'enemies within', we should look to find new suitable friends (Scott, 2013):

> Far too often, in the real rather than the theoretical world, the
> response to the presence of the stranger – the application for
> entry, the beggar, the disorderly and disreputable – is to confine
> them, to segregate them, or to exclude them altogether. Prisons,
> detention centres, ghettoes and gated estates demonstrate the
> refusal of hospitality and the desire to avoid encounters with
> strangers, rather than to respond to their claims and needs.
> (Hudson, 2011: 120)

Drawing on the insights of Hudson (2011) and Dussel (2013), Scott (2016a) has
argued that liberative praxis leads us down an emancipatory path that
intimately connects debates around justice and responsibilities with the
promotion of human rights. From an abolitionist perspective, Scott (2016a)
argues that such a human rights agenda will always be 'unfinished' for it must

be forged through emancipatory struggle and acts of defiance. An 'aboltionist human rights agenda' from below will continuously evolve and should be focussed on making more visible the institutionally-structured violence of incarceration alongside broader structural inequalities that blight human life. Such abolitionist critiques must aim to reveal the ideological closure of the existing foundations of legal rights and reignite their more emancipatory potential. Abolitionist human rights agendas therefore move beyond a merely humanitarian approach reflecting the content of international covenants and grounded in the amelioration of suffering. Theirs is an agenda that reflects the liberation struggles of the powerless and contributes to emancipatory and transformative praxis. Consequently, for Scott (2016a) the aspiration of those struggling for justice and human rights must be for freedom from domination and the removal of the causes of human suffering.

For abolitionists such as Hudson (2003, 2011) and Scott (2016a) human rights must reflect our responsibilities *for* the Other rather than for the self. To protect human rights, society must learn to hear and learn to learn from the voice of the estranged Other, recognise their inherent dignity, and meet them with non-violence (Scott, 2016b). Radical alternatives should be historically immanent, in place of an existing sanction and not be grounded in authoritarian forms of domination (Scott, 2013). Non-penal interventions must reflect the normative frameworks of human rights, democratic accountability and social justice (Scott, 2013, 2016c). In this sense, the 'abolitionist real utopia' (see Scott and Bell, this volume) perspective maps directly onto the concerns of those of Wright (2010) and Dussel (2013).

For Dussel (2013), liberative justice is not just about creating freedom for victims, but also responsibility for the social, economic and political transformation of the conditions and structures which create victimhood in the first instance. In an argument reminiscent of that found in commonism, the aim of the praxis of liberation is to create symmetrical relationships resulting in mutual aid and responsibility. There is an 'ethical obligation of "transforming" the reality that produced victims' (Dussel, 2013: 288) and the creation of a new 'mutual responsibility' (ibid: 281).

> The excluded should not be merely *included* in the *old* system – as this would be to introduce the Other into the Same – but rather ought to participate as equals in a new *institutional moment* ... This is a struggle not for *inclusion*, but for *transformation*. (Dussel, 2008: 89, *emphases in the original*)

Transformation must entail direct engagement with the 'victim'. For the purposes of non-penal utopian justice, the victim here must be understood widely to include *all* victims of social injustice, whether they have broken the law and caused harm or not. The encounter with the victim, for Dussel (2013: 352) is the *'possible* utopia' (*emphasis in the original*). We must work, day-in-day-out with the people of the 'present utopia: the peripheral peoples, the oppressed classes' (Dussel, 1985: 48) Emancipatory politics and praxis must then exercise an *'ethical-utopian reason'* (Dussel, 2013: 223, *emphasis in the original*) and draw upon the 'feasibility' principle to build upon interventions that are real and viable in our historical moment.

Unleashing transformative justice
We therefore have a responsibility when developing non-penal responses to social harm to work in common with all those affected in a common endeavour to develop a just response in opposition to the often unjust responses of the State. It is an opportunity to create a counter-revolution in response to these exclusionary responses by proposing a new non-penal rationality that is genuinely transformative. A citizenship of the common, and an emancipatory politics and praxis, ought therefore to favour transformative justice. Ruth Morris (2000:3) describes transformative justice as follows:

> Transformative justice uses the power unleashed by the harm of crime to let those most affected find truly creative, healing solutions. Transformative justice includes victims, offenders and their families, and their communities, and invites them to use the past to dream of a better future ... Transformative justice recognises the wrongs of all victims, and recognises also that sooner or later, we are all both victims and offenders.

Transformative justice means handling conflicts and troubles by listening, acknowledging the victim's injury and hurt and finding ways that can lead to healing and just settlements for all. Transformative justice is victim-focused, but it recognises equally the victims of problematic and troublesome interpersonal harms and the 'victim' (Dussel, 2013) of the harms generated by 'distributive' and social injustices, multi-national corporations and state domination (Morris, 2000: 5). The focus is justice and the transformation of context and situations characterised by injustice and the facilitation of more caring, cooperative and inclusive communities. Only transformative social justice can lead to transformative non-penal justice: transformative justice is impossible in unjust contexts.

This goal of social transformation leads to an emphasis on finding answers, recognising wrong done, providing safety and security, providing an appropriate form of redress and helping the victim find new meanings and understandings (Morris, 2000). But it also means meeting needs – housing, relational, therapeutic – and reaffirming life. Transformative justice is about restoring 'world' for victims, providing them with voice and helping to create or rebuild 'vitality' – the paradigm of life (Dussel, 2013). The struggle for transformative justice is at the heart of our daily lives – interventions, direct action, writing, speaking, engaging with people about the issues that matter – living a life that connects with our principles and responsibility for Others: emancipatory politics and praxis.

Conclusion: commonism, real utopias and transformative justice

In neoliberal societies, individualism and competition constantly undermine the 'common' as the ties that bind us become weakened. As society becomes increasingly atomised, collective participation in social, institutional and political structures is limited, allowing power to become ever-more concentrated at the top. In a context of 'decollectivisation' and profound social inequality (Dardot and Laval, 2014: 15), attempts to reinvigorate communities have been unsuccessful. The discourse of individual responsibilisation has paradoxically justified the irresponsibility of communities with regard to individuals who are thought to have failed in their duties to the community. Once deresponsibilised in this way, communities have allowed the State to exercise its repressive power with regard to those who are deemed unworthy of citizenship.

A reimagined citizenship of the common offers a possibility to citizens to become genuinely active in imagining alternative social structures. Faced with the significant hegemonic power of the neoliberal model, such a concept of citizenship is unlikely to emerge spontaneously. Conscious efforts need to be made to get citizens involved in common projects to radically reimagine the way that society is currently ordered, thus fostering mutual responsibility. Dussel's concept of 'liberation praxis' allows us to imagine how we may assume responsibility for developing a *just* social order. It suggests that citizen action needs to be transformative, capable of overturning hegemonic rationalities of all kinds. In that sense, it is utopian, but it is also real, grounded in the praxis of collective action. It is through working collectively to develop common responses to social problems such as crime that the notion of a citizenship of the common can go beyond the ideal to become a practical, transformative reality, capable of generating non-penal responses to social problems.

References

Bauman, Z. (1989) *Modernity and the Holocaust* New York: Cornell University Press

Bourdieu, P. (1997) 'A Reasoned Utopia and Economic Fatalism', Speech of acceptance of the *Ernst-Bloch Preis der Stadt Ludwigshafen*

Braithwaite, J. (1989) *Reintegrative Shaming* Cambridge: Cambridge University Press

Cameron, D. (2016) 'Prison Reform', speech to the Policy Exchange, London, 8 February

Cameron, D. (2010a) Speech on the Big Society. http://www.telegraph.co.uk/news/politics/david-cameron/7897445/David-Cameron-launches-his-Big-Society.html (consulted 13 May 2016)

Cameron, D. (2010b) HC deb 3 November 2010, Volume 517, col. 921

Comaroff, J. and Comaroff, J. L. (eds) (2001) *Millennial Capitalism and the Culture of Neoliberalism* Durham: Duke University Press

Convery, U., Haydon, D., Moore, L. and Scraton, P. (2008) 'Children, Rights and Justice in Northern Ireland: Community and Custody' in *Youth Justice* Volume 8, No. 3 pp 245-263

Dardot, P. and Laval C. (2014) *Commun: Essai sur la révolution au XXIe siècle* Paris : La Découverte

Duff, R. A. (2005) 'Introduction: Crime and Citizenship' in *Journal of Applied Philosophy* Volume 22, No. 3 pp 211-16

Dussel, E. (1985) *Philosophy of Liberation* Oregon: Wipf and Stock

Dussel, E. (1998) *The Underside of Modernity* New York: Humanity Books

Dussel, E. (2008) *Twenty Theses on Politics* Durham: Duke University Press

Dussel, E. (2013) *The ethics of Liberation* Durham: Duke University Press

Dwyer, P. (1998) 'Conditional Citizens? Welfare Rights and Responsibilities in the Late 1990s' in *Critical Social Policy* Volume 18, No. 4 pp. 493-515

Etzioni, A. (1995) The *Spirit of Community* London: Fontana Press

Faulkner, D. (2003) 'Taking Citizenship Seriously: Social capital and criminal justice in a changing world' in *Criminal Justice* Volume 3, No. 3 pp 287–315

Gove, M. (2015) 'The treasure in the heart of man – making prisons work', speech delivered to the Prisoners' Learning Alliance, London, 17 July.

Hoffman, J. (2004) *Citizenship Beyond the State* London: Sage

Hudson, B.A. (1993a) *Penal Policy and Social Justice* London: Macmillan

Hudson, B.A. (2000) 'Punishing the Poor: Dilemmas of justice and difference', in Haffernan, W. and Kleinig; J. (eds) *From Social Justice to Criminal Justice* New York: Oxford University Press

Hudson, B.A. (2003) *Justice in the Risk Society* London: Sage

Hudson, B.A. (2011) 'All the people in all the world: a cosmopolitan perspective on migration and torture' in Baillet, C, and Franko-Aas, K. (eds) (2011) *Cosmopolitan Justice and its Discontents* Abingdon: Routledge

Hudson, B.A. (2012) 'Who needs justice? Who needs security' in Hudson, B.A. and Ugelvik, S. (eds) (2012) *Justice and Security in the 21st Century* Abingdon: Routledge

Hyams, E. (1979) *Pierre-Joseph Proudhon* London: John Murray

Isin, E. F. and Turner B. S. (2002) 'Citizenship studies: An introduction' pp 1-10 in Isin, E. F. and Turner B. S. (eds) *Handbook of Citizenship Studies* London: Sage

Jordan, B. (1993) *Theory of poverty and social exclusion* Cambridge: Polity Press

Kelly, D. (1994) 'Introduction' in Proudhon, P.J. (1994) *What is Property?* Cambridge: Cambridge University Press

King, R. and Morgan, R. (1980) *The Future of the Prison* Farnworth: Gower Publishing Ltd

Marshall, T. H. (1950) *Citizenship and Social Class*; reprinted in T.H. Marshall, (1963 [1950]) *Sociology at the Crossroads* London: Heinemann

Mathiesen T. (1974) *The Politics of Abolition* New York: John Wiley and Sons

May, T. (2002) 'Speech to the Conservative Party Conference', http://conservative-speeches.sayit.mysociety.org/speech/600929

Morris, R. (2000) *Stories of Transformative Justice* Toronto: Canadian Scholars Press

Proudhon, P.J. (1989) *General Idea of Revolution in the Nineteenth Century* London: Pluto Press

Proudhon, P.J. (2011) 'Justice in the Revolution and in the Church' in McKay, I. (ed) (2011) *Property is Theft* Edinburgh: AK Press

Proudhon, P.J. (2011b) 'What is property?' in McKay, I. (ed) (2011) *Property is Theft* Edinburgh: AK Press

Reiner, R. (2010) 'Citizenship, Crime, Criminalization: Marshalling a Social Democratic Perspective' in *New Criminal Law Review* Volume 13, No. 2 pp 241-261

Scott, D. (2001) 'Prisoners' Rights and the "Responsibilities and Justice Paradigm": Which Rights? Whose Responsibility? What Justice?' in *Strangeways* pp 5-7

Scott, D. (2009) 'Punishment' in Hucklesby, A. and Wahidin, A. (eds) (2009) *Criminal Justice* Oxford: Oxford University Press

Scott, D. (2013) 'Visualising an Abolitionist Real Utopia: Principles, policy and praxis' in Malloch, M. and Munro, B. (eds) *Crime, Critique and Utopia* London: Palgrave

Scott, D (2016a) 'Regarding rights for the Other: Abolitionism and human rights from below' in Weber, L. et al (eds) (2016) *Routledge Handbook of Criminology and Human Rights* Abingdon: Routledge

Scott, D. (2016b) 'Hearing the Voice of the Estranged Other: Abolitionist ethical hermeneutics' *Kriminolosches Journal*, to be published

Scott, D. (2016c) *Emancipatory Politics and Praxis* Bristol: EG Press

Shantz, J. (2013) *Commonist Tendencies* New York: Punctum Books

Swaaningen, R. van (1997) *Critical Criminology* London: Sage

Winstanley, G. (1649 /2010) *The New Law of Righteousness* London: EEBO Editions

Woolf, L.J, (1991) *Prison disturbances* London: TSO

Wright, E.O. (2010) *Envisioning Real Utopias* London: Verso

Wright, E. O. (2009) *Envisioning Real Utopias*, http://citeseerx.ist.psu.edu/viewdoc/download?doi=10.1.1.152.6099andre p=rep1andtype=pdf

Realistic Utopianism and Alternatives to Imprisonment: The ideology of crime and the utopia of harm

Lynne Copson[1]

Abstract

This article investigates the question of how we might begin to move beyond critique and towards the development of radical, yet realistic, alternatives to penal practices. In so doing an argument is made for the advancement of a zemiological 'transpraxis' as a primary site for realising meaningful change. Situating this discussion in the contemporary climate of penal dystopianism, the article first explores how the contemporary impulse is one largely born in critique. Highlighting a tension between the desire to effect meaningful change and the danger of legitimising the status quo, the article points to attempts to resolve this tension through a burgeoning interest in the concept of utopia as a form of praxis. However, by drawing on Mannheim's distinction between 'ideology' and 'utopia', the article proceeds to demonstrate that, despite their normative ambitions, efforts to realise 'realistic utopias' within contemporary criminal justice systems necessarily tend towards 'ideology' and reification of the existing system rather than alternatives to it. Highlighting parallels between Mannheim's concepts and Foucault's idea of 'regimes of truth', the article makes its central argument: that responding differently to crime begins by thinking and talking differently. It concludes by offering the discourse of social harm as a primary site of 'transpraxis', encouraging us to think beyond contemporary linguistic and conceptual frameworks to understand social problems, arguing that it is only through the adoption of a 'replacement discourse' of harm that we can start to build realistic utopias and meaningful alternatives to imprisonment.

---

[1] Lynne Copson is Lecturer in Criminology at The Open University. Contact: lynne.copson@open.ac.uk

Introduction

Concerns about the use of imprisonment, its pains and inadequacies and the search for better and more effective alternatives have been a central theme within criminology for much of its history. Belief in the possibility of realistic alternatives to prison, however, has waned from its heyday with the birth of abolitionism in the 1960s. That is not to say that such beliefs or the struggle for alternatives have disappeared. However, optimism in the possibility of their practical realisation has become muted, particularly in a contemporary climate of rising incarceration rates and increasingly punitive responses to crime (see Simon, 2014). At the same time, the contemporary climate of knowledge production has seen an increasingly uncomfortable relationship develop between government and the funding of criminological research (see Hillyard et al, 2004a; Walters, 2011), disciplinary specialisation and the suppression of normative theorising in social scientific research. This has led to a growing polarisation between, on the one hand, radical ideals with no means of effective translation and, on the other, practical reforms which seek to reform the existing system in a piecemeal fashion. Emerging from this context has been a renewed interest in the idea of utopianism as a means of realising genuine alternatives to the dominant discourse of crime and justice that resist simply becoming 'add-ons' to existing systems (Mathiesen, 1986; Mathiesen and Hjemdal, 2011/this volume).

Against this backdrop, this article explores the extent to which such approaches offer a realistic strategy for challenging dominant paradigms of criminal justice. It situates the emergence of calls for more utopian theorising within criminology against a backdrop of increasing awareness of the inadequacies and harms of contemporary criminal justice which become all the more pressing in a climate of increasing rates of imprisonment, and the perceived absence of alternatives. Within such a climate, it argues, normative theorising becomes increasingly detached from issues of practical reform. Charting one response to this as lying in burgeoning interest in the concept of utopia, and particularly, an implicit notion of utopia as a form of praxis, particularly amongst penal theorists, the article highlights how the concept of 'real utopias' (Wright, 2010) has been identified as one possible means of transcending existing approaches to criminal justice and penal reform, to offer meaningful alternatives. However, drawing on Mannheim's distinction between ideology and utopia, the main argument is that, despite the best of intentions, such attempts are ultimately likely to serve ideologically to reinforce the *status quo* rather than to transcend it. Specifically, it is maintained that, so long as we take the criminal justice system as the starting point of our critique and the locus for the construction of alternatives, reforms are destined to reinforce and legitimise the contemporary 'regime of truth' (Foucault, 1980) and dominant constructions of crime, harm and justice. Therefore, it is argued that it is only by identifying a different starting point and developing a new 'replacement discourse' (Henry and Milovanovic, 1991) for conceptualising social problems (and hence, means of their reform) that we can hope to move beyond the ideology of crime. Finally, the developing zemiological or 'social harm' approach is identified as a potential candidate for doing so.

Contemporary criminal justice: a paradigm of inadequacy

The harms and inadequacies of the criminal justice and penal systems are well-documented. Not only do these systems fail to reduce reoffending (see, for example, Hillyard and Tombs, 2007: 14), but the penal system in particular, has long been recognised as a system of 'pain delivery' (Christie, 1981) which serves to dehumanise and inflict harm upon some of the most vulnerable members of society. However, these problems are arguably rendered more pressing within a contemporary context, in which increasing rates of imprisonment culminate in a crisis of mass incarceration (see Simon, 2014). That this should come at the same time as we are witnessing *falling* rates of crime (Garland, 2002; Office for National Statistics, 2016) arguably highlights the extent to which contemporary approaches to addressing crime, especially the use of imprisonment, have become detached from normative questions of what constitutes 'justice'.

Consequently, the criminal justice system is increasingly recognised as an 'industry' (see Hillyard and Tombs, 2007). Rather than offering an impartial, objective means of addressing harm and delivering 'justice', it is argued that the criminal justice system provides a specific lens through which harmful acts are shaped and constructed in particular ways (Pemberton, 2007), with particular implications for the imagining of appropriate responses and 'justice' (see also Hillyard and Tombs, 2007). Whilst this has constituted a key theme in abolitionist thinking (see, for example, Hulsman, 1986), this critique has been developed more recently through the emerging perspective of zemiology (Hillyard et al, 2004b; Dorling et al, 2008).

The individualising logic of criminal justice

Proponents of the zemiological perspective, in particular, have highlighted the individualising logic of criminal justice, which serves to hold individuals to account for their behaviour at the expense of the broader contexts of inequality, exclusion and social marginalisation in which the majority of offending occurs (Hillyard and Tombs, 2007: 15-16). Reinforced by a penal system which focusses on individual education and reform as the means of rehabilitation, this has led to claims that, not only is the criminal justice system essentially doomed in its quest to tackle offending, but that it operates ideologically to recast wider social problems as individual failings (see Carlen and Tombs, 2006).

The neglect of victims

The criminal justice system has also been criticised in its failure to address adequately the needs of victims, at worst contributing to their secondary victimisation (see Hoyle and Zedner, 2007). Moreover, it plays an important role in determining legitimate victimhood in the first place, with a number of commentators pointing out that many of those harms that are recognised through the criminal justice system are often relatively trivial events which 'would not score particularly high on an imaginary scale of personal hardship' (Hulsman, 1986: 65) when compared with many, arguably more significant harms we are likely to face during our lifetime (Hillyard and Tombs, 2007).

Thus the contemporary criminal justice system arguably constitutes a paradigm of inadequacy on a number of grounds: it fails to realise its own explicit *raison d'être* in terms of tackling crime; it functions as a system of pain delivery which fails to recognise the needs of victims and offenders alike; and constructs particular harms – and the solutions to these – in particular, individualised ways.

Contemporary penal dystopianism

Despite recognising these inadequacies within the criminal justice and penal systems, however, the contemporary impulse is one born largely in critique. It appears that, as critical scholars, activists, and citizens, we are far better at deconstructing existing systems than positively constructing meaningful alternatives (Lippens, 1995; Zedner, 2002). Even where evidence of an impulse toward the latter exists, this is often diluted over time via its translation into routine politics.

Part of the problem, no doubt, is the dominance of the criminal justice paradigm itself. As Shapland et al argue:

> western criminal justice has, through the state adoption of powers of trial and punishment, removed not only responsibility for the future from participants, but even the need and the habit of thinking about the future consequences of offending. (2006: 515)

Accordingly, even where attempts are made to offer potentially radical alternatives to the existing criminal justice apparatus, these are typically co-opted 'add-ons' (Mathiesen, 1986: 86; Mathiesen and Hjemdal, 2011: 225), offering piecemeal reforms at best, and/ or forms of 'transcarceralism' at worst (see Carlen and Tombs, 2006). Therefore, they typically ultimately serve to reify the *status quo* rather than fundamentally engage with, or challenge the underlying normative premises of that system. This has implications both for how harms are constructed and are to be addressed, with emphasis placed upon individual reform as the solution to crime.

Recognising victims within the criminal justice system

An example can be seen with the increasing inclusion of victims within conventional justice apparatuses via the development of the *Code of Practice for Victims of Crime* (Home Office, 2015), and growing use of Victim Personal Statements (Ministry of Justice, 2013; see also Hoyle and Zedner, 2007).

However, these have arguably resulted in the increasing incorporation of victims and restorative justice within conventional justice apparatuses, rather than the development of genuine *alternatives* (see Marshall, 1996; Shapland et al, 2006). For example, the use of Victim Personal Statements sees them deployed only *after* the guilt of an offender, within the conventional criminal justice system, has been determined and they do not permit the views of the victim on an appropriate punishment to be considered. If they are read in court, it is also for the court to determine which sections are to be presented (Ministry of Justice, 2013), such that, at every step, victim experience is channelled within existing frameworks of justice. Such measures therefore, whilst seeking to give voice to victims' experiences, only do so to the extent to which they are compatible with existing criminal justice frameworks.

Restorative Justice

Similarly, there has been increasing research into restorative justice processes within the criminal justice system, particularly in relation to juvenile crimes (cf. Home Office, 2002; Youth Justice Board, 2006; Muncie, 2009: 326-331). Restorative justice has been promoted as a means of salvaging conflicts from the processes of criminal justice, which construct them in particular ways to the exclusion of those directly involved in them and a consideration of the broader social contexts (see Christie, 1977).

However, just as victim statements are only employed post-conviction, in existing practices of restorative justice '[t]he relevant stage in criminal justice is[...] sentencing or the penal process, not the trial process/determination of guilt' (Shapland et al, 2006: 507). Because of this, those involved in restorative justice find themselves already cast in the roles of victim and offender. This has the effect of already closing down alternative ways of framing conflicts and developing responses that might go beyond the views of 'justice' and concerns of the criminal justice system, such as the traditional focus on individual reform for preventing future offending (see ibid: *passim*). Again, the use of such measures *within* the criminal justice system is criticised for its implicit reification of the normative frameworks of the dominant criminal justice paradigm.

This is not to deny that strategic advances have been made, nor the potential of such measures to 'influence and even slightly moderately transform criminal justice' (Shapland et al, 2006: 523). Indeed, evaluations of restorative justice within youth justice, for example, have highlighted 'the more positive lines of communication that have been opened up between offenders, parents, victims and communities' (Muncie, 2009: 330) despite recognising its problems and limitations. Therefore, one can recognise that the danger of a tendency to describe anything short of wholesale radical reform as serving an ideological function is that this may legitimise stagnation and inaction in addressing immediate problems for 'fear of buttressing an unjust[...] system' (Loader, 1998: 204).

At the same time, there is still a concern that without more effective translation of specific policy reforms into a broader positive politics of change, even the most critical approaches to contemporary criminal justice are destined to act as no more than a 'scientific "alibi"' (Garland, 1992: 404) for existing criminal justice and penal practices.

Reimagining vs. reifying the criminal justice system

This tension between effecting meaningful change and legitimising the existing system is increasingly recognised by critical criminologists and penal scholars alike (see Barton et al, 2011; Loader and Sparks, 2011; Young, 2011). It is a tension that strikes at the very heart of the criminological project itself, reflecting criminology's normative concern with questions of 'justice', and its practical project concerned to develop policies to address crime and/ or harm (Copson, 2013: 116-117).

It is also a tension that has been well-recognised by those advocating reform of criminal justice in general, and penal systems in particular (see Mathiesen, 1986; Mathiesen and Hjemdal, 2011; Scott, 2013). As Scott and Gosling highlight:

> There are many difficulties when attempting to promote alternatives to prison varying from net widening [...] to falling through the net [...]. Radical alternatives must be able to incorporate both an engagement with the problems and possibilities of our historical moment, whilst simultaneously disrupting punitive and other ideologies which facilitate social inequalities. (2016: 53)

Accordingly we appear to reach an impasse between propping up the *status quo* through practical, but small-scale reforms to the existing system and advocating radical social reform without offering any means of doing so. It is this impasse that, perhaps, largely explains the contemporary tendency towards penal dystopianism – even, in some cases, anti-utopianism – and an emphasis on critique, without a positive politics for social change.

The importance of critique in inspiring social change should not be overlooked and the reluctance to impose change reflects an implicit recognition of the dangers of doing so: as history has taught, too often reforms that have been imposed for the greater good have come at great cost to others (see Copson, 2013: 119-121, [forthcoming]). However, the result has been a loosening of normative theorising within criminology, from the practical project of addressing crime, as refuge is sought in small-scale improvements which, whilst leaving untouched the broader structure of society, do not run the risk of making things much worse than the *status quo*. However, they are unlikely to make it vastly better either.

However, we are currently witnessing increasing calls for a recoupling of these strands as a means of moving beyond this impasse (see, for example, Zedner, 2007; Loader and Sparks, 2011; see also Copson, 2013, 2014, and [forthcoming]). There appears to be a renewed commitment to more normative theorising within social science in general (see Wright, 2010; Levitas, 2013), and criminology in particular. This is seen as crucial to moving beyond contemporary penal dystopianism and enabling us to connect normative ideals with practical reforms in a way that will enable us to move beyond reification of the contemporary regime. Included within this has been a burgeoning interest in the field of utopianism (see Young, 1992; Lippens, 1995; Malloch and Munro, 2013; this issue).

Ideology and Utopia

Since its introduction as the title of Sir Thomas More's (1516) work, the term 'utopia' has negotiated an ambiguous and often contested terrain. Coined as a pun playing on the terms *outopia* ('no place') and *eutopia* ('good place'), the term simultaneously juxtaposes questions of possibility with conceptions of desirability (Levitas, 1990: 2).

Whilst space denies justice to a full account of the ambiguity and contestation that characterises the history of attempts to use and define 'utopia' – though see Levitas (1990) for an excellent account of this – one definition identifies utopia with a blueprint for realising a proposed good society (see also Levitas, 2013), reflecting, perhaps, ambiguity as to whether More's utopia was intended as a serious proposal for the instantiation of the good society (Carey, 1999: 38-39). Another, and perhaps the most common, approach has been to restrict the definition of utopia to a literary form (see, for example, Kumar, 1991).

However, despite its proliferation as a common definition, there remain those suspicious of confining utopia to a literary form (see Jameson, 2007). This is particularly so given a contemporary context in which fictional and holistic outlines of the good society typical of the utopian literary genre are arguably in decline (see for example, Kumar, 2003). Moreover, the general identification of utopia as literary fiction has typically been undertaken in order to facilitate discussion of its role as a means of critical reflection upon contemporary society, rather than 'an exercise of the literary imagination in and for itself' (Kumar, 1991: 24).

Common to both accounts of utopia as a blueprint for social change and the identification of the literary genre as a means of critically engaging with the established social world is, arguably, the idea of utopia as a form of *praxis*. Through the presentation of alternative forms of society, it is suggested,

> Utopia's value lies not in its relation to present practice but in its relation to a possible future. Its 'practical' use is to overstep the immediate reality to depict a condition whose clear desirability draws us on, like a magnet [...] so utopia's 'nowhereness' incites the search for it. (Kumar, 1991: 3)

Accordingly, some theorists, and particularly those who deploy the term in the context of social theory and research, define 'utopia' as a form of praxis and a drive to practical action.

An example of this is offered by Karl Mannheim who sought to distinguish ideas that serve to legitimate the *status quo* from those that bring about social change. Mannheim distinguishes utopia from ideology, arguing that this distinction lies in the transformative potential of utopia and the instantiation of an alternative social order it realises (Mannheim, 1960 [1936]: 173).

It is this conception of utopia as a form of *praxis* that contemporary criminologists are apparently invoking in their calls for more normative theorising and utopianism within criminal justice research (see, in particular, Young, 1992). This can be seen in the emphasis that has been placed on the imagining of 'realistic utopias' in response to the perceived inadequacies of the existing criminal justice and penal systems (see, for example, Loader, 1998; Scott, 2013; Scott and Gosling, 2016). At the same time, the tension highlighted between effecting meaningful change and reinforcing and legitimating the *status quo* that emerges in contemporary calls to imagine alternatives to imprisonment arguably reflects the key distinction drawn by Mannheim between ideology and utopia.

Both terms 'ideology' and 'utopia' have frequently become political labels used to discredit opposing ideas: ideology being used to suggest an individual is unaware of reality, misguided and a slave to the ideas of a powerful faction, with utopia being invoked, at times, to suggest naïveté – admirable in intention but impossible in reality. However, Mannheim distinguishes between ideological and utopian ideas in terms of their capacity for effecting social change. Whilst both 'transcend the reality within which they occur' (Levitas, 1990: 68) utopias 'tend to shatter, either partially or wholly, the order of things prevailing at the time' (Mannheim, 1960 [1936]: 173). Ideological ideas, by contrast, are those which, even whilst appearing to transcend the existing social order, ultimately reaffirm the *status quo*. They are

> the situationally transcendent ideas which never succeed *de facto* in the realization of their projected contents. Though they often become the good-intentioned motives for the subjective conduct of the individual, when they are actually embodied in practice their meanings are most frequently distorted. (Mannheim, 1960 [1936]: 175)

As such, the extent to which a form of thought can be considered ideological or utopian will depend upon the extent to which it questions the very premises upon which one's own position is based. For, as Mannheim argues:

> As long as one does not call his [*sic*] own position into question but regards it as absolute, while interpreting his opponents' ideas as a mere function of the social positions they occupy, the decisive step forward has not yet been taken. (Mannheim, 1960 [1936]: 68)

The tension between creating meaningful alternatives to current penal regimes and reinforcing dominant contemporary paradigms within contemporary criminal justice can thus be seen as a reflection of the distinction between ideology and utopia in Mannheim's work. The question then becomes one of how we can escape this tension in order to construct 'realistic utopias' that take us beyond the provision of new forms of ideology and reinforcement of the *status quo*.

Foucault argues that '[e]ach society has its régime of truth, its 'general politics' of truth: that is, the types of discourse which it accepts and makes function as true' (1980: 131). As these 'regimes of truth' are necessarily predicated upon, and reinforcing of, the current social system, an alternative regime of truth is only possible by changing the current social structure. Thus,

> The essential political problem for the intellectual is not to criticise the ideological contents supposedly linked to science, or to ensure that his own scientific practice is accompanied by a correct ideology [...]. The problem is not changing people's consciousness – or what's in their heads – but the political, economic, institutional régime of the production of truth'. (Foucault, 1980: 133)

In this way, our lived social reality and contemporary 'regime of truth' can be considered mutually reinforcing, such that it is ultimately the structure of society that must be transcended if we are to realise a genuine alternative to the *status quo*.

This arguably resonates to some degree with Mannheim's distinction between ideology and utopia. Although recognising the very different philosophical positions to which Foucault and Mannheim respectively belong, we may nevertheless argue that it is only through altering the social context of production of discourses that they may realise their utopian potential, rather than lapse into ideological reinforcement. At the same time, however, owing to the dialectical relationship between regimes of truth and the socioeconomic and political systems to which they correspond, it is also through altering the discourses available to us that we may create a genuine alternative to the existing system.

Thus, whilst critical scholars have sought numerous ways in which we might seek to move beyond existing approaches and offer meaningful alternatives to contemporary penal regimes in practice, so long as they remain wedded to the language of crime and criminal justice they arguably cannot help but lapse into ideological reinforcement by leaving unquestioned the premises upon which traditional conceptions of crime and justice have been based.

The ideology of crime?

Scott (2013), for example, invokes Erik Olin Wright's (2010) calls to 'envision real utopias' as a means of engaging with and realising meaningful social change. Suggested by Wright as a means of reflecting the 'tension between taking seriously emancipatory aspirations for a radically more humane and just world, and confronting the hard constraints of realism' (2007: 27), Scott employs this concept as a means of developing what he terms an 'abolitionist real Utopia' (2013: 91), coupling a normative commitment to the abolition of criminal justice with a practical strategy of reform. He seeks to move 'beyond' contemporary criminal and penal justice frameworks by subverting them from within by 'exploiting gaps, cracks and crevices within existing policy and practice' (Scott, 2013: 92). In doing so, his approach is offered as an antidote to the contemporary retreat to critique of the existing system without a positive politics of reform (*ibid*: 97).

Scott situates his approach in an abolitionist critique of contemporary criminal justice and penal systems, arguing that in order to challenge the dominant paradigms of criminal justice and penality what is needed is

> a deconstruction of the 'reality' assembled through criminal processes and the adoption of the meanings and understandings derived from the situational wisdom of the life world where the conflict emerged, alongside the promotion of alternative means of conflict handling that recognise dignity, equality and social justice. (2013: 97)

To build this in practice, Scott identifies a need to develop alternatives guided by 'an abolitionist compass' (*ibid*: 98). This compass is underpinned by a commitment to: protecting human dignity and minimising suffering; social justice; alternatives that challenge and contradict established practices; a genuine alternative to criminal justice; legal protections and accountability for any alternatives; and meaningful and relevant interventions which allow active participation in creating norms (Scott, 2013: 97-100).

Whilst in the longer term, Scott suggests a number of 'historically immanent policies, practices and designs' (2013: 101) to address the material inequalities in society and thereby reduce recourse to punishment, he identifies five key alternatives which he regards as the primary concern for developing for 'the actual visualisation of abolitionist real Utopia pragmatic interventions' (*ibid*: 103). These involve:

1. Putting the victim of crime at the heart of responses
2. Using alternative models to the criminal law for handling conflicts
3. Providing more effective social support to help prevent crime from even occurring (through skills training, housing, healthcare etc.)
4. Providing more voluntary treatment programmes to divert those who come into contact with the criminal justice system through 'illness'
5. Creating intentional communities for lawbreakers, thereby providing a more meaningful context to develop new skills and responses to problematic behaviours (Scott, 2013: 103-107)

These are undoubtedly laudable and practical aims and one can see how, through their development, we might be able to begin to meaningfully reform the dominant criminal justice and penal responses. Moreover, one can appreciate the need for pragmatic and practical measures if we are not to retreat into abstract theorising of alternatives with no means of their practical realisation, or anti-utopian acceptance of the *status quo*. However, it remains unclear how such measures will necessarily resist co-option within the existing criminal justice framework.

This is a danger Scott himself acknowledges elsewhere, in his discussion of Therapeutic Communities as a radical alternative to prison (Scott and Gosling, 2016). To avoid co-option it is suggested, alternatives must be deployed '*beyond* the criminal process', specifically '*before* and *instead of* a prison sentence' (*ibid*: 63). However, one could argue that similar aims have historically underpinned restorative justice approaches also, and yet they have all-too-frequently become adjuncts of criminal justice as noted above.

The problem here is that, so long as criminologists and abolitionists take the criminal justice and penal systems as their primary concern or the starting point against which they offer 'alternatives', they cannot help but reify that system and its associated conceptual frameworks.

This is not to undermine the important role that such contributions can play in improving conditions within prisons or reforming the criminal justice system. However, so long as such measures fail to question the very context of their production, they can only ever reinforce the contemporary 'regime of truth'. Indeed, the overwhelming danger is that the discourses we use, including the discourse of crime and justice which characterises contemporary society, are not merely ideological constructions as has often been recognised (see, for example, Box, 1983). Rather, they are predicated upon and reaffirm a particular 'regime of truth' and way of understanding the world, with particular implications for responding to crime and understanding justice.

This is evident, for example, in accounts of restorative justice. In their research into restorative justice programmes within the criminal justice system, Shapland et al found that:

> participants, [...] are bringing to it their similar, normative assumptions about justice, offenders and victims, which are propelling them culturally to similar activities and expressions. (2006: 522)

This highlights the importance of context in shaping normative discussion. Similarly, it seems that so long as we invoke the language of crime and criminal justice, or penal abolitionism, we invariably set those systems as the normative yardstick against which alternatives will implicitly be measured.

As Henry and Milovanovic, in their articulation of 'constitutive criminology' have argued:

> discursive practices produce texts (narrative constructions), imaginary constructions, that anchor signifiers to particular signifieds, producing a particular image claiming to be reality. These texts become the semiotic coordinates of action, which agents recursively use and, in so doing, provide a reconstruction of the original form. (1991: 300)

Therefore, it is a central premise of the argument put forward here that the search for meaningful and genuine *alternatives* in responding to crime must start by thinking and, ultimately, talking differently about crime.

The utopia of 'harm'?

The premise that the search for meaningful and genuine *alternatives* in responding to crime must start by thinking and, ultimately, talking differently about crime is both inspired by and reflected in the emergence of 'zemiology' or 'a social harm perspective' (see Hillyard et al, 2004b; Dorling et al, 2008). Within this perspective, the idea of social harm has increasingly been deployed as part of an attempt to highlight the shortcomings of criminology's focus on crime and as a basis upon which to establish a more holistic framework for understanding and addressing harm.

Deconstructing criminology
The roots of the zemiological approach can be located in the development of an increasingly critical orientation towards criminology itself in response to the renewed focus on criminal justice and preventative techniques of crime control with the advent of administrative criminology and criminal justice science in the late twentieth/early twenty-first century. There has been an increasing concern to deconstruct the discipline of criminology, pointing to its formation within existing structures of power (see Tifft and Sullivan, 2001) which, it is argued, has reinforced conventional constructions of both crimes and criminals (see, for example, Matthews and Kauzlarich, 2007). As Smart notes, '[t]he thing that criminology cannot do is deconstruct "crime"' (1990: 77). Therefore, whilst critical criminology has highlighted the differential construction and deployment of legal constructions of crime, Hulsman notes, 'the ontological reality of crime, has not been challenged' (1986: 66).

Consequently, we remain 'stuck in a catascopic view of society in which our informational base [...] depends mainly on the institutional framework of criminal justice' *(ibid*: 67-68).

Thus, contemporary approaches to crime and justice have increasingly sought to 'decriminalise criminology' (Muncie, 2000) and 'decentre crime' from public discourse (*ibid*) through the positing of 'harm' as a more useful concept for understanding social phenomena (see also Milovanovic and Henry, 2001; Tifft and Sullivan, 2001).

'Beyond' the discourse of crime

Presenting an explicit shift away from focussing on crime, key proponents of the zemiological perspective identify a number of critiques of criminology which reiterate existing critical criminological critiques regarding the social construction of crime and the operations of the existing criminal justice system, but also seek to move beyond them.

A central thesis of the perspective is that the discourse of crime excludes a whole host of harmful experiences for which no discrete cause or causal agent can be identified, neglecting the way in which apparently individualised, monocausal harms may be located in wider networks of systemic harm such as capitalism, racism, or patriarchy. It also reinforces a false dichotomy between legality and illegality which, when taken to its extreme, implicitly legitimates non-criminalised harms by virtue of the absence of sanction (and thus formal recognition) against it. In so doing, it ultimately implicitly reinforces, rather than challenges, the criminal justice agenda set by the State (Hillyard and Tombs, 2007).

Therefore, central to this perspective is the argument that the discourse of 'crime' and criminal justice structures our interpretations and responses to social phenomena in particular ways. Thus, so long as we continue to talk in the language of 'crime' and criminal justice, we cannot escape the perspective or 'truth' such language both requires and perpetuates.

By contrast, as Muncie (2000) notes,

> [t]he redefining of crime as harm opens up the possibility of dealing with pain, suffering and injury as conflicts and troubles deserving negotiation, mediation and arbitration rather than as criminal events deserving guilt, punishment and exclusion.

Drawing attention away from legally defined crimes and locating criminal harms in broader systems of socioeconomic inequality and injustice, critical criminology challenges the capacity of the penal system to realise justice. It also encourages the development of alternative policies better able to address the harms people experience and to realise the crime-free society.

Social harm: a replacement discourse
With this in mind, proponents of the social harm perspective point to the power of using an alternative discourse around 'harm' as a means of mobilising the 'subjugated knowledges' of harm excluded by the contemporary criminal justice regime (Hillyard and Tombs, 2007: 21). They point to the need for methodological tools 'to "debunk" the persuasive narratives of "crime" and create the discursive spaces where the marginalized can articulate their lived experience of harm without persistent reference to the notion of "crime"' (Pemberton, 2007: 33).

By changing the language according to which we come to articulate and understand social phenomena, through the offering of a 'replacement discourse' (Henry and Milovanovic, 1991) to that of 'crime', policy responses can be devised and implemented to more effectively prevent and address harms people experience 'from "cradle to grave"' (Pemberton, 2007: 34) than either current penal policy or the penal reforms with which critical criminologists have typically been preoccupied (see also Hillyard and Tombs, 2007). Such an approach can still admit that conventional 'crimes' are harmful, but also allow a more nuanced conception of the harmful nature of the systems that generate them. Whilst contemporary approaches to criminal justice reform have long recognised the way in which criminal harms are often premised on structures of inequality, marginalisation and exclusion, so long as the focus of reform remains on existing processes and institutions, as we have seen, the risk is that the solutions to structural problems become recast as individual 'treatments' through the individualising logic which underlies both the concept of crime and, by extension, criminal justice.

Thus, whilst underlying this approach is a commitment to developing a more socially just, safe, and equitable society in which social harm is significantly reduced if not eradicated, the shift towards a language of harm demands a broader policy focus which transcends existing specialisms to address a whole host of issues across institutions, rather than on improvements to the criminal justice system. The creation of alternative discursive spaces for articulating harm outside the conceptual framework of crime, it is advocated, will facilitate the remedy of such harms by a more joined-up and comprehensive social policy approach (Pemberton, 2007: 33; see also Pantazis and Pemberton, 2009 for examples of specific policies).

Realistic utopianism?

By shifting to the language of harm as a 'replacement discourse' (Henry and Milovanovic, 1991), zemiology and the discourse of social harm can be seen as offering an important means of realising 'realistic utopias' that take us beyond the ideology of crime and criminal justice. However, if the history of the co-option of alternatives to conventional criminal justice has taught us anything it is that the power of existing structures of thought is not easily resisted, particularly in a climate where all too often academic research is shaped by issues of access to funding. As many have noted, the contemporary climate of academic funding and research means that often the research agenda is shaped by external forces and interests (including those of government) which can, in turn, feed into the replication of existing discourses around crime (see Hillyard et al, 2004a; Walters, 2011). Such forces are not easily resisted. Even in those cases where they have been, we bear witness to the costs of doing so.

The high-profile dismissal of Professor David Nutt from the Government's Advisory Council on the Misuse of Drugs offers a prime example of the strength of resistance to attempts to present a 'replacement discourse'. This dismissal followed Nutt's analysis of the harms of recreational drugs (see Tran, 2009) and resulting claims that many of those drugs we criminalise are less harmful than those we do not, such as alcohol and tobacco (Nutt, 2009). Such potential costs would make many researchers, especially those at the start of their career without the security of an established position or international acclaim, think twice about radically challenging the conventional wisdom on a given issue.

There is also a danger of holding out the discourse of 'harm' as a panacea to eradicating the problems of 'crime' and replication of the *status quo*. Immediate questions, acknowledged by proponents of the zemiological perspective themselves, stem from concerns as to whether 'harm' is any less socially constructed than 'crime', and the possible dangers of majoritarianism and relativism in any attempt to define harm (see Hillyard et al, 2004b: 271-275; Pemberton, 2007; 35-37).

Another danger, arguably neglected by proponents of the social harm perspective, is the extent to which the discourse of crime permeates our very perceptions of harmfulness. For example, there is a sense in which people perceive 'crimes' as 'worse' than other harms (see Ashworth, 1986: 105).

Similarly, the individualising tendency identified as underlying the concept of crime arguably constitutes a framework of understanding, reflected in broader attitudes that often seek to blame clear, identifiable individuals for harms. For example, reflecting on his analysis of jury decision-making concerning the awarding of damages in civil cases in the US, Feigenson suggests that people 'may be inclined to think about accidents in simplified, personalized, and moralized ways because that is a predominant way in which the culture at large constructs its accounts of accidents and many other kinds of events' (2000: 14).

Mannheim distinguishes 'relative' from 'absolute' utopias, where a relative utopia is one 'which seems to be unrealizable only from the point of view of a given social order which is already in existence' (Mannheim, 1960 [1936]: 177). Given the cultural and political power of the discourse of crime within contemporary society (see Loader and Sparks, 2011), a practical zemiological application must take seriously its 'relative' impracticability within a contemporary context if it is to offer a realistic alternative discourse.

That said, as Foucault has noted, challenging the existing 'regime of truth' is 'not a matter of emancipating the truth from every system of power [...] but of detaching the power of truth from the forms of hegemony, social, economic and cultural, within which it operates at the present time' (1980: 133). The democratic commitment of the zemiological perspective to the unearthing of 'subjugated knowledges' therefore arguably provides the means through which we can conceptualise the translation of the discourse of social harm as a means of constructing 'realistic utopias'.

From abolitionist praxis to zemiological transpraxis
The discourse of crime, as the history of critical strands of criminology has demonstrated, reflects the interests of those with the social power to define it. It is a discourse which, in Foucault's words, reflects 'the status of those who are charged with saying what counts as true' (1980: 131). As such, it is inexorably linked to the current *status quo*, the current 'regime of truth', and precisely those 'forms of hegemony, social, economic and cultural, within which [the power of truth] operates at the present time' (*ibid*: 133).

By contrast, zemiology, with its ideal of democratic unearthing and articulation of experiences of harm, without reference to the discourse of crime, as the basis for social policy may be seen as the first step towards realising this emancipation from the current 'regime of truth'. This discourse operates not merely at the superficial level but presents a form of 'transpraxis' whereby:

> If praxis is taken to be purposive social activity born of human agents' consciousness of their world, mediated through the social groups to which they belong [...] Transpraxis assumes that critical opposition must be aware of the reconstitutive effects – the reproductions of relations of production – in the very attempts to neutralize or challenge them. (Henry and Milovanovic, 1991: 295)

Conclusion

Therefore, whilst the endeavours of critical scholars engaged in the search for 'realistic utopias' within the current penal system reflect an idea of utopia as *praxis*, they nevertheless cannot help but tend towards Mannheimian ideology. This is because, so long as they take crime and criminal justice as their starting point, they implicitly reify a 'regime of truth' that constructs 'crime' and processes of criminal and penal justice as the most pressing social issue and primary site for effecting social change, a position that has historically been supported and sustained by the very discipline of criminology itself. By contrast, it is only by engaging in strategies that challenge the very premises upon which these approaches are based, by offering alternative discourses and starting points, defined outwith existing disciplinary confines, that we can make the shift towards *transpraxis* and from 'ideology' to 'utopia'. As such, a perspective conceived around giving voice to subjugated experiences of harm typically excluded from academic theorising offers a genuinely 'new' starting point for conceptualising and responding to social problems. In this way, the zemiological perspective presents a means for moving beyond the existing context of knowledge-production and challenging the current 'regime of truth' in a way that radical perspectives *within* criminology cannot hope to. By challenging the primacy of crime, criminal justice and penal responses it opens up a horizon in which genuine and meaningful alternatives to these systems can be imagined, beyond the reification of the systems it seeks to oppose.

In conclusion, as this paper has sought to demonstrate, whilst the inadequacies and harms of the criminal justice and penal systems are well-recognised, interest in utopianism as a form of *praxis* has emerged as a means of challenging contemporary penal anti-utopianism. However, current attempts at meaningful reform are limited. These are undeniably important as a challenge to contemporary dystopianism and anti-utopianism amongst critical scholars, and a necessary antidote to the increasing specialisation and polarisation between radical normative theorising and practical projects of piecemeal reform within criminal justice research. However, so long as they take these systems and their failings as their starting point, such attempts will necessarily tend towards ideology and legitimation of the existing 'regime of truth' owing to their implicit reification of criminal justice discourse. It is therefore only by seeking a 'replacement discourse', such as that offered by social harm and zemiology, that we can find a new starting point outside criminology. It is only by transcending the ideology of crime and its normative underpinnings that we may take the first steps towards realising the practical utopia of harm.

References

Ashworth, A. (1986) 'Punishment and Compensation: Victims, Offenders and the State' in *Oxford Journal of Legal Studies* Volume 6, N° 1 pp 86-122

Barton, A., Corteen, K., Scott, D. and Whyte, D. (eds) (2011) *Expanding the Criminological Imagination* Abingdon: Routledge

Box, S. (1983) *Power, Crime and Mystification* Abingdon: Routledge

Carey, J. (ed) (1999) *The Faber Book of Utopias* London: Faber and Faber Ltd

Carlen, P. and Tombs, J. (2006) 'Reconfigurations of Penality: The Ongoing Case of Women's Imprisonment and Reintegration Industries' in *Theoretical Criminology* Volume 10, N° 3 pp 337-360

Christie, N. (1977) 'Conflicts as Property' in *British Journal of Criminology* Volume 17, N° 1 pp 1-15

Christie, N. (1981) *Limits to Pain* Oxford: Martin Robertson

Copson, L. (2013) 'Towards a Utopian Criminology' in Malloch, M. and Munro, B. (eds) *Crime, Critique and Utopia* Basingstoke: Palgrave Macmillan

Copson, L. (2014) 'Penal Populism and the Problem of Mass Incarceration: The promise of utopian thinking' in *The Good Society* Volume 23, N° 1 pp 55-72

Copson, L. (forthcoming) 'After Penal Populism: Punishment, Democracy and Utopian Method' in Dzur, A., Loader, I. and Sparks, R. (eds) *Democratic Theory and Mass Incarceration* Oxford: Oxford University Press

Dorling, D., Gordon, D., Hillyard, P., Pantazis, C., Pemberton, S. and Tombs, S. (eds) (2008) *Criminal Obsessions* (Second Edition) London: Centre for Crime and Justice Studies

Feigenson, N. (2000) *Legal Blame* Washington DC: American Psychological Association

Foucault, M. (1980) 'Truth and Power' in Gordon, C. (ed) *Power/Knowledge*. Harlow: Longman

Garland, D. (1992) 'Criminological Knowledge and its Relation to Power: Foucault's Genealogy and Criminology Today' in *British Journal of Criminology* Volume 32, N° 4 pp 403-22

Garland, D. (2002) *The Culture of Control*. Oxford: Oxford University Press

Henry, S. and Milovanovic, D. (1991) 'Constitutive Criminology: The Maturation of Critical Theory' in *Criminology* Volume 29, N° 2 pp 293-316

Hillyard, P. and Tombs, S. (2007) 'From "Crime" to Social Harm?' in *Crime, Law and Social Change* Volume 48, N° 1-2 pp 9-25

Hillyard, P., Sim, J., Tombs, S. and Whyte, D. (2004a) 'Leaving a 'Stain Upon the Silence: Contemporary Criminology and the politics of dissent' in *British Journal of Criminology* Volume 44, N° 3 pp 369-390

Hillyard, P., Pantazis, C., Tombs, S. and Gordon, D. (eds) (2004b) *Beyond Criminology* London: Pluto Press

Home Office (2002) *Justice for All* London: The Stationery Office, https://www.cps.gov.uk/publications/docs/jfawhitepaper.pdf (consulted 13 May 2016)

Home Office (2015) *The Code of Practice for Victims of Crime*, https://www.gov.uk/government/uploads/system/uploads/attachment_data/file/476900/code-of-practice-for-victims-of-crime.PDF (consulted 13 May 2016)

Hoyle, C. and Zedner, L. (2007) 'Victims, Victimisation and Criminal Justice' in Maguire, M., Morgan, R. and Reiner, R. (eds) *The Oxford Handbook of Criminology* (4th Edition) Oxford: Oxford University Press

Hulsman, L. (1986) 'Critical Criminology and the Concept of Crime' in *Contemporary Crises* Volume 10, N° 1 pp 63-80

Jameson, F. (2007) 'Varieties of the Utopian' in *Archaeologies of the Future: The Desire Called Utopia and Other Science Fictions* London: Verso

Kumar, K. (1991) *Utopianism* Milton Keynes: Open University Press

Kumar, K. (2003) 'Aspects of the Western Utopian Tradition' in *History of the Human Sciences* Volume 16, N° 1 pp 63-77

Levitas, R. (1990) *The Concept of Utopia* New York: Philip Allen

Levitas, R. (2013) *Utopia As Method* Basingstoke: Palgrave Macmillan

Lippens, R. (1995) 'Critical Criminologies and the Reconstruction of Utopia' in *Social Justice* Volume 22, N° 1 pp 32-50

Loader, I. (1998) 'Criminology and the Public Sphere: Arguments for Utopian Realism' in Walton, P. and Young, J. (eds) *The New Criminology Revisited*. Basingstoke: Palgrave

Loader, I. and Sparks, R. (2011) *Public Criminology?* Abingdon: Routledge

Malloch, M. and Munro, B. (eds) (2013) *Crime, Critique and Utopia* Basingstoke: Palgrave Macmillan

Mannheim, K. (1960 [1936]) *Ideology and Utopia* Abingdon: Routledge and Kegan Paul

Marshall, T. (1996) 'The Evolution of Restorative Justice in Britain' in *European Journal of Criminal Policy and Research*, Volume 4, N°4 pp 21-43

Mathiesen, T. (1986) 'The Politics of Abolition' in *Contemporary Crises* Volume 10, N° 1 pp 81-94

Mathiesen, T. and Hjemdal, O. (2011) 'A New Look at Victim and Offender – An Abolitionist Approach' in Bosworth, M. and Hoyle, C. (eds) *What is Criminology?* Oxford: Oxford University Press

Matthews, R. and Kauzlarich, D. (2007) 'State Crimes and State Harms: A Tale of Two Definitional Frameworks' in *Crime, Law and Social Change* Volume 48, N°1-2 pp 43-55

Milovanovic, D. and Henry, S. (2001) 'Constitutive Definition of Crime: Power as Harm' in Henry, S. and Lanier, M. (eds) *What Is Crime?* Oxford: Rowman and Littlefield Publishers, Inc.

Ministry of Justice (2013) 'Making a Victim Personal Statement', https://www.gov.uk/government/publications/victim-personal-statement (consulted 13 May 2016)

Muncie, J. (2000) 'Decriminalising Criminology' in *British Criminology Conference: Selected Proceedings*, Vol. 3, http://www.britsoccrim.org/volume3/010.pdf (consulted 13 May 2016)

Muncie, J. (2009) *Youth and Crime* (Third Edition) London: Sage

Nutt, D. (2009) *Estimating Drugs Harm: A Risky Business?* Eve Saville Memorial Lecture , Briefing 10 (October 2009). London: Centre for Crime and Justice Studies

Office for National Statistics (2016) *Statistical Bulletin: Crime in England and Wales: Year Ending September 2015*, http://www.ons.gov.uk/peoplepopulationandcommunity/crimeandjustice/bulletins/crimeinenglandandwales/yearendingseptember2015 (consulted 13 May 2016)

Pantazis, C. and Pemberton, S. (2009) 'Nation States and the Production of Social Harm: Resisting the hegemony of "TINA"' in Coleman, R., Sim, J., Tombs, S., and Whyte, D. (eds) *State Power Crime* London: Sage

Pemberton, S. (2007) 'Social Harm Future(s): Exploring the Potential of the Social Harm Approach' in *Crime, Law and Social Change* Volume 48, N° 1-2 pp 27-41

Scott, D. (2013) 'Visualising an Abolitionist Real Utopia: Principles, Policy and Praxis' in Malloch, M. and Munro, B. (eds) *Crime, Critique and Utopia.* Basingstoke: Palgrave Macmillan

Scott, D. and Gosling, H. (2016) 'Before Prison, Instead of Prison, Better than Prison: Therapeutic Communities as an Abolitionist Real Utopia?' in *International Journal for Crime, Justice and Social Democracy* Volume 5, N°1 pp 52-66

Shapland, J., Atkinson, A., Atkinson, H., Colledge, E., Dignan, J., Howes, M., Johnstone, J., Robinson, G. and Sorsby, A. (2006) 'Situating Restorative Justice within Criminal Justice' in *Theoretical Criminology* Volume 10, N° 4 pp 505-532.

Simon, J. (2014), *Mass Incarceration on Trial* London: The New Press

Smart, C. (1990) 'Feminist Approaches to Criminology or Postmodern Woman Meets Atavistic Man' in Gelsthorpe, L. and Morris, A. (eds) *Feminist Perspectives in Criminology* Buckingham: Open University Press

Tifft, L. and Sullivan, D. (2001) 'A Needs-Based, Social Harms Definition of Crime' in Henry, S. and Lanier, M. (eds) *What Is Crime?* Oxford: Rowman and Littlefield Publishers, Inc.

Tran, M. (2009) 'Government Drug Adviser David Nutt Sacked' *The Guardian*, Friday 30 October 2009

Walters, R. (2011) 'Critical Criminology and the Intensification of the Authoritarian State' in Barton, A., Corteen, K., Scott, D. and Whyte, D. (eds) *Expanding the Criminological Imagination* Abingdon: Routledge.

Wright, E. (2007) 'Guidelines for Envisioning Real Utopias' in *Soundings* Volume 36, pp 26-39

Wright, E. (2010) *Envisioning Real Utopias*, London: Verso

Young, J. (2011) *The Criminological Imagination* Cambridge; Malden, MA: Polity

Young, P. (1992) 'The Importance of Utopias in Criminological Thinking' in *British Journal of Criminology* Volume32, N° 4 pp 423-437

Youth Justice Board (2006) *Developing Restorative Justice* London: Youth Justice Board, http://yjbpublications.justice.gov.uk/en-gb/Resources/Downloads/RJper cent20Actionper cent20Plan.pdf (consulted 13 May 2016)

Zedner, L. (2002) 'Dangers of Dystopias in Penal Theory' in *Oxford Journal of Legal Studies* Volume 22, N° 2 pp 341-366

Zedner, L. (2007) 'Pre-Crime and Post-Criminology?' in *Theoretical Criminology* Volume 11, N° 2 pp 261-281

What Is To Be Done? A reconsideration of Stan Cohen's Pragmatic Utopianism

Bill Munro[1]

Abstract

Visions of Social Control *(1985) is an important but unconventional work within British criminology. Its academic unconventionality is perhaps most clearly displayed in the final chapter* What is to be Done? *in which Cohen appeals to criminologists to be intellectual adversaries in projects of demystification and institutional reform. While the book's overall aim is explicitly utopian the narrative is one of an underlying pessimism. A question at the heart of Cohen's 'pragmatic utopianism' is whether social science can provide a more effective theoretical understanding of the institutions of social control in relation to their location in the social and physical space of the city? This paper will outline the key arguments of Cohen's* Visions of Social Control, *offer an account of his pragmatic utopianism and consider what a pragmatic utopianism may look like under today's changed historical conditions.*

> *So you can understand that our knowledge*
> *Will be entirely dead, after the point*
> *At which the gate of the future will be shut.*
> Dante, Inferno X

Introduction

Visions of Social Control (1985) is an important but unconventional work within British criminology. Its academic unconventionality is perhaps most clearly displayed in the final chapter *What is to be Done?* in which Cohen appeals to criminologists to be intellectual adversaries in projects of demystification and institutional reform. However the unconventional strangeness of the work is deeper than the unusualness of such a politicised appeal to activism within the structure of what appears on the surface to be an academic work. The incongruity of *Visions of Social Control* lies in an antagonism between the book's aims, its ideal if you like, and its definitive narrative. While its overall

---

[1] Bill Munro is Lecturer in Criminology at the University of Sterling, Scotland.

aim is explicitly utopian – '[m]y preference is to be pragmatic about short-term possibilities but to be genuinely utopian about constructing long-term alternatives' (Cohen, 1985: 252) – the narrative is one of an underlying pessimism. In this it follows Gramsci's (1996) appeal for a pessimism of the intellect combined with an optimism of the will. This antagonism, alongside the work's unconventional structure, is, I would argue, a strength of the book as a whole and not a limitation, as it provides a means of reading what we may regard as being the work's moral vision against the very real social constraints of what is possible.

In Stan Cohen's (1979/2013) earlier work *The Punitive City: Notes on the Dispersal of Social Control,* which in many respects lays the foundation of *Visions of Social Control,* he asks the two questions, one pragmatic, one theoretical, which lie at the heart of his pragmatic utopianism. The first asks whether the new forms of community intervention that emerged in the late 70s and early 80s, can be clearly distinguished from the old institutions that they were intended to replace, or whether they merely reproduced within the community the very same coercive features of the older system. The second question asks whether social science can provide a more effective theoretical understanding of the institutions of social control in relation to their location in the social and physical space of the city. In both *The Punitive City* and *Visions of Social Control* Cohen provides a compelling yet pessimistic answer to the first question. At the end of *The Punitive City* he writes that his argument is tilted towards a rather bleak view of social change and the undesirable consequences of the emerging social control system. The second question Cohen leaves hanging. It is in this question however that an implied utopianism is ambiguously articulated. Cohen's punitive city has much in common with Foucault's (1991) equally pessimistic account of the carceral dystopia yet, unlike Foucault's vision, Cohen's narrative offers a brief utopian light within this heart of darkness. When Cohen writes about 'blurring the boundaries' it is not only the blurring of the once clear spatial boundaries of the prison – the spatial logic of an institution as thing or object – to the unclear and ambiguous limits of community corrections, he writes also about the ambiguity and ingenuity of language, and the blurring of meaning in relation to the processes of social control. This slippage from a real place to that of a semiotic, or signifying space is what makes *The Punitive City* and *Visions of Social Control* unique, in the sense that space and the social use of space is conceptualised as a problem of syntax. This movement between the real and the semiotic outlines the utopian trace both within his own work, but also in relation to a broader theme of the emancipatory aspect of social science in general. An area that is central to Cohen's question on whether social science can provide a more effective theoretical understanding of the institutions of social control in relation to their location in the social and physical space of the city. Like Virgil who guided Dante through the gates of hell and purgatory in *The Divine Comedy*, Cohen in *The Punitive City* and *Visions of Social Control* uses the metaphor of the city to guide his readers through contemporary visions of hell and the contradictions between the reality and the rhetoric of crime control policies and practices in Western jurisdictions. This paper will outline the key arguments of Cohen's *Visions of Social Control*, offer an account of his pragmatic utopianism and consider whether his pragmatic utopianism can be developed under today's changed historical conditions. In considering this latter question the paper will explore Olin Wright's (2010) model of a 'real utopia', as a contemporary lens within criminological discourse (see Scott, 2013), which as a framework for an emancipatory social science shares Cohen's concern with seeking to demystify dominant narratives by providing a systematic diagnosis of our time, as well as the desire to envision viable alternatives.

The Central Argument

The blurring of meaning and the slipping from a real to that of a signifying space is a constant theme in *Visions of Social Control*. Cohen (1985: 13) writes in his discussion of the master patterns of social control in Western industrial societies that there have been two transformations, 'one transparent, the other opaque, one real, the other eventually illusory'. The first of these transformations or shifts took place between the end of the eighteenth century and the beginning of the nineteenth and laid the foundations of all subsequent systems of social control. The first shift was accompanied by increased rationalisation and bureaucratisation within the penal system. The increased power of the modern nation state meant that punishment was regulated and administered by central government agencies, which in turn lead to the growth in the scale of the penal infrastructure. Modernisation of the penal system also led to increasing professionalism and standardisation within the institutions of punishment. Since the 1790s punishment had become increasingly 'rational', to use the eighteenth century meaning of that term, i.e. based on a normative social contract theory. By the late nineteenth century, however, the rationality of punishment had taken on a different meaning; here it meant that penalties be administered in a rule-governed, routine and impassive fashion (see also Garland 1991). The rule-governed and scientific administration of punishment was reflected in the development of rule-governed and scientific explanations of crime. The positivist development of classificatory schemes and explanations of criminal behaviour as being determined by individual pathology all lay the foundations for the development of a scientific penology based on therapy where the mind replaced the body as the object of penal repression. The increased differentiation and classification of deviants into separate types and categories, each with its own body of knowledge and accredited experts, was replicated physically by the increased segregation of those deviants into asylums, mental hospitals, penitentiaries, reformatories and prisons, the latter emerging as the dominant institution for normalising problematic behaviour as well as the preferred form of punishment.

The second transformation, which is the subject of Cohen's book, was understood by many people (see Skull 1977; Bottoms, 1983) as representing a questioning, or even a reversal of the first transformation, reducing state involvement in crime control, replacing prison with 'community alternatives', decentralising and diverting deviants away from the criminal justice system, reducing professional dominance, re-establishing classical 'justice' principles, and reintegrating offenders into the community. Cohen (1979/2013: 1985), as did other authors (Mathiesen, 1983; Hudson, 1984) challenged the 'decarceration' thesis that attempted to explain this second transformation and investigated the gap between the reality and the rhetoric of this shift in penal control (see also Cavadino et al 2013). Cohen argues that this master pattern is more illusory than real and is merely the continuation and intensification of the first. Evidence shows that state intervention has been strengthened and extended, and that both old and new forms of social control have expanded. Not only have old and new forms of control increased but the focus of control has become dispersed and diffused, and the boundaries between those under control and those not under control have become blurred.

> The technological paraphernalia previously directed at the individual, will now be invested in cybernetics, management, systems analysis, surveillance, information gathering and opportunity reduction. This might turn out to be the most radical form of behaviourism imaginable – prevention of the act of crime

by the direct control of whole populations, categories and spaces.
(Cohen, 1985: 147)

Cohen describes how, as control mechanisms are dispersed from the prison into the community, they penetrate more deeply into the social fabric, blurring the boundaries between different types of deviants and between deviants and non-deviants. It is the boundary blurring and the absorption of the community by the control system that, Cohen argues, enables the system to camouflage its activities.

The answer Cohen provides as to whether the new forms of community intervention that emerged in the late 70s and early 80s merely reproduced within the community the very same coercive features of the older system, is pessimistic and offers little means to resist the emerging social control system. Cohen's second question asks whether social science can provide a more effective theoretical understanding of the institutions of social control and the gap between the reality and the rhetoric of those institutions.

A Pragmatic Utopian Social Science?

Cohen's project of understanding the phenomena of crime and punishment in modern society and linking this understanding to a strategy that can facilitate progressive reform within the penal system is at the heart of both a critical and pragmatic criminology. Cohen's (1985) preference to be pragmatic about short-term possibilities and genuinely utopian about constructing long-term alternatives follows Nils Christie's vision which, in abandoning utilitarian attempts to change the offender or to inflict a just measure of pain, favours a clear moral position that bases its programme within a historical critique of the dominant ideologies of social control. From this perspective, discussions on utopia are by necessity entangled in debates concerning the relationship between history and consciousness, historical understanding and actual social practices. This link between history and utopia was fundamental to the rehabilitation of the concept of utopia within Marxism by authors such as Ernst Bloch. In his writings on utopia, Bloch (1986; 1988) makes a distinction between abstract and concrete utopia. For Bloch, abstract utopia is wishful thinking, or a form of daydreaming, and as such is not accompanied by the desire to bring the dream to realisation; the world in this form of thinking remains as it is. The problem of abstract Utopia, according to Bloch, is one of immaturity and a consequent tendency to become lost in fantasy and memory rather than being oriented to real possibility. Abstract utopia is a form of thinking that is not only compensatory in its aim, but has also, according to Bloch, discredited the concept of utopia, 'both in pragmatic political terms and in all other expressions of what is desirable'. In abstract utopianising, the utopian function is only immaturely present, and as a consequence it is easily led astray (Bloch, 1986: 145). In this way social science has the responsibility to be realist and to establish what is concrete and possible. Concrete utopia is therefore not compensatory but anticipatory, it is directed towards what Bloch calls a 'Real-Possible' future. Bloch calls concrete utopia 'the power of anticipation' and is a form of *wilful* thinking. He argues that it embodies the essential utopian function of both anticipating and affecting the future simultaneously. While abstract utopia may express a compensatory desire it does not express hope; only concrete utopia can achieve this. The process of extracting concrete utopia from its abstract trappings results in what Bloch describes as the 'unfinished forward dream' – *docta spes,* or educated hope. It is a 'methodical organ for the New, an objective aggregate form of what is coming up' (Bloch, 1986: 157). Concrete utopia can be understood as both latency and tendency. It is historically present and refers forward to an emergent future.

Bloch (1988) makes an important distinction between two forms of concrete utopia: social utopias where representations are constructed in which there are no labouring and burdened people; and natural law, in which there are no humiliated and insulted people. This distinction between social and legal utopias is mirrored in Cohen (1985: 248) when he writes about 'doing good' versus 'doing justice'. Cohen uses this distinction to make a similar appeal to focus utopian practice on the historical and concrete as opposed to the ideological and the abstract as a means of avoiding the 'theoretical crudity of the idealist separation of theory and practice which is so continually striking in the history of crime control'. The consequences of such a separation is an ideological commitment to either one of the dominant modes of 'doing good' (in the form of the rehabilitative models surrounding 'community alternatives'), or 'doing justice' (the return of a 'justice model' of penal reform), while ignoring their historical and political contexts.

> We are told that, instead of giving way to despair, liberals should realise that rehabilitation is the only ideology which can be used to resist conservative policy and the only one which commits the state to care for the offender's needs and welfare. It is not enough for justice-model liberals to talk about the 'right' to decent conditions and treatment, nor to proclaim humanity as an

end in itself. This would only open criminal-justice politics to a struggle which the powerless are bound to lose. (Cohen, 1985: 247)

Cohen (1985: 247-48) argues that while being a persuasive programme – and if he were interested in defending traditional liberalism he would have no hesitation in joining this campaign – he also would have had no hesitation in doing the opposite and attacking rehabilitation in the late sixties and upholding the value of justice. He might also have encouraged the Fabian version of rehabilitation in Britain at the end of the fifties, supported the Progressives in the twenties, as well as the child-saving movement at the end of nineteenth century. He may even have joined the ranks of the original asylum and penitentiary founders. Cohen outlines the complexity involved in resolving the contradictions between what we learn from history and the values and principles entrenched in our theories: however, to hold to those values and principles despite the historical and political contexts in which we find ourselves is to court defeat. Cohen (1985: 248) talks about the persistent assumption when faced with such defeat, that theories are always beautiful until the barbarians make them ugly. However, it is not the barbarians that make them ugly but changed historical circumstances.

Earlier in *Visions of Social Control* Cohen argues that such theoretical models are not just competing abstract explanations or schools of thought to be purchased in the academic supermarket, but that they are connected to a corresponding system of power. Norrie (1991) raises a similar concern when he considers the re-emergence of the 'justice model' in the 1970s and early 80s. Criminology up until that time had taught that 'classical criminology' was part of the pre-history of valid knowledge, yet here it was back on the agenda. How was this intellectually possible? Are ideas recyclable in such a reductive way as to be detached from their original social contexts and applied to new ones? Can thought be dictated through the negation of intellectual enquiry and by social and political circumstance alone? Norrie argues that there were clear political reasons why classicism was making a comeback at that time, but raised serious concerns about the uncritical reductionism of such forms of idea formation and intellectual practices. In terms of Cohen's 'doing good' distinction, Bottoms (1977) also questions the dangers of uncritically adopting discredited models to deal with new situations when he writes on the renaissance of dangerousness in penal policy in the 1970s. Only a few years before his article, the concept of dangerousness would have seemed to him, as to most others concerned with penal policy in Britain, to be very remote from the language of debate typically used in discussion of penal matters. He argued that the renaissance of dangerousness was heavily dependent on the conceptual framework of positivism, a perspective at that time on the retreat within academic criminology and sociology. In particular, Bottoms highlighted that the positivist endorsement of the scientific was problematic as it returned to a belief that crime is a naturalistic category and that the analysis of social meaning attached to it could therefore be ignored. Again, the political reasons as to why recommendations by a discredited penal philosophy should make a resurgence in the late 70s was clear in a resurgence of conservative anti-rehabilitation which dominated penal policy at that time. As Cohen (1985: 147) notes, the 'renaissance of the concept of dangerousness in contemporary penology depends on the decline of the rehabilitative ideal'. Yet despite this, these ideas continued to influence the so called 'progressive' rehabilitation debates surrounding 'what works' during the 1990s to the present. What links both the 'doing good' and the 'doing justice' models is that the 'notion of progress is always present in the sense that things can obviously be better' (Cohen, 1985: 89). Organisations which try to implement each model start with their own interests and generate stories (based on their respective ideologies) that are in turn 'located in a particular social structure or political economy'. Although not explicitly presented as such, the 'doing good' and the 'doing justice' models contain, respectively, the conservative totalising utopias of social stability and law and order.

Utopian ideas therefore cannot be made through specifying the content of the good society or the just society, as content is dependent on social conditions. The wish images of the justice model or the rehabilitative model can be discussed individually only according to the degree to which present conditions allow for their realisation. What is required therefore is not content, but instead, what Bloch (1988: 7) terms a 'topos of an objective real possibility'. In other words, one must not offer a picture of utopia in a positive manner. Any attempt to describe or portray utopia in a simple way, i.e., it will be like this, should be avoided in order to guard against 'the cheap utopia, the false utopia, the utopia that can be bought' (Bloch, 1988: 11). On the content of the utopian 'there is no *single* category by which utopia allows itself to be named' (Bloch: 1988: 7). At the heart of Cohen's book, as there is in Bloch's, is the imperative 'Thou shalt not make a graven image'. 'Much self-consciously intellectual work is needed if we are to wake up from the dream of beautiful theories untouched by the pragmatics of power' (Cohen, 1985: 248).

Utopia and the City

As mentioned earlier, when Cohen writes about 'blurring the boundaries' it is not only the blurring of the once clear spatial boundaries that separated a prison from a community or the classificatory boundaries that separate deviants from non-deviants; he writes also about the ambiguities and cunning of language in this process. Boundary blurring is a result of how we talk about control systems and their mechanisms and it is how we talk about them that enables the system to camouflage its activities. The role of language in the blurring of boundaries is mirrored in Stan Cohen's own work when he blurs the social and physical space of the city into representational space and imaginary space. The slippage from real space to that of a semiotic or signifying space is carried out in chapter six in his discussion of Utopia:

> Cities, then, have never been just places, almost as soon as they were invented, they spawned a phantom version of themselves; an imaginative doppelganger that lived an independent life in the imagination of the human species at large. In other words, they stood for something. In the ancient world and then again with the re-emergence of city life in the later middle ages, the city tended to be conceived as a metaphor of order. The patterning of the city, its spatial arrangements, hierarchies, functional specifics, served as a mirror image of what the wider social reality could and should be like. (Cohen, 1985: 206)

Cohen is writing not only about the influence of language and syntax in how we structure the world but how there is a functional unity between a system of signs and human experience situated on an empirical and historical terrain. In other words, spaces of representation are mental inventions (codes, signs, 'spatial discourses', utopian plans, imaginary landscapes, and even material constructs such as symbolic spaces, particular built environments, paintings, museums) that imagine new meanings or possibilities for spatial practices (see also Harvey, 1990). Cohen argues that the semiotic effects, the meaning-constructions of imaginary representations of the city, are anchored in the coercive realities of a concrete historical society itself.

Earlier in the chapter Cohen writes that the beginning and end of the nineteenth century marked two utopian moments in the history of crime control. At the beginning of the first transformation of the master patterns the founders of the American and European penitentiary system were confident that they had not only found a solution to the crime problem, but one that would also lead to a better society. An explicit utopian thinking not only informed their design but also was reflected in the faith in scientific progress in the new 'science' of criminology which also emerged at that time. Although such optimistic views on the abilities of science and technology to solve social problems and create a new social order came under assault from more pessimistic narratives within the social sciences, an optimistic, utopian element in crime control thinking has always been a constant trope,

> the countervision of order, regulation and security which will replace the imminent threat of breakdown and chaos. This vision appeared in the early penitentiary movement, in the idealistic excesses of scientific positivism, in the Continental social-defence school and today, in the bland technicist criminology peddled by international agencies to the Third World. (Cohen, 1985: 202)

The metaphor for the utopia of community corrections, of social stability, the fulfilment of private life, law and order, was the city. Hall et al (1978: 145) make a similar point with regards to the imaginary power of the city as a metaphor of social hygiene when they write that 'the state of the city' is 'in a sense, the tide-mark of civilisation; it embodies our level of civilisation and the degree to which we are successful in maintaining that level of achievement'. The patterning of the city, its spatial arrangements and hierarchies not only served as a mirror image of what society could and should be like, but reinforced the idea that social problems can be solved merely by reordering physical space. The ordered city was a system for holding chaos at bay, an idealised form of the actual city where an imaginary order was embodied in every ritual and practice. The impending problem of social control was brought alive through this imaginary order by the work of planners and visionaries in the form of the closed institution. Here then was constructed a working model of what society should look like. Cohen draws on Foucault (2001) to show how leprosy and the plague provided the models and technologies of control for this imaginary. Leprosy through the rituals of exile, banishment and exclusion and the plague through the technologies of examination, classification and discipline. The control of both diseases left behind the models for the Great Incarcerations. The prison was a space of exclusion, but it was also a space within which people were observed, partitioned, subject to timetables and disciplines. Here also was a form of 'moral architecture' – buildings designed not as ostentatious signs of wealth and power, nor as fortresses for defence, but for the fabrication of virtue. Power and order in its pure utopian form. Foucault fantasized the 'punitive city' as the utopia of the early judicial reformers 'at the crossroads, in the gardens, at the side of roads being repaired or bridges built, in workshops open to all, in the depths of the mines that may be visited, will be hundreds of tiny theatres of punishment' (Cohen, 1985: 209). However, this utopian fantasy was never realised and in its place emerged the disciplinary society where Foucault 'visualised "panopticicm" as a generalised principle, extended and dispersed throughout the social network' (Cohen, 1985: 209). For Foucault, the city was not a place for other metaphors but a powerful spatial metaphor itself, a metaphor of 'geopolitics' (city, archipelago, maps, streets, topology, vectors, landscapes) that he used to describe the dispersal of discipline.

While the utopian ideal of order and control had never passed out of existence, its imaginary representations have. Cohen asks what are the utopian after images of the emerging control system? Here he draws on Mumford's vision where today's good city in the form of a collective human machine is haunted by its dehumanised dark shadow, *the invisible machine* of the modern technocratic state. The power of this new imaginary, or imaginaries, does not draw from its visible parts but from 'the minute, intangible assembly of science, knowledge and administration' (Cohen, 1985: 210). *The invisible machine* has two contrasting modes of control which fitted its particular imaginaries. The first was *inclusion*: its utopia was of the invisibly controlling city with its metaphors of penetration, integration and absorption, and its apparatus of bleepers, screens and trackers. The second was *exclusion*: its utopia was of the visibly purified city with its metaphors of banishment, isolation and separation, its apparatus of walls, reservations and barriers. *The invisible machine* is no longer an agent for creating the ideal city, but itself becomes the utopia which is worshipped and perpetually expanded. Cohen argues that it was in response to the horror of *the invisible machine* that produced the romantic, anti-industrial impulses and visions of the 1960s including, paradoxically, the radical destructuring movements themselves. However, 'so invisible was the machine that its most benign parts (therapy, social work, humanitarianism) hid its most repressive operations' (Cohen, 1985: 210).

The anxiety that sustains this imaginary is the fear of what lies 'outside' of its representations, 'in the chaos of urban life, in the desolate city streets abandoned to the predators, lies the ultimate horror – chaos, disorder, entropy' (Cohen, 1985: 210). The city of the present in the streets of which lie the clearest mirrors of dystopian imagery (the iconography of crime, violence, pollution) is the society of the future. In 1985 Cohen speculated as to whether *the invisible machine* was breaking down by itself and was being replaced by a new imaginary influenced by the fear of what lay 'outside'. Since then much criminological debate has focused on the fear of crime as a metaphor for other types of urban unease or a displacement of other fears (Young 1999). The increasing public fear of what Cohen termed the predator is also informed by what Garland (2001) has called the criminology of the dangerous other. This criminology typically depicts crime in dramatic and moralising terms and frames its analysis in the language of war and 'zero tolerance'. The relationship of this criminology of the 'other' to *the invisible machine* is that while it still draws from the apparatus of science, knowledge and administration and the bifurcation between the categories of inclusion and exclusion, these categories are now more refined and are focussed more minutely on those groups of offender who are politically and governmentally demonised and excluded. The utopia for this new imaginary can be found in the actuarial language of risk and the probabilistic calculations of the risk society.

What is to be done?

In chapter 7 of *Visions of Social Control: What is to be Done?* Cohen appeals to criminologists to be intellectual adversaries in projects of demystification and institutional reform and it is here also that he makes explicit the utopian aim of his book. That such a dark and pessimistic book drew on the trope of utopia might seem to some paradoxical only if we understand utopia in its more discredited forms. It is also paradoxical that a work which claims to be 'genuinely utopian about constructing long-term alternatives' (Cohen, 1985: 252) should consist largely of a sustained critique of utopia. However, it is often in the examination of our darker constraints that the trace of utopia appears to guide our orientation as a society towards not only the present conjuncture but also our future. The quotation by Dante at the start of this article outlines the important relationship between knowledge and the future, not in the sense of how knowledge may allow us to predict the future (the abstract utopia of positivism) but how it allows us to be conscious of and understand our present as a society within history and oriented towards an emergent future. This it would seem to me to be at the heart of the pragmatic utopianism outlined in the book and is similar to what Bloch (1986) called educated hope. It was this historically-based and future-oriented hope that linked his question as to whether social science can provide a more effective theoretical understanding of the institutions of social control with his pragmatism about the possibilities of reform.

Institutional reform, however pragmatic, is not possible without the project of demystification promised by the social sciences. Given the importance of historical context in the construction of a pragmatic utopianism, it is striking that Cohen's question as to whether the social sciences can provide a more effective theoretical understanding of the institutions of social control was focussed very specifically on those institutions' relationship to their location in the social and physical space of the city. Soja (1989: 15) points out that an overdeveloped historical contextualisation of social life within social theory often 'actively submerges and peripheralizes the geographical or spatial imagination'. However it is the persistent movement from a real historical space to that of a signifying or imaginary space throughout *Visions of Social Control* that not only gives the book its analytical strength in distinguishing the real from the illusory, the transparent from the opaque, but allows Cohen to avoid the 'theoretical crudity of the idealist separation of theory and practice which is so continually striking in the history of crime control' (Cohen, 1985: 248). As we have seen, one of the consequences of such a crude separation of theory and practice is an ideological commitment to what Cohen (1985: 248) called 'beautiful theories', theories which in themselves often contain traces of conservative utopias. Cohen's utopia lies not in the dreams of the future but in the waking up from such dreams. He argues that the semiotic effects of such dreams mask the coercive realities of a concrete historical society.

Cohen's ability to link the spatial with the historical in order to separate the concrete from the imaginary is close to Michel Foucault's (1986) notion of heterotopias. Like Cohen, Foucault's utopias do not have a content and cannot be developed into programmes of change. Heterotopias, according to Foucault, are the spaces in which we live and in which the erosion of our lives, our history, occurs. Unlike the totalising Utopias of social stability and law and order, heterotopias are heterogeneous spaces; in other words, spaces which are irreducible to one another and not fully superimposable on to one another. Unlike the law and order Utopia these spaces are messy, ill-constructed, disorganised and chaotic yet also provide the context where the dominant fantasies can be resisted and remodelled according to different patterns of action and forms of construction. Like Cohen's pragmatic utopianism, it is not to be found in the beautiful theories of justice or rehabilitation, but in the resistance to the dominant fantasies of the system.

The task for criminologists is still to be intellectual adversaries in projects of demystification and institutional reform but under the new historical conditions of today. Today there is an incoherent and contradictory range of developments occurring in penal policy and practice. O'Malley (1999) argues that this 'volatility' which, for many, reflects a crisis in the institutions of punishment, has been explained by criminologists in different ways: as evidence of the limits of the sovereign state (Garland, 1996); as the result of the emergence of neo-liberalism and 'new right' politics (O'Malley, 1999, 2004); and as a sign of a postmodern disintegration of penal modernity and the rehabilitative ideal (Pratt, 2000). Many of these themes were captured by Cohen as they first emerged in the late 1970s, early 80s but now, due to hindsight, can be more clearly seen as influenced by neo-liberal ideas relating to individual responsibility and discourses on risk (Garland, 2001). These so called 'new penologies' reflect a reconfiguration of the relationship between the individual and the State. More specifically, a shift from the modernist/welfare project distinguished by commitment to rehabilitation towards one characterised by a focus on managerial efficiency (Feely and Simon, 2003).

The continuity of the new penology with what Cohen called *the invisible machine* is its close association with criminological positivism, that is, it has a reliance on expert knowledge and 'knowledge professionals'. Its divergences from *the invisible machine* lies in the technologies of classification, a shift from individual to aggregate categories of offenders, a greater focus on preventive measures and an emphasis on social segregation (Feeley and Simon, 2003). It could perhaps be argued, however, that these new penologies, like the second great transformation outlined by Cohen, are merely the continuation and intensification of that first transformation that took place between the end of the eighteenth century and the beginning of the nineteenth and laid the foundations of all subsequent systems of social control. State intervention again has been strengthened and extended, social control has expanded and increasingly dispersed and diffused, and the boundaries between those under control and those not become increasingly blurred. What has happened is that the mask has finally slipped from the illusory destructuring rhetoric.

So what does this mean for Cohen's utopianism with his preference for pragmatic short-term possibilities and genuine utopian thinking about constructing the long-term alternatives? As mentioned earlier, while the utopian ideal of order and control has never changed, its imaginary representations have. The new fantasies of the system still require to be demystified and resisted and a clear moral position that bases its analysis within a historical critique of the dominant ideologies of social control still requires to be developed. However, such a critical project that aims to contribute to and influence significant change within the penal system has recently been in retreat. As most critical scholars are all-too-painfully aware, although the range and scope of writing within critical criminology has expanded, the present conjuncture within modern capitalist society has erected major economic, political and social constraints on such broad political aims, both in relation to intellectual critique and activist involvement. Any commitment to a 'reflexive' praxis between knowledge and a strategy for radical social change is today seen as wildly utopian in the negative sense of that term.

It is perhaps because of this that there has been a renewed interest in the concept of Utopia, not only as a political perspective within recent social science discourses, but one that opposes abstract wishful thinking with an empirical or realist utopian commitment. Olin Wright (2006, 2010), for example, develops the theme of a realist utopia to present a framework for an emancipatory social science which seeks both to generate the knowledge necessary for opposing human oppression and for enabling the conditions in which human beings can live fulfilling lives. From a perspective similar to Cohen's pragmatic utopianism, Olin Wright (2006, 2010) argues that social science still has a role to play in demystifying dominant institutional narratives and outlines three fundamental tasks for social science: to elaborate a systematic diagnosis and critique of the world as it exists; to envision viable alternatives; and to understand the obstacles, possibilities and dilemmas of transformation. Both Cohen and Olin Wright's insights into pragmatic/real utopias also inform Scott's (2013: 92) 'abolitionist real Utopias'. For Scott, the 'abolitionist real Utopia' must diagnose and critique the power to punish, 'identifying the hurt, suffering and injuries inherent within, and generated through, criminal processes and critically reflecting upon the legitimacy of the deliberate infliction of pain'. It must advocate for the provision of radical alternatives that engage with the possibilities for action within a specific historical conjuncture. Lastly, it must have a 'clear strategy of emancipatory change to reduce social inequalities and current penal excess'. Following Cohen's unstated imperative 'Thou shalt not make a graven image', Scott (2013: 110) argues against the notion of a 'blueprint' for change but advocates 'explorations of potentialities that sensitise the imagination to what is possible'.

The utopian focus on the uses of the imagination in rethinking penal practices is also explored in different ways in the work of Carlen (2008) were the imagination was contrasted with the concept of the imaginary to show how various political and populist ideologies on punishment and justice structure a representation, or image, of penal policy and practice (see also Sim (2008); Barton, et Al (2007) and Hudson (2008)). The utopian contrast between the imagination and the imaginary is a means of thinking through the impasse brought about by the closing off of alternative, more imaginative discourses on justice and penal practice within contemporary neo-liberal penality. In a period in which alternative ways of being and means of transformation are so opaque, positions that in the past were perhaps viewed as moderate and achievable are now considered utopian. This is a paradox that Jameson (2005: xii) eloquently expressed when he said, 'there is no alternative to Utopia'. The renewed interest in the concept of utopia therefore has less perhaps to do with a greater clarity of vision or the existence of an identified agent for social change, and more to do with grasping those obstacles and explaining the resilience of the present constraints to change. Therefore today, the proscription against any actual Utopian effort to create a new society is also a proscription against any effort to *imagine* doing so. To attempt to imagine social change, or in some cases even limited reform, outside the trope of utopia is therefore to risk losing not only our orientation as a society towards the future but also our present. In other words, in not addressing the utopian, we risk becoming a society without historical consciousness, a society without history (Jameson, 1994).

When it comes, the resistance to this de-historicised society and its forms will come from those outside the dominant imaginary and who inhabit those disorganised and chaotic spaces where the system can be resisted and transformed according not only to different patterns, maps and forms of construction but also in a different language. As Cohen (1985) reminds us, much self-consciously intellectual work is still needed if we are to wake up from the dreams of the law and order utopias.

References

Barton, A, Corteen, K., Scott, D and Whyte, D. (2007) *Expanding the Criminological Imagination* Cullompton: Willan Publishing

Bloch, E. (1986) *Principles of Hope* Oxford: Blackwell

Bloch, E (1988) *The Utopian Function of Art and Literature* Cambridge: MIT Press

Bottoms, A.E. (1977) 'Reflections on the Renaissance of Dangerousness' in *Howard Journal of Criminal Justice* Volume 16 pp 70-96

Bottoms, A.E. (1983) 'Neglected Features of Contemporary Penal Systems' in Garland, D. and Young, J. (eds) *The Power to Punish* London: Heinemann

Carlen, P. (ed) (2008) *Imaginary Penalities* Cullompton: Willan Publishing

Cavadino, M. Dignan, J. and Mair, G. (2013) (Fifth edition) *The Penal System* London: Sage

Cohen, S. (1985) *Visions of Social Control* Cambridge: Polity Press

Cohen, S. (2013) 'The Punitive City: Notes on the dispersal of social control', in McLaughlin, E. and Muncie, J. (eds) *Criminological Perspectives* London: Sage.

Feely, M. and Simon, J (2003) 'The New Penology' in McLaughlin, E., Muncie, J. and Hughes, G. (eds) *Criminological Perspectives* (2nd edition) London: Sage

Foucault, M. (1986) 'Of Other Spaces' in *Diacritics* Volume 16, No. 1 pp 22-27

Foucault, M. (1991) *Discipline and Punish: The Birth of the Prison* Harmondsworth: Penguin

Foucault, M. (2001) *Madness and Civilization* Oxon: Routledge.

Garland, D. (1991) *Punishment and Modern Society: A Study in Social Theory* Oxford: Clarendon Paperbacks

Garland, D. (1996) 'The Limits of the Sovereign State: Strategies of Crime Control in Contemporary Society' in *The British Journal of Criminology* Volume 36, No. 4 pp 445-471

Garland, D. (2001) *The Culture Of Control: Crime and Social Order in Contemporary Society* Oxford: Oxford University Press

Gramsci, A. (1996) *Letters from Prison* London: Pluto

Hall, S. Critcher, C. Jefferson, T. Clarke, J. and Roberts, B. (1978) *Policing the Crisis: Mugging, the State, and Law and Order* London: Macmillan Press

Harvey, D. (1990) *The Condition of Postmodernity* Oxford: Blackwell

Hudson, B. (1984) 'The Rising Use of Imprisonment: The Impact of "Decarceration" Policies' in *Critical Social Policy* Volume 11 pp 46-59

Hudson, B. (2008) 'Re-imagining Justice: Principles of Justice for Divided Societies in a Globalised World' in Carlen, P. (ed) *Imaginary Penalities*, Cullompton: Willan Publishing

Jameson, F (2005) *Archaeologies of the Future: The Desire Called Utopia and Other Science Fictions* London: Verso

Jameson, F (1994) *The Seeds of Time* California: Columbia University Press

Mathiesen, T. (1983) 'The Future of Control Systems – the Case of Norway' in Garland, D. and Young, J. (eds) *The Power to Punish* London: Heinemann

Norrie, A. (1991) *Law, Ideology and Punishment: Retrieval and Critique of the Liberal Ideal of Criminal Justice* London: Kluwer Academic Publishers

O'Malley, P. (1999) 'Volatile and Contradictory Punishment' in *Theoretical Criminology* Volume 32 pp 175-195

Pratt, J. (2000) 'The Return of the Wheelbarrow Men: or, The Arrival of Postmodern Penality?' in *The British Journal of Criminology* Volume 40 pp 127-145

Scott, D. (2013) 'Visualising an Abolitionist Real Utopia: Principles, policy and practice' in Malloch, M. and Munro, B. (eds) *Crime, Critique and Utopia* Basingstoke: Palgrave Macmillan

Scull, A. (1977) *Decarceration: Community Treatment and the Deviant – A Radical View* New Jersey: Prentice-Hall

Sim, J. (2008) 'Pain and Punishment: the Real and the Imaginary in Penal Institutions' in Carlen, P. (ed) *Imaginary Penalities* Cullompton: Willan Publishing.

Soja, W. (1989) *Postmodern Geographies: The reassertion of space in critical social theory* London: Verso.

Wright, E.O. (2006) 'Compass Points' in *New Left Review*, Volume 41 pp 93-124

Wright, E.O. (2010) *Envisioning Real Utopias* London: Verso

Young, J. (1999) *The Exclusive Society* London: Sage

What Lies Beyond Criminal Justice? Developing transformative solutions

J.M. Moore and Rebecca Roberts[1]

Abstract

Criminal justice failure has been well-documented. The traditional response to this failure has been to seek out alternatives. However, by their very nature, alternatives are usually conceived and positioned in relation to the failed criminal justice interventions they seek to replace. In this paper we focus on an initiative, Justice Matters, which seeks to provide a model, not for developing alternatives to criminal justice failure, but instead the creation of transformative solutions to a range of social problems. To illustrate the potential of this approach we explore two examples: drugs and violence against women.

Central to our argument is that for nearly all social problems, solutions already exist. But they exist beyond the boundaries of criminal justice and its experts. By drawing on appropriate knowledge – health for drugs and feminism for gendered violence; – aligned to a political commitment to social justice, we argue it is possible to develop transformative solutions which can provide the foundation for a society that lies beyond criminal justice.

Introduction

To talk about a world without prisons, police and the penal law – a post-criminal justice future – is to risk being accused of being idealistic, utopian or, worst of all, unrealistic. Nowhere is the belief that 'there is no alternative' more universal than when it comes to the agencies of criminal justice and the legal framework in which they operate. However much the failure of penal law is demonstrated (and indeed this failure is almost universally accepted,) all responses must be kept within the boundaries of criminal justice. In rejecting the limitations of such thinking and by daring to imagine how we can move beyond criminal justice we are simultaneously rejecting and embracing

---

[1] J.M. Moore is senior lecturer in criminology at Newman University, Birmingham. Contact: jmmoore911@outlook.com or on Twitter - @Moore_J_M. Rebecca Roberts is Senior Policy Associate at the Centre for Crime and Justice Studies and Senior Visiting Research Fellow at the Open University. Contact: rebecca.roberts@crimeandjustice.org.uk or on Twitter - @reberrama.

utopian thinking. We reject the utopian thinking that believes in an imagined perfect world – a world without crime and harm – that can be imposed on society, or utopian thinking which refuses to accept failure and maintains, against all the evidence, that institutions of criminal justice can be reformed. However, we argue that utopia as the use of the imagination to construct a better future is essential for the achievement of social justice and human emancipation (Levitas 2013). Utopian thinking provides the tools required to construct real social change on our own terms (Wright 2010). Such utopian thinking is about the deployment of values and principals and as such is inevitably always unfinished and indeed accepts and embraces failure (Mathiesen 1974; Dilts 2016).

Erik Olin Wright (2010) has called for the envisaging of real utopias. This requires, he argues, firstly identifying 'the ways in which existing social institutions and social structures systematically impose harms on people' and in this essay we therefore start with a critique of existing criminal justice arrangements (ibid:11). This is intentionally brief as it is well trodden ground and we wish to focus our attention more on the development of transformative solutions. As Wright (2010:20) has correctly pointed out, critique, although essential, is not enough, it must be combined with the development of 'alternatives to existing institutions and social structures that … eliminate, or at least significantly mitigate the harms and injustices identified in the diagnosis and critique'. Those who reject criminal justice face the inevitable question: 'so what would you replace it with?' This is a legitimate question. Social problems are real and need solutions; the harms experienced, particularly by the most marginalised, are frighteningly real; and conflicts likewise are very real. They all require concrete responses and solutions. To do this, the second section focuses on a specific initiative, *Justice Matters,* which is seeking to develop a practical blueprint for generating social justice solutions to conflicts, harms and social problems.

In the third section we explore two examples – drugs and violence against women – to illustrate the potential of the *Justice Matters* approach. Alcohol and drugs were two of the 'main drivers of crime' (out of six) recently identified by a UK Government Minister (Bates cited in Hansard 2015).[2] For those in the political mainstream, alcohol and drugs are a social problem that is central to the functioning of criminal justice, an approach we argue is not only ineffective but generates more harms. There are more effective and just

---

[2] The other four were 'the effectiveness of the criminal justice system; opportunity; profit; and character'.

ways of responding. Given the endemic and serious nature of gendered violence, we use this as our second example. Demands that violence against women be taken seriously have led many activists and campaigners to develop a Janus-like approach to the State and criminal justice. The public and political debate has become narrowly focused on what criminal justice could do better despite there being a wealth of international research and practice that focuses on solutions that sit outside of criminal justice. These brief examples, we argue, demonstrate how 'real utopias', which offer transformative solutions, can be developed. Because these solutions are *social justice* interventions, developed independently of criminal justice, we argue, in the conclusion, they are far less vulnerable to the colonisation and incorporation often experienced by interventions which have been developed specifically as 'alternatives' to criminal justice.

Criminal justice as failure and criminal justice as success

The criminal justice system is both a failure and a success. It is a notorious failure when it comes to preventing crime and dealing with the needs of those who have been harmed. There exists an extensive and persuasive literature identifying the failure of criminal justice at a number of levels: it inadequately responds to victims' needs (Christie 1977); it is unable to address the underlying social problems it claims to be a response to (Davis 2003); it is highly sensitive to power, repeatedly allowing the serious harms of the powerful to escape sanction (Box 1983; Tombs 2015a); it focuses attention on a narrow range of predominantly minor harms, deflecting attention away from many other more serious harms (Hillyard and Tombs 2004); and it tends to create and reinforce social inequality through its focus on the poorest and most marginal communities in our societies (Chapman 1968; Sim 2009). In particular, a careful evaluation of punishment's stated justifications – deterrence, rehabilitation, retribution, and incapacitation – has shown that criminal justice fails (Mathiesen 1990).

Indeed, there is considerable agreement that criminal justice in general and prison in particular is failing. Despite this, mainstream penal reform (under the guise of humanitarian or crime fighting objectives) has sought to fix the criminal justice system and those people held inside it. These liberal reforms have resulted in incremental changes to policing, sentencing, probation and prison policy. However, such reform has done little to understand or address

ilures and contradictions of the penal law and criminal justice
, Harris (1991:91) has observed:

> Existing structures, institutions, relations, and values create the
> problems that we then turn around and ask them to solve — or
> rather, control — using the very same structures, forms and
> values, which in turn leads to more problems and greater
> demand for control.

The failure of these 'reformist' reforms have repeatedly reinforced the
legitimacy of punishment as a response to a wide range of social problems and
indeed contributed to the expansion of the penal system.

Governments and criminal justice agencies are fully aware that penal law is
unable to prevent and manage most harm or crime in society. However, they
still parade it as the one-size-fits-all solution to public concerns about security
and safety. This commitment to a system which, in its own terms, fails so
spectacularly, needs exploring. Drawing on a range of sociological studies, JM
Moore (2015) has highlighted that the prison performs a number of important
functions remarkably successfully. As an instrument for highlighting the (minor
and relatively harmless) 'crimes' of the powerless whist hiding the (much more
serious) harms of the powerful (Hillyard and Tombs 2004); as a mechanism for
reinforcing existing power structures and disciplining the poor (Wacquant
2013); as a tool for disposing of the homeless, mentally ill and other
marginalised sectors of society (Bauman 2004); as an illusory device for
creating an appearance of the state's concern for citizens' security (whilst
allowing it to implement austerity, a programme that causes real insecurity)
(Neocleous and Rigakos 2011; Reiman 2007); as a strategy for electoral
support (Pratt 2006); and as an institution that can generate profits for the
increasing number of corporations involved in the commercial delivery of pain
(Flateau 1996); prison works. Similarly, writing about the USA, Angela Davis
(2016: 6) has highlighted the prison's success 'as a strategy of deflection of the
underlying social problems — racism, poverty, unemployment, lack of
education, and so on'. These observations, although primarily directed at
prisons, can be applied to the whole of the criminal justice system. Whilst it
fails in terms of its stated aims, it performs important social functions tied to
the maintenance and consolidation of the current social order. It is this real
and insidious purpose of criminal justice which explains both its
imperviousness to the damning critiques of its failure to achieve its official
purpose and its tendency to incorporate and distort progressive reforms.

Ultimately, criminal justice is a system whose primary function is the maintenance of an unjust social order. In terms of this function it must be considered a success.

Imaging and creating solutions: *Justice Matters*

It is because the criminal justice system both succeeds (at least in terms of promoting the interests of the powerful) and fails (at least for those who aspire to social justice) that we wish to shift the focus away from it. Whilst we are guided by abolitionist thinking (Christie 1981; Davis 2003; Lamble 2011; Mathiesen, 1974) and a strong critique of reformist goals (Mathiesen, 1990), both, in very different ways, place the criminal justice system at the centre of their agendas. Reformism seeks to fix criminal justice, something we believe impossible, and abolitionism seeks to do away with it, something we believe cannot occur without alternatives that sit outside the existing 'footprint' of prisons, punishment and penal law. What is needed are programmes and approaches that ultimately make *reform unnecessary* and *abolition inevitable*. In this paper, we argue that by creating 'social justice' solutions, criminal justice as a system becomes unnecessary and obsolete. This is about transformation rather than reform, abolition or alternatives.

One initiative, that we are both involved in, that seeks to put this approach into practice is *Justice Matters*, launched in 2013 by the Centre for Crime and Justice Studies, London. It is motivated by the understanding that the over-reliance on policing, prosecution and punishment is socially harmful, economically wasteful and, rather than a source of justice, largely a source of great injustice. Three key elements were identified as part of a *Justice Matters* approach: Downsize; Build; and Transform.[3] The idea was to look beyond criminal justice and build partnerships and collaborations to identify both visionary objectives and concrete solutions. In the 'downsize' phase of the project, the Centre invited written contributions, asking people to identify which element of criminal justice practice could be radically downsized, or done away with altogether. The Centre was inundated with suggestions on elements of the system that could be downsized, or abolished altogether. Examples included the police, youth courts, drug criminalisation, children's imprisonment, women's imprisonment, measuring 'reoffending', short prison sentences and psychological services.[4] These contributions were helpful in

---

[3] Inspired by Critical Resistance (n.d.) who identify three 'frames' as part of their abolitionist strategy: 1. Dismantle. 2. Change. 3. Build.

identifying areas of criminal justice activity that could be withdrawn, but on their own were insufficient in answering questions about how to best protect people and resolve harm.

Contributions on the 'build' and 'transform' aspect were then invited and a number were brought together in *Discussing Alternatives* (Allison and McMahon 2015). Contributions to the what 'I would build' comment series included: 'An alternative to the corporation' (Tombs 2015); 'A new liberal politics' (Bell 2015); 'Schools instead of prisons' (Pike 2015); 'Collective capacity for policy change' (Drake and Samota 2014); 'Stronger communities' (Daddow 2015); 'A movement to engage men in preventing violence against women and girls' (Duggan 2015); and 'A blueprint for change' (Roberts 2015). The Centre continues to receive and publish short online articles. These contributions helped to provide a broad base of options to build on. It was clear that there were many who shared a critical understanding of the failures of criminal justice and the limitations of reform.

While there was a real appetite for finding alternatives, one of the main stumbling blocks for the project was in developing a programme for social justice solutions that truly sat outside of criminal justice. This became clear at a central London event attended by more than 80 activists, practitioners and researchers. There was a consensus on *what not to do* but an impasse when it came to what *to do*. Discussions gravitated to criminal justice improvements. This paralysis was rooted in the fact that these conversations were often amongst criminal justice experts; people who had in-depth knowledge of the criminal justice system. Added to this was a sense of helplessness that very little could be done in the absence of huge changes required to tackle structural inequalities and social arrangements. Criminal justice sceptics (ourselves included) are usually very good at identifying what isn't working. But it is important to complement critique of criminal justice with the expansion of (non-criminal justice) interventions and approaches that promote wellbeing, health, stability, security and safety in people's lives. Whilst criminal justice experts usually start with the area they know best – criminal justice reform – the project of building safer and healthier societies must be the task of a much wider group of social justice experts and activists.

The next step in the *Justice Matters* initiative was to attempt to create resources or tools to help frame coherent and constructive discussions about

---

[4] To read the various contributions to the 'I would give up' series see :
http://www.crimeandjustice.org.uk/search/node/Iper cent20wouldper cent20giveper cent20up

'radical alternatives'. In late 2015, in collaboration with a small group of activists and researchers, work commenced on developing a toolkit and visual aids. This toolkit is intended to encourage the creation of thinking and practice that responds to social harm and conflicts without recourse to criminal justice and punishment. By taking participants through a series of steps, the workshop is structured to identify policy and practice that in the short, medium and longer term may resolve harm and ultimately make criminal justice irrelevant, unnecessary and obsolete. With the assistance of a working group, work is ongoing to develop a prototype kit including poster, infographics and worksheets as a resource that can be used by people in a range of settings for discussions about how we move 'from criminal justice to social justice'.

The infographic below offers a visual representation. Shaped as a 'J' for justice, on the left hand side we see criminal justice options: police; courts; and punishment. Moving to the right, we see multiple options, of many different kinds. These are simply illustrative and used as a basis for workshop discussions. They indicate the breadth of possible options that might be explored once you move 'beyond criminal justice'.

In using this model in workshops participants are asked to identify a social harm or social problem. Rather than discuss 'alternatives', the workshop is focused on identifying 'solutions'. The problem identified is open – and could be wide-ranging – from rape and sexual violence, through to burglary and theft, or workplace injury. Participants are then grouped together according to the problem they would like to discuss and asked to focus on a scenario and identify who is harmed. This is followed by a discussion about the current criminal justice response to identify the problems with, and limitations of, such an approach. Participants are then invited to focus on 'doing things differently' with prompts such as 'what would a social justice approach look like?' At various points, the discussion groups are encouraged to consider whether the responses or approaches they are identifying are focused on an individual, institutional or systemic level; whether they challenge or alleviate patterns of inequality; and who benefits? This is followed by a discussion of 'risks' – whether the proposals replicate any of the problems inherent within criminal justice approaches – and how it might be possible for them to be subverted or captured by criminal justice. The final part of the workshop invites participants to discuss how change can happen, concrete examples, quick wins, and how the proposals fit on a timeline. What becomes clear is that even within a short workshop, the opportunities exist for radically different solutions to social problems. Many alternatives do exist.

Justice Matters: Building social justice solutions
(January 2016 draft)

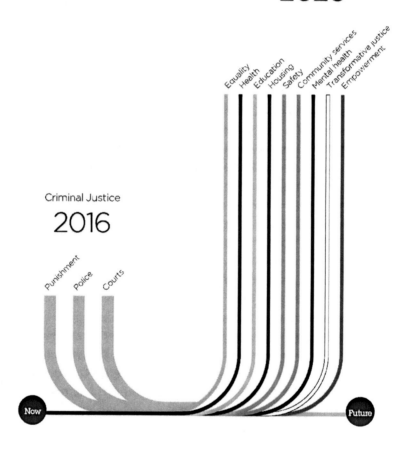

Transformative Alternatives: Drugs

It is no exaggeration to describe criminal justice as drug-fuelled. The association between violence and alcohol is well established. The Crime Survey of England and Wales 2013/14 estimated that 53 per cent (704,000 out of 1,327,000) of violent incidents involving adults were alcohol-related (ONS 2015a). Whilst the correlation was closest for violence between strangers (64 per cent) it was also a factor in an estimated 36 per cent of incidents of domestic violence (ibid). Significantly, the association between alcohol and violence increases as the evening (and drinking) progresses. Alcohol is linked to 23 per cent of violent incidents that occur between noon and 6pm, rising to 83 per cent of incidents between 10pm and midnight (ibid). This suggests that the amount of alcohol consumed is a significant factor. For heroin, cocaine and other 'illegal' drugs, the criminal justice system predominately responds to 'crimes' related to fundraising. Whilst most consumers of (both illegal and legal) drugs have incomes sufficient to pay for their purchases, the consumption of a significant minority is funded through illegal activity: shoplifting; burglary; or robbery. A confidential British Government report in 2003 estimated that out of a total of 64 million crimes some 53 million were committed by people who reported consuming illegal drugs in the previous 30 days (SU Drug Project 2003:22). They estimated that some 36 million (56 per cent) of these offences could be defined as 'motivated by drug use' (ibid:22).

The harms experienced by victims of violence and acquisitive crimes are substantial and serious. However they are only some of the harms caused by (legal and illegal) drugs. By focusing on 'crime', criminal justice limits its responses to policing and punishment. These responses are not only inadequate but a generator of further harms. A social justice approach has the capacity to address the harms related to all drugs as well as to focus on developing solutions which promote the construction of safer and healthier societies. The starting point of such an approach would be to concentrate on substances' harms rather than their legality. Drug harms can broadly be divided into three groups: the inherent harms of the substances (direct harms); the harms consumers of them cause to others (indirect harms); and the harms generated by the production, distribution and retailing of the substances (market harms). The potential direct harms of various substances are well-documented (Nutt et al 2010). The harm caused by alcohol in particular is extensive. In 2013 there were 8,416 alcohol related deaths registered in the UK (ONS 2015b:1). In terms of health, these deaths are only the tip of the iceberg, with alcohol-related chronic ill health affecting hundreds of thousands people in the UK. However, alcohol is not the most harmful drug, that is tobacco smoking which in 2013 resulted in 79,700 deaths and an estimated 460,900 hospital admissions in England (HSCIC 2014:46,45). Deaths linked to illegal drugs are significantly less, with their consumption being associated with 1,957 deaths in England and Wales in 2013 (ONS 2014:2). A further 998 deaths were associated with other 'legal' drugs (ibid).

The potential indirect harms of drugs vary by substance and are closely linked to their current legal status. The indirect harms of tobacco are the most substantial with second-hand smoke killing over 12,000 people and causing around 165,000 new cases of diseases in children each year in the UK (CRUK 2015). Although the indirect harms of alcohol are less substantial, they tend to be more dramatic, particularly the alcohol-related violence associated with the night time economy of town centres. The main indirect harms of illegal drugs are the estimated 36 million offences caused by acquisitive fundraising crime detailed above. Market harms are evident in all categories of drugs. For 'legal drugs' such as tobacco and alcohol these are closely associated with the promotion of their commercial interests by the drugs industries. To optimise profits, they seek to maximise sales and minimise regulation. With all drugs, but particularly with alcohol and tobacco, the associated risks of harms (both direct and indirect) increase with higher rates of consumption. However, it is users consuming high and dangerous amounts that are the focus of the commercial strategies of the tobacco and alcohol industries. Whilst in recent years the UK has seen the tobacco industry subjected to increased regulation prioritising public health over profits, the alcohol industry has been progressively deregulated. Increased availability – facilitated by the removal of restrictions on sales and a reduction in taxation to reduce cost – have led to increased consumption (Brennan et al 2016). Big alcohol has effectively gained control of its own regulation (Hawkins and Holden 2014) resulting in an increase in both direct and indirect harms (as well as alcohol industry profits).

For illegal drugs, the market harms are more complex and are closely linked to the substances' legal status. By prohibiting substances, states effectively choose not to regulate their production, distribution or retailing. This means no quality control, which increases the direct harms of, for example, overdoses; market participants' exclusion from civil law resolutions, generating the indirect harms of violence which characterise illegal drug markets (Dills et al 2008); high prices – particularly of heroin and (crack) cocaine – which generate high levels of acquisitive crime; the criminalisation of consumers, a harm that falls disproportionately on black and minority ethnic communities

(Eastwood et al 2013); and, at an international level, the political destabilisation of (poor, underdeveloped) producer and transit countries.

An alternative social justice response to the 'problem' of drugs (including both those currently legal and prohibited) would start by a recognition that people, for a variety of good and bad reasons, wish to consume them. However, we need to adopt a framework which allows consumption to occur whilst simultaneously minimising harms. Both direct and indirect drug harms are best addressed through the paradigm of public health. This requires a clear analysis of the respective risks associated with different substances to provide a scientific base for policy development. However, this can only occur within the context of an effectively regulated legal market. So a social justice approach to developing transformative solutions will require fundamental changes to the markets for all drugs, legal and illegal. The interests of the producers, distributors and retailers of drugs need to be made subservient to those of public health. Although a controlled market provides the framework for effective regulation, different drugs carry different risks – and have different social meanings – so the exact regulatory regimes will not be uniform. However, regulation is likely to be characterised by price controls (high enough to deter excessive use but not so high as to promote acquisitive crime); the promotion of lower strength products; restrictions on sales to children; supply through prescription for drugs linked to dependence; bans on branding, advertising and other promotional activities; safe consumption facilities; and education based on enabling consumers to make informed choices (Transform 2009).

Whilst such policies represent a major departure from the existing war on drugs and deregulation of the alcohol industry they are all approaches with histories. These are not speculative proposals but are based on an existing body of evidence. For example:

- Cannabis legalisation in a number of US states and South American countries has ended the excessive harms of criminal justice regulation without any evidence of an increase in any other harms (Drug Policy Alliance 2015)
- The decriminalisation of the personal consumption of all drugs in Portugal has not only seen a dramatic decrease in criminal justice harms but has also seen a reduction of the problematic use of previously illicit drugs (Gonçalves et al 2015).
- Alcohol regulation in early twentieth century Britain, through pricing (via taxation) and limiting availability (through licencing

restrictions), saw a significant reduction of both direct and indirect harms (Greenway 2003).

- The British system of prescription, which operated until the 1970s, whereby those with a drug dependency (particularly opiates) were prescribed them (Farrell and Hall 2015).
- The provision of shooting-up galleries and other safe consumption spaces which have significantly reduced overdose deaths and other harms in a number of countries including Switzerland (Hendrich 2004).

Limited space does not allow us to further expand on these or indeed explore innovative new approaches – such as David Nutt's (2006) proposal to develop a safer form of alcohol – effectively prohibited under the existing framework. However, what is clear is that there are effective ways of reducing significantly the direct, indirect and market harms of all (legal and illegal) drugs. What they all have in common is a rejection of the current reliance on criminal justice, which not only fails to address harms but directly contributes to them.

Transformative Alternatives: Gendered Violence

Violence against women is an endemic harm deserving of serious attention when thinking about moving beyond criminal justice and creating 'social justice' solutions. Mills et al (2015) offer a gendered analysis of the failures of criminal justice approaches, highlighting how in the case of violence against women, the system often replicates violence and inequality. Although the scale of violence against women is impossible to know, *End Violence Against Women* (2014) estimate that approaching three million women in the UK experience violence every year. This is likely to be an underestimate, as Helen Mills (2015) has pointed out:

> many incidents will not have been recognised as violence (including by those experiencing it). Others will not have fitted a formal crime classification. Even when recognised as violence by the person at the receiving end of it, the complex, usually intimate, context means underreporting is chronic.

Women experience violence routinely in the form of everyday sexism. A focus on violence defined as crime ignores the daily experience of leers, whistles, looks, comments, being followed and other routine harassments that remind women daily of the ever-present potential of gendered violence. Such events are rarely perceived, defined or recorded as crimes and, although they can be dismissed as 'minor', this classification is only apparent 'in retrospect' (Kelly and Radford 1987:242).

When gendered violence most obviously fits the category of 'crime', in cases of sexual violence, the criminal justice system still fails spectacularly. The Crime Survey for England and Wales, estimated that there are annually between 60,000 and 95,000 victims of rape and 430,000 to 517,000 victims of sexual offences (ONS 2013:7). This compares with 1,070 people convicted of rape and 5,620 people convicted of other sexual offences (ibid). These figures indicate a 'clear-up' rate for the CJS of less than two per cent for rape and just over one per cent for other sexual offences.[5] Such endemic failure often provokes the question 'what can criminal justice agencies do to respond better?' While this is a legitimate question to ask, it has been asked before and in response the criminal justice system has been subject to widespread reform, particular in respect of its responses to sexual violence. However, the failure detailed above occurred *after* these reforms, suggesting a much more fundamental problem. Demands for the police and courts to respond to every instance of violence against women would require a huge shift in approach and a vast investment in policing and investigation resources. Even then, they would largely focus on responding to violence after it had occurred. Crime *detection* and *reaction/response* should not be confused with *prevention*.

Whilst feminist campaigners and activists have been successful in raising the level of debate and awareness about violence against women, and this has resulted in some policing agencies recognising the hidden and harmful nature of this form of violence, there is a danger that the stick has bent too far. Mimi Kim (2013:1278), in an analysis of anti-violence work and criminalisation, argues that the 'constraining logic of criminalisation' has resulted in 'the alignment of the anti-domestic violence movement with the criminal justice

---

[5] These figures are not directly comparable and underestimate the clear-up rate. Whilst they contain all convictions irrespective of the age of the victim the estimated prevalence is based on self-reporting by women aged 16 to 59. Given the particular vulnerability of girls and older women, the frequency of sexual violence is far greater. Recent figures (ONS 2016) illustrate this: over 30 per cent of victims in rape prosecutions are under 16, as are over 50 per cent of victims of 'other sexual offences'. Based on this data, the likely clear up rate, for women between the ages of 16 and 59, for rape is at best 1 per cent and for other sexual offences under 0.5 per cent. For women who may not fit the 'ideal' profile of a woman (for example, women with uncertain immigration status, lawbreakers), as well as black and ethnic minority women, the clear-up rate is considerably lower. In fact such women are routinely further victimised and traumatised by criminal justice agencies' responses.

system' which in turn has 'foreclosed alternative conceptual frames and remedies'. Indeed, despite the criminal justice system accommodating many feminist demands, there remains, as Laureen Snider (1998:2) has highlighted, 'no persuasive evidence that reliance on criminal justice has made the female complainant safer or the male offender less violent'. Sadly, for most women, contact with the criminal justice system following an experience of sexual violence runs the risk of ending with them 'being humiliated, discredited, disbelieved, and even reviled for their efforts' (Leander 2013:357).

If focusing on, and directing resources through, criminal justice is ineffective, then we need an alternative approach. A social justice approach would be fundamentally different and would involve 'divert(ing) resources from the traditional axis of criminal justice and into adequate, stable sources of funding for women's services' (Hall and Whyte 2003:14). The eye-catching and powerful protests and actions of Sisters Uncut, a UK based feminist group taking direct action to defend domestic violence services, have gained widespread media attention and raised awareness about the impact of austerity on domestic violence services. Writing for the *Justice Matters* initiative, Sisters Uncut activist, Lauren White (2015), highlights the immediate need for well-funded refuges and specialist services. White connects the short-term needs to longer term demands, outlining a range of interventions, responses and conditions required to build a society in which all women are safe from male violence. She argues that not only should there be sufficient refuge spaces for all women and children fleeing violence but that these should include specialist services for Black and Minority Ethnic (BAME) women, women affected by the criminal justice system, trans women and women with disabilities. They should also create refuges where actively using and recovering substance users can live safely and access support to address their substance use. In addition, all women should have access to legal aid and, to reach the most socially excluded and vulnerable women in society, there should be drop-in services for street homeless women.

Whilst such services would ensure the immediate needs of women experiencing violence are met, these, White argues, should be accompanied by a wider programme aimed at both promoting social justice and engaging with the underlying causes of gendered violence. It is important to also:

> Teach girls they are important, that their voices, their thoughts, their bodies, matter. Teach young people about respect and consent. Link our struggles, and our successes, with our sisters

and brothers around the world in the fight against misogyny, racism, incarceration and neo-capitalism. (White 2015)

Such approaches focus on an agenda largely shaped by the needs of women rather than those of state agencies. Other groups have sought to construct a transformative justice approach based on 'a pragmatic recognition that (the) available institutional remedies would not lead to desired outcomes' (Kim 2012:17). These involve developing community strategies to address gendered violence that do not involve the criminal justice system. These approaches are particularly appealing to BAME communities whose encounters with criminal justice have been characterised by institutional racism. In the United States INCITE!, an organisation of radical feminists of colour, has sought ways of addressing the multiple forms of violence they experience. This includes both violence *against* their communities (for example from the police) and violence *within* their community (such as gendered violence). Having realised that the agencies of the criminal justice system are generators rather than preventers of violence, INCITE! (2014) argues that effective responses to violence require the development of alternative community based strategies which should seek to:

- Create and affirm values and practices that resist abuse and oppression and encourage safety, support, and accountability
- Develop sustainable strategies to address community members' abusive behaviour, creating a process for them to account for their actions and transform their behaviour
- Commit to ongoing development of all members of the community, and the community itself, to transform the political conditions that reinforce oppression and violence
- Provide safety and support to community members who are violently targeted that respect their self-determination

This is clearly an ambitious and long term strategy which will involve overcoming considerable obstacles. However, if we want to generate transformative change we need to be 'building models today that practice how we want to live in the future' (Lamble 2011:252). More immediately, White's (2015) suggestions above show that there are many available responses to supporting women that are simple and achievable. In the longer term we need to face up to the reality that a dramatic reduction in gendered violence requires more fundamental change. Tackling root causes can only be achieved by removing 'the social and economic disadvantage experienced by women and their dependents' (Bumiller 2008:163) and discovering 'how communities can be restructured and dominant masculinities and identities changed' (Snider: 1998:28), 'something the State fundamentally refuses to do' (Mathews 1994:165). Whilst some may accuse such an approach of being idealistic or utopian, it is important to highlight that both the immediate achievable objectives and the more fundamental long term ones are based on a wealth of professional and academic knowledge about how best to eliminate violence against women, knowledge which can be found in the fields of public health, anti-violence, feminism, epidemiology, economics, and other disciplines.

Conclusion: Beyond Radical Alternatives – Developing transformative solutions

These two examples have shown that the potential exists for developing transformative solutions. In fact, for many social problems, harms and conflicts the answers can often be found within existing knowledge and practice. The argument that criminal justice and penal law are essential demonstrates an incapacity to think outside the crime paradigm: we don't realise we know the answers because we insist on asking the wrong questions. The *Justice Matters* initiative, by framing the question in terms of creating socially just transformative solutions to specific scenarios rather than seeking to create alternatives to criminal justice interventions, allows the right questions to be asked, questions to which we often already have the answers. It also attempts to extend involvement beyond the usual, top-down, 'experts' of practitioners, policy makers and academics to build on every day experience.

A focus on transformative solutions builds on the abolitionist tradition and attempts to address the weaknesses of many apparently progressive 'alternatives to criminal justice': the danger of administrative incorporation into – and ideological colonisation by – the very system they have sought to replace (Mathiesen 1974; Mills et al 2015). Rather than allow people to escape the harshest aspects of penal sanction, these alternatives have allowed the criminal justice system to widen its net and draw additional people into its control. An example that illustrates this is restorative justice that, despite being based on progressive principles, by locating itself (as an alternative) *within* the criminal justice system, has found itself being increasingly used in a punitive manner and targeted at people who previously were, by and large, outside the grasp of penal law (Takagi and Shank 2004; Wood 2015). This paradox, the need for alternatives to make moving beyond criminal justice credible combined with the criminal justice system's capacity to incorporate and corrupt alternatives is transcended by the approach of developing *transformative solutions* rather than *alternatives* (radical or otherwise) to criminal justice. As Nils Christie (2011:78) has warned us 'experts are sometimes dangerous people' and so integral to our approach is a belief in the participation of those communities and individuals directly affected by social problems. It is their knowledge, experiences and wisdom, rather than that of experts and policy makers that will create solutions designed to solve real social problems, meet real human needs and respond to real harms and conflicts. Transformative solutions therefore need to be democratic, both in their development and in their implementation. Framed in this way, they are not alternatives to criminal justice but much broader, offering the concrete building blocks for real utopias. If they are developed democratically along principals of social justice they are ideologically incompatible with criminal justice's function of maintaining an unjust social order. Transformative solutions can be the scaffolding for the building of 'a better way of living and of being' (Levitas 2013:4).

References

Allison, C. and McMahon, W. (2015) *Discussing alternatives to criminal justice* London: Centre for Crime and Justice Studies, http://www.crimeandjustice.org.uk/sites/crimeandjustice.org.uk/files/Disc ussingper cent20alternativesper cent20toper cent20criminalper cent20justice.pdf

Bauman, Z. (2004) *Wasted Lives: Modernity and its Outcasts* Cambridge, Polity

Bell, E. (2015) 'I would build... a new liberal politics', *Centre for Crime and Justice Studies*, http://www.crimeandjustice.org.uk/resources/i-would-build-new-liberal-politics (consulted 13 May 2016)

Box, S. (1983) *Power Crime and Mystification* Abingdon: Routledge

Brennan, A., Meier, P., Purshouse, R., Rafia, R., Meng, Y., and Hill-McManus, D. (2016) 'Developing policy analytics for public health strategy and decisions - the Sheffield alcohol policy model framework' *Annals of Operational Research* Volume 236, No. 1 pp149-76

Bumiller, K. (2008) *In an Abusive State: How Neoliberalism Appropriated the Feminist Movement against Sexual Violence* Durham: Duke University Press

Chapman, D. (1968) *Sociology and the Stereotype of the Criminal* London: Tavistock Publications

Christie, N. (1977) 'Conflicts as property' in *The British Journal of Criminology* Volume 17 pp 1-15.

Christie, N. (1981) *The Limits of Pain* Oxford: Martin Robertson

Christie, N (2011) 'Reflections from the Periphery' in *British Journal of Criminology* Volume 51, No. 4 pp 707-710

Critical Resistance (n.d.) 'CR Structure and Background', http://criticalresistance.org/about/cr-structure-background/ (consulted 13 May 2016)

CRUK (2015) 'Passive Smoking' *Cancer Research UK*, http://www.cancerresearchuk.org/about-cancer/causes-of-cancer/smoking-and-cancer/passive-smoking (consulted 13 May 2016)

Daddow, R. (2015) 'I would build... stronger communities'. *Centre for Crime and Justice Studies*, http://www.crimeandjustice.org.uk/resources/i-would-build-stronger-communities (consulted 13 May 2016)

Davis, A. Y. (2003) *Are Prisons Obsolete?* New York: Seven Stories Press

Davis A. Y. (2016) *Freedom is a Constant Struggle: Ferguson, Palestine, and The Foundation of a Movement.* Chicago: Haymarket Books.

Dills, A.K., Miron, J.A. and Summers, G. (2008) 'What do economists know about crime' *National Bureau of Economic Research Working Paper* Series No:13759

Dilts, A. (2016) 'Justice as Failure' in *Law, Culture and the Humanities,* http://lch.sagepub.com/content/early/2016/01/05/1743872115623518.abstract (consulted 13 May 2016)

Drake, D. and Samota, N. (2014) 'Building collective capacity for policy change' *Reclaim Justice Network,* https://downsizingcriminaljustice.wordpress.com/2014/12/01/building-collective-capacity-for-policy-change/ (consulted 13 May 2016)

Drug Policy Alliance (2015) 'Status Report: Marijuana Legalization in Washington After 1 Year of Retail Sales and 2.5 Years of Legal Possession', http://www.drugpolicy.org/sites/default/files/Drug_Policy_Alliance_Status_Report_Marijuana_Legalization_in_Washington_July2015.pdf (consulted 13 May 2016)

Duggan, M. (2015) 'I would build... a movement to engage men in preventing violence against women and girls' *Centre for Crime and Justice Studies,* http://www.crimeandjustice.org.uk/resources/i-would-build-movement-engage-men-preventing-violence-against-women-and-girls (consulted 13 May 2016)

Eastwood, N., Shiner, M and Dear, D. (2013) *The Numbers in Black and White: ethnic disparities in the policing and prosecution of drug offences in England and Wales* London: Release, http://www.release.org.uk/sites/default/files/pdf/publications/Releaseper cent20-per cent20Raceper cent20Disparityper cent20Reportper cent20finalper cent20version.pdf (consulted 24 February 2016)

Farrell, M and Hall, W (2015) 'Heroin-assisted treatment: has a controversial treatment come of age?' in *The British Journal of Psychiatry* Volume 207, No.1 pp 3-4

Flateau, J. (1996) *The Prison Industrial Complex: Race, Crime and Justice* New York: Medgar Evers College Press

Gonçalves, R., Lourenço, A. and da Silva, S.N. (2015) 'A social cost perspective in the wake of the Portuguese strategy for the fight against drugs' in *International Journal of Drug Policy* Volume 26 pp 199-209

Greenaway, J. (2003) *Drink and British Politics since 1830: A study in policy-making* Basingstoke: Palgrave: Macmillan

Hall, T. and Whyte, D. (2003) 'At the Margins of Provision: Domestic violence, policing and community safety' in *Policy and Politics* Volume 31, No. 1 pp 3-18.

Hansard (2015) 'Offenders' Literacy' *House of Lords Written Question* http://www.parliament.uk/business/publications/written-questions-answers-statements/written-question/Lords/2015-12-21/HL4764/ (consulted 13 May 2016)

Hawkins, B and Holden, C. (2014) 'Water dripping on stone? Industry lobbying and UK alcohol policy' in *Policy and Politics* Volume 42, No. 1 pp 55-70

Hedrich, D. (2004) 'European report on drug consumption rooms' in *European Monitoring Centre for Drugs and Drug Addiction*, http://www.emcdda.europa.eu/attachements.cfm/att_2944_EN_consumpt ion_rooms_report.pdf (consulted 13 May 2016)

Hillyard, P and Tombs, S. (2004) 'Beyond Criminology' in Hillyard. P, Pantazis, C., Tombs, S. and Gordon, D. (eds) *Beyond Criminology: Taking harm seriously* London: Pluto

HSCIC (2014) 'Statistics on Smoking: England 2014' *Health and Social Care Information Centre.* http://www.hscic.gov.uk/catalogue/PUB14988/smok-eng-2014-rep.pdf (consulted 13 May 2016)

INCITE! (2014) *Community Accountability: How do we address violence within our communities?* http://www.incite-national.org/page/community-accountability (consulted 13 May 2016)

Kelly, L. and Radford, J. (1987) 'The Problem of Men: Feminist Perspectives on Sexual Violence' in Scraton, P. (ed) *Law, Order and The Authoritarian State: Readings in Critical Criminology* Milton Keynes: Open University Press

Kim, M. E. (2013), 'Challenging the Pursuit of Criminalisation in an Era of Mass Incarceration: The Limitations of Social Work Responses to Domestic Violence in the USA', *British Journal of Social Work* Volume 43, No. 7 pp 1276–1293.

Kim, M.E. (2012) 'Moving Beyond Critique: Creative Interventions and Reconstructings of Community Accountability' in *Social Justice* Volume 37, No. 4 pp 14-35

Lamble, S. (2011) 'Transforming Carceral Logics: 10 Reasons to Dismantle the Prison Industrial Complex Using a Queer/Trans Analysis', in Stanley, E.A. and Smith, N. (eds) *Captive Genders: Trans Embodiment and the Prison Industrial Complex* Oakland: CA: AK Press

Lamble, S. (2014) 'The marketisation of Prison Alternatives' in *Criminal Justice Matters* Volume 97, No. 1.

Leander, K. (2013) 'The Decade of Rape', in Gilmore, J., Moore, J.M. and Scott. D. (eds) *Critique and Dissent* Ottawa: Red Quill Books.

Levitas, R. (2013) *Utopia as Method: The Imaginary Reconstruction of Society* Basingstoke: Palgrave Macmillan

Mathiesen, T. (1974) *The Politics of Abolition* New York: John Wiley and Sons

Mathiesen, T. (1990) *Prisons on Trial* London: Sage

Matthews, N.A. (1994) *Confronting Rape: The Feminist Anti-Rape Movement and the State* Abingdon: Routledge

Mills, H. (2015) 'Addressing violence against women beyond criminal justice' in Mills, H., Roberts, R. and Townhead, L. (eds) *Empower, resist, transform: A collection of essays* London: Centre for Crime and Justice Studies, http://www.crimeandjustice.org.uk/sites/crimeandjustice.org.uk/files/Emp owerper cent20Resistper cent20Transformper cent20Januaryper cent202015_0.pdf (consulted 13 May 2016)

Mills, H., Roberts, R. and Townhead, L. (2015) *Empower, Resist, Transform: A collection of essays* London: Centre for Crime and Justice Studies, http://www.crimeandjustice.org.uk/sites/crimeandjustice.org.uk/files/Emp owerper cent20Resistper cent20Transformper cent20Januaryper cent202015_0.pdf (consulted 13 May 2016)

Moore, J.M. (2015) 'Reframing the "Prison Works" Debate: For whom and in what ways does prison work?' *Reclaim Justice Network*, https://downsizingcriminaljustice.wordpress.com/2015/03/10/reframing-the-prison-works-debate-for-whom-and-in-what-ways-does-prison-work/ (consulted 13 May 2016)

Neocleous, M. and Rigakos, G.S. (2011) *Anti-Security*. Ottawa: Red Quill Books

Nutt, D.J. (2006) 'Alcohol alternatives--a goal for psychopharmacology?' In *Journal of Psychopharmacology* Vol. 20, No.3.

Nutt, D.J., King, L.A. and Phillips, L.D. (2010) 'Drug harms in the UK: A multicriteria decision analysis' in *The Lancet* Volume 376 pp 1558-65.

ONS (2013) 'An Overview of Sexual Offending in England and Wales' *Ministry of Justice, Home Office and the Office for National Statistics*, https://www.gov.uk/government/uploads/system/uploads/attachment_data/file/214970/sexual-offending-overview-jan-2013.pdf (consulted 13 May 2016)

ONS (2014) 'Deaths Related to Drug Poisoning in England and Wales, 2013', *Office for National Statistics*, http://www.ons.gov.uk/ons/dcp171778_375498.pdf (consulted 13 May 2016)

ONS (2015a) 'Five facts about alcohol-related violence' *Office for National Statistics*, http://www.ons.gov.uk/ons/rel/crime-stats/crime-statistics/focus-on-violent-crime-and-sexual-offences--2013-14/sty-facts-about-alcohol-related-violence.html (consulted 13 May 2016)

ONS (2015b) 'Alcohol-related Deaths in the United Kingdom, Registered in 2013', *Office for National Statistics*, http://www.ons.gov.uk/ons/dcp171778_394878.pdf (consulted 13 May 2016)

ONS (2016) 'Experimental Statistics 1: New data on police recorded violent and sexual offences, year ending March 2015', *Office for National Statistics*, http://www.ons.gov.uk/ons/dcp171778_432746.pdf (consulted 13 May 2016)

Pike, G. (2015) 'I would build...schools instead of prisons' in *Centre for Crime and Justice Studies*, http://www.crimeandjustice.org.uk/resources/i-would-buildschools-instead-prisons (consulted 13 May 2016)

Reiman, J. (2007) *The Rich Get Richer and the Poor Get Prison: Ideology, class and criminal justice* (8th edition) New York: Macmillan

Roberts, R. (2015) 'I would build...a blueprint for change', *Centre for Crime and Justice Studies*, http://www.crimeandjustice.org.uk/resources/i-would-builda-blueprint-change (consulted 13 May 2016)

Sim, J. (2009) *Punishment and Prisons: Power and the Carceral State* London: Sage

Snider, L. (1998) 'Towards Safer Societies: Punishment, Masculinities and Violence Against Women' in *British Journal of Criminology* Volume 38, No. 1 pp 1-39

SU Drugs Project (2003) *Phase 1 Report: Understanding the Issues*, No. 10 Strategy Unit Drugs Project. Leaked to *The Guardian*, http://image.guardian.co.uk/sys-files/Guardian/documents/2005/07/05/Report.pdf (consulted 13 May 2016)

Takagi, P. and Shank, G. (2004) 'Critique of Restorative Justice' in *Social Justice* Volume 31, No. 3 pp 147-163

Tombs, S. (2015a) *Social Protection after the Crisis: Regulation without enforcement* Bristol: Policy Press

Tombs, S. (2015b) 'I would build...an alternative to the corporation', *Centre for Crime and Justice Studies*, http://www.crimeandjustice.org.uk/resources/i-would-buildan-alternative-corporation (consulted 13 May 2016)

Transform (2009) *After the War on Drugs: Blueprint for Regulation* Bristol: Transform Drug Policy Foundation

Wacquant, L. (2013) 'Crafting the Neoliberal State: Workfare, prisonfare and social insecurity' in Scott, D. Why Prison? Cambridge: Cambridge University Press

WHO (n.d.) 'Tobacco' *World Health Organisation*, http://www.who.int/trade/glossary/story089/en/ (consulted 13 May 2016)

White, L. (2015) 'I would build a society where all women are safe from male violence', Centre for Crime and Justice Studies, http://www.crimeandjustice.org.uk/resources/i-would-buildpercentE2per cent80percentA6-society-where-all-women-are-safe-male-violence (consulted 13 May 2016)

Wood, W.R. (2015) 'Why Restorative Justice Will Not Reduce Incarceration' in *British Journal of Criminology* Volume 55, No. 5 pp 883-900

Wright, E.O. (2010) *Envisioning Real Utopias* London: Verso

A New Look at Victim and Offender:
An abolitionist approach[1]

Thomas Mathiesen and Ole Kristian Hjemdal[2]

Abstract

Since the 1980s prison populations have increased dramatically in most Western countries. Criminology has proposed several approaches to reverse this development, but with only meagre success. Treatment programmes based on individual explanations of crime conducted inside prisons have not been able to overcome the negative effects of the prison-life; programmes conducted outside prisons have often been supplements and add-ons rather than alternatives; and strategies of incapacitation based on an understanding of social and societal risk factors have often shown themselves to be both repressive and ineffective. Mere criticism of the prison system, as ineffective and repressive, along with proposals to reduce the number of prisons and decriminalise drug use are important, but not enough to tear down the prison walls and significantly reduce prison populations.

To effectively reduce the number of prisoners and prisons, an abolitionist approach which more fundamentally transcends the existing boundaries of current criminal policy is necessary. This abolitionist approach may be seen not only as a stance, an attitude of saying 'no', but also as an important academic exercise, where you can express and develop your idea of abolition of the penal system, and as a more practical and activist strategy directed at key points in our prison and penal policies and culture. This is the line we advocate for a new criminology.

At the core of this criminology is a new look at the relationship between victim and offender. The point of departure is the understanding that it serves

---

[1] This is a revised and updated version of 'A New look at Victim and offender - An Abolitionist Approach', by the two of us, in M. Bosworth and C. Hoyle (Eds.) What is Criminology? (pp 223-234) Oxford University Press. The basic idea on the relationship between victim and offender, in the latter part of this paper, was first presented by sociologist Ole Kristian Hjemdal. The idea was further developed in the Norwegian edition of Thomas Mathiesen's book Prison on Trial (1990). The idea was not presented in the English edition, and was developed for the first time in English in What is Criminology? The remainder of the paper contains joint perspectives

[2] Thomas Mathiesen is Professor Emeritus of the Sociology of Law at the University of Oslo. Ole Kristian Hjemdal is senior researcher at the Norwegian Centre for Violence and Traumatic Stress Studies.

neither the victim nor the offender much to have the offender reported to the police and possibly imprisoned. What we propose is to make the victim rather than the offender the object of criminal policy and that the efforts of society should shift from adjusting the right punishment to the crime committed by the offender to adjusting the correct help to the needs of the victim. This concentration on help to the victims could conceivably take three general forms: firstly, symbolic rehabilitation and comfort, secondly, material compensation and restoration and thirdly, social support, and if possible, reconciliation. More details will be outlined below concerning these points. The crux of the matter is that a concentration on the victim brings in something which is 'real' - it is even to some limited extent relied on in practice today. Yet it is still 'utopian' in that it will not be an option on a large or major scale in actual practice instead of prisons for a very long time. In this sense it constitutes 'a non-penal real utopia' in relation to present-day prison affairs, and a way to think of prison abolition.

Old News

It is old news in criminology that prison figures are soaring in many countries. The World Prison Population List of 2015 (Walmsley, 2016), states that probably more than 11 million people are now held in penal institutions throughout the world, either as pre-trial detainees/ remand prisoners or having been convicted and sentenced. Since about the year 2000 the world prison population total has grown by almost 20 per cent, which is slightly above the estimated 18 per cent increase in the world's general population over the same period. There are considerable differences between the continents, and variation within continents. The total prison population in Oceania has increased by almost 60 per cent and that in the Americas by over 40 per cent; in Europe, by contrast, the total prison population has decreased by 21 per cent. The European figure reflects large falls in prison populations in Russia and in central and Eastern Europe. In the Americas, the prison population has increased by 14 per cent in the USA, by over 80 per cent in Central American countries and by 145 per cent in South American countries (ibid).

There are nuances, the Netherlands and Sweden in fact have some empty prisons now, and Norway is renting a whole Dutch prison for inmates from Norway to alleviate the waiting list for those waiting to serve sentences. But despite the nuances, and a slight decrease after 2008 (Allen, 2015), the total increases since 2000 are marked. And the trends go further back, at least until the 1980s. What should we do about it?

Various Approaches

Criminology provides various approaches. One of them may be called *boundary acceptance*. The boundaries of the prison are kept intact. The conditions which are part and parcel of the penal and prison system are accepted as boundaries to be taken for granted. Attempts are made to find and underscore the kinds of criminology that governments are listening to and responding to in penal policy, without the boundaries being crossed or violated. Criticism may occur, but only within these boundaries, literally these walls.

One variety of boundary acceptance is based on *individual explanations* of deviance and crime. The hope is that genetics, biology, psychology, various pedagogical approaches like cognitive skills programmes, anger management programmes, cognitive behavioural therapies and the like are called in, which may improve things on the individual level. Strategies of individual incapacitation, in which risk assessments based on a variety of techniques have a prominent place, have likewise gained prominence. A wide range of studies in the 'What Works' (Martinson, 1974) tradition, a treatment-orientation which has supplanted the 'Nothing Works' thinking from the 1960s and 1970s, have re-kindled hope (Lipsey, 1995). Alternatives such as community sentences, conflict resolution boards and electronic surveillance in the home are being tried in some countries.

The trouble with the various trends and studies based on an individual understanding of crime is that their effectiveness in terms of recidivism is to a very considerable extent scant (Mathiesen, 2007). Under rigorous controls, various carefully designed measures based for example on psychological and pedagogical preconditions may work to some extent, but such rigorous controls and carefully designed measures are rarely present in our prisons. Our closed prisons are to a large extent boisterous and unruly places where drugs are taken in large quantities.

Furthermore, alternatives such as community sentences and conflict resolution boards tend to become add-ons to the prison system rather than true alternatives to it. In the eleventh hour parliaments will vote in such a manner that the measures will be opened not primarily as alternatives to unconditional sentences, but rather as alternatives to conditional sentences or even more lenient control efforts. This is a story which goes far back into the history of 'alternatives'. As Stanley Cohen (1985) has pointed out so eloquently, the total control system seems to swell rather than shrink, at least in many places. To be sure, important exceptions exist (McMahon, 1992), but this is a general trend. It might be added that reliance on the fiscal crisis, arguing that it is too expensive to build or maintain prisons (which has recently become a line of thinking in the US state of California), appears likely to be only a short term method which will melt away when the economy changes. It is not based on an intrinsic wish to decrease prison figures.

A second variety of boundary acceptance is based on *social or societal explanations* of crime and delinquency. Reference is made to collective morality (which presumably is waning), class conflict and status discords, demography, ethnicity (often combined with class), geography and culture and so on – as well as their practical applications in terms of strategies of collective incapacitation – where whole groups or categories are targeted. As in the case of boundary acceptance of the individual variety, the intentions may partly be humanistic and critical of important societal dimensions (class and ethnicity are cases in point), but it is difficult to see the practical results, and measures are often strongly repressive and quite ineffective. In Norway, two related examples come to mind: A so-called 'VIC project', in which 'Very Important Criminals' are closely monitored and taken off the streets when apprehended; and a 'broken windows project' imported from New York, which is another variety of the same. In New York as well as in Norway the 'broken windows' approach is one of many examples of repressive measures which do not yield desired results. Demographic factors and other factors are at work. The crime rate has gone down in cities and towns also where a 'broken windows' approach is not applied.[3]

A third and final variety of boundary acceptance, where the prison as such is not attacked, but rather accepted, should also be mentioned. We are thinking here of various *critical approaches* to the existing prison system, which keep the boundaries up and the prison as a solution intact. Arguments like; the prison does not work as a preventive measure, the costs of control are greater than the gains, crime is a cultural construction which remains uninfluenced by prison, the number of prisons should be reduced, there should be more open prisons and fewer closed ones, certain behaviour

---

[3] A Norwegian version of the criticism of the 'broken windows' strategy is discussed in Elisabeth Myhre Lie: 'Lov og orden i New York' ('Law and Order in New York'), *Aftenposten* 23 September 2009. Lie works at the Norwegian Police University College in Oslo.

patterns which currently are criminalized (the use of softer drugs) should be decriminalized, and the like are fair enough as criticisms, but do not tear down the walls. Generally speaking, criticisms and proposals like these are well meaning, they may be mustered by enthusiasts with good intentions. We cannot shrug them off like many of us did in the 1970s. Reforms may be important to prisoners, and they may also have some positive long-term functions. But, by keeping boundaries up, the authorities may easily ward them off as methods to significantly reduce prison populations.

Abolitionism

If the goal is to reduce the number of prisoners and prisons effectively, a much bolder attack on the prison which can transcend system boundaries is in order. It must follow a line of thinking which is as broad as possible, essentially demanding a sea of change in Western criminal policy, which in its current form is at a dead end. This is the crux of an *abolitionist* approach to criminal and penal policy.

An abolitionist, whether a scientist, a teacher or a person practising his/her trade, is not a person who is preoccupied with what we would call system justification. He/she is not a person who is preoccupied with refining the existing. His/her wish is to get rid of the existing, like some people, close to two thousand years ago, got rid of (the remnants of) the Roman Empire, or like others, more recently, in many countries got rid of slavery and the death penalty. To be sure, many forces operated in the direction of these major historical examples of abolitions. Also, in quite a few places slavery and the death penalty are not abolished. In addition, you do find examples of their return under new names. Nevertheless, in many places they may be seen as major, more or less full scale abolitions.

More concretely, and having worked with the issues involved in abolitionism in the realm of penal and prison policy for roughly 40 years, we have over time delineated several different *lines* of abolitionist thinking. Here we will briefly mention three of them.

Firstly, *abolitionism may be seen as a stance*. It is the attitude of saying 'no'. This does not mean that the 'no' will be answered affirmatively in practice. A 'no' to prisons will not occur in our time. But as a *stance* it is viable and important. This does not mean that we have not been preoccupied with concrete abolitions. In the Norwegian context, we have been strongly engaged in getting forced labour for alcoholic vagrants abolished (it was in fact abolished in 1970), likewise the borstal, or youth prison, abolished (they were in fact abolished in 1975). We have done this through our work in the Norwegian prison movement (KROM – the Norwegian Association for Penal Reform, established in 1968 and still going strong). But we have (also in the context of KROM) been preoccupied with fostering and developing an abolitionist stance (in Norwegian *holdning*, and in German the much better word *Stellung*); a constant and deeply critical attitude to prisons and penal systems as inhumane solutions.

Many forces, at the work place as well as in the private sphere, operate in the direction of softening the abolitionist stance, and you therefore have to be on constant alert to maintain and develop it.[4]

Secondly, *abolitionism may be seen as an important academic exercise*. While maintaining and advocating an abolitionist stance to penal and prison matters in the external world, the abolitionists who are engaged academically have the academic site as a concrete work place. In the academic world, in contrast to life outside which is full of compromises, pressures, pitfalls and loud noise, it is possible to think in a clear and principled way. The main point with abolitionism as an academic exercise is that the context provides an opportunity to think and loudly express new ideas, think and loudly express what may be imagined although it is not yet anywhere near practical policy. It was possible for example for Louk Hulsman to ponder deep questions such as what will it take to have not only prisons, but also penal policy as a whole, abolished? Is it possible to develop a new language supplanting the criminal justice language, and to have criminal law supplanted by civil law? Is it possible to create a civil rather than penal frame of reference in society?

The pressures within the academy to follow the mainstream and remain within a criminal law and penal frame of reference are very strong indeed. Producing research grants, getting tenure as well as a whole range of other social pressures are at work in favour of the mainstream. But in the Western world the academy is one of the few places where basic views outside the mainstream may be upheld and loudly voiced.[5]

---

[4] For a further understanding of this line of abolitionism, see Thomas Mathiesen: 'The Abolitionist Stance', paper presented at the International Conference on Penal Abolition (ICOPA XII), 23 July 2008, printed in *Journal of Prisoners on Prisons*, Vol. 17 No. 2 2008, pp 58-63. See also his *The Politics of Abolition Revisited*, Routledge, 2015 pp 31-36

[5] The present brief statement about abolitionism as an academic exercise is inspired by, but partly different from, Louk Hulsman's conception of 'academic abolition'. Hulsman takes academic abolition to mean i.a. the development or reconstruction of a different language with which to talk about 'problematic situations'; see his 'Themes and Concepts in an

Abolition as a stance and academic abolitionism are two forms of abolitionism at a time where the actual abolition of prisons lies in the future, out of our reach. Both are viable and important. But there is also another possibility, a third form of abolitionism, which is as viable and important as the others. It brings in a third dimension, where a retreat to the safe haven of the academy or a mere dimension of a staunch *no* is combined with 'expeditions' and actions favouring basic change in the outside world, *notably at key points in our prison and penal policies and culture*. This third form of abolitionism crosses boundaries with stamina and resolve, brings in deep and prolonged interaction with those who are subject to the so-called criminal justice system – the prisoners, and is up to a point practical. But it consciously leaves aside many of the practical technicalities and compromises which all too quickly make system boundaries arise once again.[6] It is an art.[7]

This is the line we advocate for *a new criminology*, as a non-penal real utopia, to counterbalance the very strong tendency in the discipline towards boundary acceptance of one or more of the kinds indicated earlier in this article. 'Real utopia' refers to a situation where an idea is presented which may in principle be carried out in practice, but which is utopian in the sense that it for various reasons will not become a major reaction for a very long time. A transfer from punishment of the offender to various escalations of aid to the offender is such a 'real utopia'. It is an idea which may be carried out in principle (and which is carried out to some extent in practice), but which for various reasons will not become a major option for a very long time.

An example is in order.

Victim and Offender

The relationship between *victim and offender* strikes at the core of criminal policy. Though victimless crime certainly abounds, the relationship is key. Turn the key, and another criminal policy may emerge.

Abolitionist Approach to Criminal Justice', Dordrecht 22 September 1997, http://www.loukhulsman.org/Publication/

[6] New debates and conflicts over abolition may occur when academics and prisoners become engaged in a common social movement. However, it is our experience, after 40 years of work in KROM (see above) that many such conflicts may be solved in a long term perspective.
[7] See for example Nils Christie: *A Suitable amount of Crime*, London: Routledge 2004.

The victim has received increasing attention over the past couple of decades. The plight of the victim, or of his or her relatives, is often compared with the situation of the offender. In public debate it is frequently said that while the offender receives large doses of help and support, the victim receives next to nothing. This, it is maintained, is out of balance and an unjust arrangement. Presumably, the tables should be turned: The victim should receive much more support of various kinds and the offender less, so that the relationship between victim and offender is brought into balance.

We propose a different way of looking at the relationship between victim and offender. We have in mind victims of offenders who today serve time in prison, or of offenders who would have served time in prison if they had been caught. Our analysis is meant as a sketch, an idea which needs further development, and is in line with an abolitionist way of thinking.

Our point of departure is that it serves the victim little to have the offender reported to the police and possibly imprisoned. Firstly, the victim largely receives little or nothing from it. An exception would be the minimum pleasure of naked revenge on the part of the victim. Though such a sentiment is understandable, we do not accept it as a legitimate function of imprisonment. Secondly, revenge is an 'open' feeling: as a sentiment, it is never fully satisfied and legal punishment of the perpetrators does not reduce the victims' feelings of revenge (Orth, 2014); stiffer sentences usually lead to further demands for revenge, and so on in an unending circle. Thirdly, our present system is of rather marginal importance to most victims. Few victims (in Norway, 15-20 per cent) report cases of violence to the police, and when property crimes are reported the main reason is to release the insurance rather than having the offender sentenced. The main reason for not reporting violence is that victims do not think it will be of any help (which by the way is quite correct as the chances of being exposed to further violent episodes is not influenced by reporting to the police (Hjemdal, 2002)). Also in cases where crimes against the person are in fact reported, sentencing does not usually follow. For example, over 80 per cent of all reported rapes charges are dropped for various reasons. To use the victim as an argument for a more repressive policy misses the target completely, not only because it does not help the victim to have the offender imprisoned, but also because the large majority of victims are out of reach of present-day criminal policy.

On the side of the prisoner, and again contrary to popular opinion, it serves the offender little to be imprisoned. The pains of imprisonment are sharp, often as knives, and prisons are not service institutions but disciplinary control systems. Those who are imprisoned systematically constitute one of the most poverty-stricken strata in society, and remain so after serving a prison sentence.

Imprisonment, then, is a solution for neither victim nor offender.

'Victimology' has, through the past couple of decades, become an important research area. Nevertheless, criminal policy does not cease to focus on the offender. The offender is the object of criminal policy. He or she is to blame, and he or she is to be punished.

We take the position that a radical change should take place in the very focus of criminal policy. The position may be seen as a concrete implementation of an abolitionist approach, as non-penal real utopia (Scott, 2013). Our proposal is to *move the focus of attention in criminal policy completely away from the offender, and over to the victim.*

Traditionally, the offender and the victim are seen in relation to each other. They are two sides of the same coin. What we propose, is to untie the relationship between the two. We propose to use Ockham's razor[8] on the tie, and make the victim *rather than* the offender the object of criminal policy.

This idea is fundamentally different from the more traditional notion of restorative justice. At the core of restorative justice is the understanding of crime as a conflict relationship between a victim and an offender. In restorative justice the role of the criminal justice system is to prepare the parties for solving the conflict between themselves. The main objective of restorative justice is to repair the damage and restore the relationship between the parties. Our notion presupposes a much stronger role on the part of the State, in which – to repeat – the State moves the very focus away from the offender and over to the victim [9]. But conflict resolution may come in as one of the many ways of providing a new social dignity on the part of the victim (and offender). We return to this later.

Our notion means that the efforts of society should not consist of adjusting the right punishment to the crime committed by the offender, but that the efforts of society should rather consist of adjusting the correct help to the victim. The measures taken by society should not be escalated, in the form of pain or punishment, relative to the guilt and damage done by the offender, but the measures taken by society should be escalated, in the form of help,

---

[8] Ockham's razor can be popularly stated as 'when you have two competing theories that make exactly the same predictions, the simpler one is the better'. The principle is attributed to 14th-century English logician and Franciscan friar, William of Ockham.

[9] In this sense it is different from the model of restitution proposed by Randy Barnett in 1977.

relative to the situation and damage done to the victim. In short: rather than operating with a scale of punishment related to the offence, we should operate with a scale of help related to the harm experienced by the victimised person.

It is a foreign thought, and we should therefore acquaint ourselves with it. Once again, the heart of the matter is to adjust the efforts of society as help to the victim *rather than* punishment of the offender. The crux of the matter is to escalate the measures of society as help relative to the situation and damage on the part of the victim *rather than* escalating them as punishments relative to the offender's guilt and damage done.

The heart of the matter, then, is a brand new criminal policy, a criminal policy which also would decrease anxiety in society, something which traditional criminal policy does not do. As Box and Hale have suggested, law makers and courts may be seen as 'anxiety barometers', as institutions which, through their decisions, reflect the anxiety of society (Box et al, 1982; Box and Hale, 1985). But they *do* nothing to the anxiety. The policy which we propose would *do* something with the anxiety by the shifting of attention mentioned above.

Such concentration on help to the victim could conceivably take three general forms:

Firstly, the *symbolic form.* Symbolic rehabilitation is important in a number of cases. Institutionalized sympathy, rituals expressing sorrow, stronger forms of rehabilitating honour through personal and public conversations and forms of being together, adequate resources for treatment in a wide sense of the word where *this* is wanted. And peace and quiet, no interference, where *that* is wanted.

Secondly, the *material form.* Life insurance in the real sense of the word is important. Here this means that all members of society automatically, from birth on, are economically insured against crime, and that the insurance is released in very simple ways, without complicated and degrading efforts on the part of the victim. It is fantastic that our advanced social democratic state has not already instituted this, but has left it to private initiative. A general life insurance from birth onwards would among other things have wiped out the class differences which exist today as far as insurance goes. The poverty of imprisoned offenders usually makes it impossible for offenders to compensate damages, at least when the damages are more than trivial. It would have to be a state insurance. A low insurance tax for all citizens from birth onwards would make it possible for the State to pay damages, at least in cases where the damages are above a certain level.

Today's state compensation to victims of violent crimes is only a beginning. Over and above economic insurance and standard compensation, concrete support for rehabilitation of material structures which have been damaged, similar support for rehabilitation of the human situations which have been damaged, would be important. You can say that it is not always easy to rehabilitate, even when it is in the material sense. But within today's system *nothing* is rehabilitated or rebuilt, and much can after all be done in this respect.

Thirdly, *the social form*. This is the place where a new contact between victim and offender could be relevant. It presupposes an active interest on the part of both parties.

Today's conflict resolution boards could be one model. Generally crime, at least of the traditional kind, may be viewed as a communicative act, a side-tracked attempt to say something. When we consider it important that what is being said is in fact said in a manner which is acceptable, further communication may be facilitated, and arrangements for that purpose should be established. But at times, or often, such communication is not desired by one or both parties, or impossible to arrange for other reasons. Obviously you cannot establish communication of this kind as long as the offence remains undetected or not cleared up. Nevertheless the social form is far from being exhausted as a way of thinking. For those who have been exposed to street violence, the establishment of networks of a protective and rehabilitative kind, especially in the sense of reducing anxiety, would be important. For those who have been subjected to violence in the private sphere, today's crisis centres for battered women and men could provide a model. As violence in the private sphere is being uncovered, we understand how important the establishment and further development of protective centres would be, and how important it would be to give those who are employed there all the resources they need for running the centres. For battered women and men and for those who have been exposed to more subtle but threatening victimisation, it would be important (as supplements to the protective centres) to develop roles for persons who could be called in and act as go-betweens. Roles of this kind are almost totally lacking in our society today.

These are just suggestions – a whole host of social measures as well as symbolic and material methods may be envisaged. But what about the cost? We have mentioned a life insurance against criminal damages for all citizens from birth, which would imply a small insurance tax on everyone. The insurance would be a non-profit matter, so the tax would be low. But it would require an administrative bureaucracy (a danger would be that this bureaucracy could grow large; this would have to be prevented), and the many other arrangements which would be relevant and necessary would be costly. Who would pay, over and above the insurance tax?

Keep clearly in mind our point of departure: the crux of the matter is to escalate the measures of society as help relative to the situation and damage on the part of the victim, *rather than* escalating them as punishments relative to the offender's guilt and damage done. In other words, the point is the development of a new kind of justice. This would lead to a drastic reduction of the prison population, which is part and parcel of the abolitionist approach. In turn this would involve a similarly dramatic reduction of costs in the construction and maintenance of prisons. We do not consider it as our task here to present a detailed budget, just to present the idea. The money saved would certainly cover the expenses of help to victims. Also of the utmost importance: it would help cover a large part of the expenses which would have to be geared towards *help to the offender*. To repeat, we know the offenders who are imprisoned are regularly extremely poor. They lack education, housing, jobs, in large numbers they are drug addicts, alcoholics and the like. Saved money would have to be divided between the ranks of victims and the ranks of offender. There would be money enough through saved prison expenses.

We hear the cry: What of protection of society? What of incapacitation of the offender, collective and selective? What of the deterrence of the offender and also of others who are not yet inside the walls? These are important questions. Our answers to them are given in detail in Thomas Mathiesen's book *Prison on Trial* (2006).[10] A large collection of data, a whole library of empirical studies, suggests that the prison is a failure in terms of all the standard justifications of imprisonment.

Perhaps there is a lower threshold or floor in terms of imprisonment which we cannot go below without doing some harm to society. In Britain, the US and many other countries we are very far indeed from that floor today. It is time to change our priorities, carving out a basically new criminal policy in our societies.

---

[10] Also out in Norwegian, Swedish, Danish, German, Italian, Spanish, and Taiwan mandarin, and has recently also been published in mainland mandarin.

We have just presented an idea to such a change. It would have to be carved out in practice. This would be a long-drawn process, with pitfalls and struggles. From the start it would involve a mode of thinking which is critical but also constructive rather than just concentrating on the difficulties. Perhaps above all, it would involve a basic change in the cultural climate of our society.

Conclusions

Quite a few years ago, the French sociologist Pierre Bourdieu coined the term *doxa* to refer to that which is taken for granted, that which is not questioned because it is common knowledge to everyone in the tribe (Bourdieu and Nice, 1977). *Doxa* has hegemony. If debates do occur *doxa* (and they often do in the Western world), they are frequently *orthodox*: while frequently sensational in terms of media coverage, the coverage often takes for granted and therefore neglects the basic issues involved. Ethnomethodologists touched on such hidden dimensions of societal communication long before Bourdieu, without using his terminology. At times, however, debates become *heterodox*, touching on deep issues. Struggles may then occur for example over critical issues in criminal policy. Heterodox opinions are often relegated to marginal journals and newspapers outside the mainstream. But sometimes they become threatening to basic dimensions of a *doxa*. They become real battles. Such struggles may make the world better, but also worse – there are historical examples of both. It is our hope that our new look at the victim and offender makes (some) people think outside of standardised patterns, outside of *doxa*, to make the world better. It would also help open up for a new and exciting science of criminology, which thinks outside the box, and which is not restricted by boundaries.

References

Allen, R. (2015) *Global Prison Trends 2015* London: Penal Reform International

Barnett, R.E. (1977) 'Restitution: A new paradigm of criminal justice' in *Ethics* Volume 87 pp 279-301

Bosworth, M. And Hoyle, C. (2011) *What is Criminology?* Oxford: OUP

Bourdieu, P. and Nice, R. (1977) *Outline of a Theory of Practice* Camridge: Cambridge University Press

Box, S. and Hale, C. (1985) 'Unemployment, Imprisonment and Overcrowding' in *Contemporary Crises* Volume 9 pp 209-228

Box, S. and Hale, C. (1982) 'Economic Crisis and the Rising Prisoner Population in England and Wales' in *Crime and Social Justice* Volume 17 pp 20-35

Cohen, S. (1985) *Visions of Social Control: Crime, punishment and classification* Cambridge: Policy Press

Hjemdal, O. K. (2002) 'Holder politiets arbeidmål? ('Is the Work of the Police up to Standard?') in Skodvin, A. (ed) *Poltitjenestemann og akademiker? Forskning i praksis og politiarbeid (Police officer and Academic)* Oslo: PHS Forskning

Lipsey, M. W. (1995) 'What do we learn from 400 research studies on the effectiveness of treatment with juvenile delinquents?' in McGuire, J. and Pease, K. (eds) *What Works: Reducing reoffending – guidelines from research and practice* New York: Wiley

Martinson, R. (1974) 'What Works? Questions and answers about prison reform' in *The Public Interest* Volume 35 pp 22-54

Mathiesen, T. (2006) *Prison on Trial* Hook: Waterside Press

Mathiesen, T. (2007) 'Fra "Nothing Works" til "What Works" – Hvor store er forskjellen?' ('From "Nothing Works" to "What Works" – How great is the Difference?') in Hofer, H. V. and Nilsson, A. (eds) *Brott i välfärden: om brottslighet, utsatthet och kriminalpolitik: festskrift till Henrik Tham (Crime in Welfare. About crime, vulnerability and penal policy: Homage volume in honour of Henrik Tham)* Stockholm: Kriminologiska Institutionen

McMahon, M. W. (1992) *The Persistent Prison? : Rethinking decarceration and penal reform* Toronto: University of Toronto Press

Orth, U. (2004) 'Does perpetrator punishment satisfy victims' feelings of revenge?' in *Aggressive Behaviour* Volume 30 pp 62-70

Scott, D. (2013) 'Visualising an Abolitionist Real Utopia: Principles, policy and praxis' in Malloch, M. and Munro, B. (eds) *Crime, Critique and Utopia* Basingstoke: Palgrave Macmillan

Walmsley, R. (2016) *World Prison Populations Briefing* (11th edition) London: Institute for Criminal Policy Research, http://www.prisonstudies.org/research-publications (consulted 13 May 2016)

Justice for Women: A Penal Utopia?

Margaret S. Malloch[1]

Abstract

For more than two decades, there has been an ongoing critique of penal responses to women in the criminal justice system. Calls to reduce the female prison population have been many, and attempts at reform have been ongoing. In Scotland, a recent decision to halt the building of a new 300-350 bed prison for women was widely welcomed, although in the aftermath of this decision, the potential of 'alternative' resources appears to be creating something of a conundrum. Despite all the academic, policy and activist research over these decades, the options for radical responses seem vague and contested. This paper reflects upon utopian traces, existing in the present and drawn from the past, to consider what a radical 'alternative' for women requires in practice and, what could be implemented to address 'social harm' in this gendered context. Looking outside the criminal justice system, the impulses of critical feminist theory are examined to consider what is required for a 'just society' for women.

Introduction

It is surprising in some ways, that in 2016, a vision of true gender equality remains essentially a utopian one; the administration and experience of justice is often mediated through a gendered lens. There have been many achievements on the road to equality, yet access to justice remains an area where there is considerable potential for improvement, not only in relation to gender, but also in terms of other determining structures such as class and ethnicity. Women's encounters with the (criminal) justice system, both as victims/survivors and in conflict with the law, have been the focus of repeated campaigns over the years[2]. In response to state punishment, calls to reduce the female prison population have been many, and attempts at penal reform have been ongoing. Nevertheless, options for radical 'alternatives' (to the

---

[1] Margaret Malloch is Reader in Criminology with the Scottish Centre for Crime and Justice Research at the University of Stirling.
[2] For example, see the work of Inquest, Howard League, Women in Prison, Justice for Women, Prison Reform Trust, Fawcett Society.

prison and to criminal justice more broadly) often seem vague and potential solutions are frequently contested. In this article, I reflect upon Erik Olin Wright's (2010) proposal for 'Real Utopias' (outlined further below) and consider the importance of critical examination of current practices, the need to envision 'non-penal alternatives', and the significance of processes of transformation that remove the binary contradiction between systems of punishment and 'their alternative'. Focusing on recent developments in Scotland, I explore some of the challenges that accompany attempts to enact 'real' utopias within structural contexts that remain essentially untransformed. I argue that utopian thought can enable critique, allow us to imagine the 'not-yet' and importantly, create a hopeful space to look beyond existing limitations of the present world.

A tentative space appears to have opened up for hopeful imaginings in the administration of criminal justice and specifically, penal practices as they are applied to women[3]. Recent developments in Scotland suggest that a real reduction in the imprisonment of women is a viable and feasible possibility. In January 2015, Scottish Justice Secretary Michael Matheson announced that the development of a 300-350 bed prison for women at Inverclyde in Scotland would no longer proceed, noting that 'we need to be bolder and take a more radical and ambitious approach in Scotland'. Justice Secretary Matheson instructed officials to 'undertake a period of intensive engagement with key partners, with a view to investing in smaller regional and community-based custodial facilities across the country'. Since then, substantial additional investment in women's community services has been allocated, with Michael Matheson arguing: 'Scotland already has the second highest female prison population in Northern Europe, doubling between 2002 and 2012. This is completely unacceptable and does not fit with my vision of how a modern and progressive society should deal with female offenders' (Scottish Government, 2015).

This decision was followed in November 2015, by an announcement from George Osborne that HMP Holloway in central London was being considered for closure as part of the government's Spending Review, with penal reformers quick to demand reallocation of funds to community resources. In both Scotland and in England and Wales, there have been calls to close prisons for women and to use the money from sales of land and running costs to invest in community resources such as women's centres[4]. In place of large prisons,

---

[3] While there is much to be said about 'justice' in its broadest sense, for the purpose of this article I focus on the imprisonment of women and the 'criminal justice' context.

penal reformers have argued in favour of small custodial units for the small number of women who have committed serious and/or violent offences (for example Commission on Women Offenders, 2012; Soroptomists International and Prison Reform Trust, 2014; All-Party Parliamentary Group on Women in the Penal System, 2015). In Scotland this may happen, indeed a new concept of 'custody in the community' is now being used (Scottish Prison Service, 2015)[5]. Although current proposals appear to favour a new 80-bed national prison for women, supported by five 20-bed units established across the country, and while still retaining a sizeable number of women in custody, this is considerably smaller than the 300-350 bed unit proposed as a new national prison at Inverclyde[6]. These developments, which resulted from recommendations by the Commission on Women Offenders (2012)[7], contrast with the aftermath of the Corston Report's (2007)[8] proposals to replace the women's prison estate in England and Wales with geographically dispersed, small, multi-functional custodial centres; a recommendation that was rejected as being neither feasible nor desirable (All Party Parliamentary Group on Women in the Penal System, 2011: 8).

Could recent developments in Scotland signify a step change in policy and, if so, what might be their effect? What is a 'real utopia' in this context? Does it constitute a drastically reduced penal estate for women and fundamental change in the central position of the prison in Scottish criminal justice policy? Should we keep our sights fixed beyond this and firmly on an abolitionist horizon? How 'real' does a Real Utopia need to be?

In general, calls to significantly reduce (or indeed abolish) the prison, as it currently exists, have always had more potential when considered in relation to women. Across the UK and internationally, the female penal estate is considerably smaller than the male estate and women are less likely to have committed acts that would suggest they present a 'risk' to wider society.

---

[4] For example, see statement by Women in Prison,
http://www.womeninprison.org.uk/news-and-campaigns.php?s=2015-11-25-hmp-holloway-closure

[5] However, this is itself a problematic concept in line with similar discourse around 'community payback', 'community punishment'.

[6] Assuming that the current national prison for women, HMP and YOI Cornton Vale, does actually close as called for by the Commission on Women Offenders (2012).

[7] The Commission was established by the Scottish Government in June 2011 to look at ways to improve outcomes for women in the criminal justice system in Scotland.

[8] The Corston Report was the product of a Commission established in March 2006 by the Home Office and chaired by Baroness Corston. The remit of the Commission was to conduct a review of women in the criminal justice system who have particular vulnerabilities.

However, while new and innovative resources have been developed in local communities, the number of women imprisoned in Scotland has not decreased, nor have the severe social circumstances that many women prisoners appear to have experienced prior to their encounters with the criminal justice system. For me, the concept of a 'penal utopia' is a contradiction in terms. In my vision of utopia, there is no penal system – no prisons, no need for punishment – and I acknowledge that this vision is truly utopian in the 'no-place' sense of the word; a luxury of utopian imaginings. But I am also grounded in present realities, perturbed by questions of how to move forward, and how to imagine a different way that is not tied by cultural and ideological bonds to present circumstances (Jameson, 2005).

My interest in utopian thinking (Malloch and Munro, 2013)[9] is grounded in utopia as critique and a way of imagining things 'other-wise'. While penal 'alternatives' can be drawn upon (such as Women's Centres, 218 Project[10], Healing Lodges[11]), such attempts to provide a service which remains within the context of the criminal justice means that they remain part of that system. They may provide useful and important support for the individuals who can access these services, but they retain the penal element that, for me, underpins all initiatives that are linked to the 'criminal' justice system. My utopian aspiration, is therefore for a process of change that involves transformations of both consciousness and social structures[12].

Transformation

> It is much easier to talk about concrete ways of tinkering with existing arrangements than it is to formulate plausible radical reconstructions (Wright, 2010: x).

---

[9] We first presented our work on utopia and critique in 2010 at the 38th Annual Conference of the European Group for the Study of Deviance and Social Control, Lesvos, Greece (Malloch and Munro, 2010).

[10] The 218 Service is a Turning Point Scotland and Glasgow Addiction Service initiative that takes a person centred, approach in dealing with the issues that women offenders face (see Beglan, 2013). Providing both residential and day services for women referred by the courts, the service is designed to address issues with substance use, physical and mental health and other social needs including housing and childcare.

[11] For example, the Okimaw Ohci Healing Lodge for Aboriginal Women in Canada (see Malloch, 2013a).

[12] See Malloch, 2013b where these ideas are outlined further.

Tension between affirmative versus transformative remedies has resulted more widely, in attempts to secure institutional change rather than any 'transformation of the deep structures of capitalist society' (Fraser, 2009: 5). Economic inequality, poverty, unemployment, racism and sexism are often ignored, while solutions are sought within the individual, both in practice and theory. Chesney-Lind (2006: 9) argues: 'The centrality of both crime and gender in the current backlash politics means that feminist criminology is uniquely positioned to challenge right-wing initiatives. To do this effectively however, the field must put an even greater priority on theorising patriarchy and crime, which means focusing on the ways in which the definition of the crime problem and criminal justice practices support patriarchal practices and worldviews'. I would argue that it is essential that critical feminist perspectives take a stance that is also informed by an examination of the political economy.

Transformation requires movement within and against existing structures. How is it possible to rethink power, change institutions and structures of state as well as structures of consciousness? This requires focusing on the political rather than simply the personal, and recognising that we can only think the future differently if we think in different ways. In order to transform current systems of punishment, as they are applied to women, it is necessary to critique patriarchal structures, redistribution and reconceptualisations of power. The challenge in presenting 'real' utopias is that they too often become incorporated into existing systems: evident when considering the progressive pulse that has underpinned many developments for women in conflict with the law.

More broadly, the current international context is one of the 'globalised destruction of social safety nets' and within this context, individualising structural inequalities. Recommendations focused on the criminal justice system can result in improved services within it, but will not reduce the problems that bring women (or men) into it. The deeper social structures of society sustain the social marginalisation and disadvantage that underpin the real experiences of men and women who encounter the prison population. These issues are often seen as too overwhelming and ingrained to tackle outwith the organisational remit of reform. Calls are made instead to increase provisions in the community via criminal justice. At the same time, the 'community' is an ambiguous and contested concept that is not unproblematic for either women, or provisions for women. In this context 'community' is often assumed or presented as a solution without any real analysis of what it is or how it is gendered (Malloch et al, 2014). Transformation at the level of attitudes as well as practicalities is required.

Despite the limitations placed on many of the radical reforms proposed over the years, developments in Scotland are admirable within an international context and do create a space for optimism. Nevertheless, as Sim (2009) highlights, liberal reform groups have had limited success in making fundamental changes to dominant penal discourses, as seen across the UK, Canada and elsewhere. But there are examples of transformative practices which can be drawn upon. The 218 Centre in Glasgow, when first established, focused on 'recovery' with an emphasis on health and well-being via a trauma-informed model which aspired to 'healing'[13]. Unfortunately this was overtaken by a shift in focus to ensure the service was responsive to the courts (criminal justice) and seen as 'legitimate' by sentencers (Malloch et al, 2008). Other practices include engagement by grass-roots groups, again focused on recovery but operating to create 'communities of resistance' within local environments and providing individuals with a sense of worth (individual and collective) and meaning (see Malloch, 2011).

Anticipatory Pragmatism

Utopian thinking and visions of utopia have much to offer in influencing and driving change socially, politically and economically and this is particularly pertinent in attempts to conceptualise 'justice' (see Malloch and Munro, 2013). While theoretical explorations of utopia are often contested as being 'no-place' or idealistic imaginings, they have the potential to set out new ways of thinking and subsequently, of being. Wright (2010: 6) taking a more practical approach, defines 'real utopias' as: 'utopian ideals that are grounded in the real potentials of humanity, utopian destinations that have accessible waystations, utopian designs of institutions that can inform our practical tasks of navigating a world of imperfect conditions for social change'. His vision provides the basis for actual reform in the material world.

The 'reality' (both a highpoint and lowpoint) of attempts to achieve justice for women, is that the blueprints for 'accessible waystations' and 'utopian designs of institutions' have already been presented, argued for and, while they have paved the way for progress, still have some way to go in achieving either radical institutional or social change. If 'plausible visions of radical

---

[13] http://www.turningpointscotland.com/what-we-do/criminal-justice/218-service/

alternatives, with firm theoretical foundations, are an important condition for emancipatory social change' (Wright, 2010: 8), what is required to achieve the enactment of radical alternatives and 'emancipatory social change' in relation to justice for women? What has prevented it happening to date? The need to distinguish between 'utopian realism' (Loader, 1998) and the danger of pursuing immediately achievable goals in the short-term is that longer-term 'revolutionary' alternatives can be lost; a tension that exists within abolitionist visions (as well as utopian aspirations), and reformist practicalities, and where appeals to realism can often end up as a defence of the status quo (Ruggiero, 1992 and 2010).

Diagnosis and Critique

The starting point for Wright (2010) is to consider in what ways existing social institutions and structures systematically impose harms. This is not difficult to evidence when it comes to the imprisonment of women. It would be reasonable to say that there is a good awareness and general acknowledgement of the 'problem'. The harmful effects of current systems of imprisonment are recognised across the UK (and internationally) and, in relation to the imprisonment of women, have been reflected in a plethora of 'official' reviews, reports and inquiries, informed by academic research and third sector agencies, which have set out practical recommendations for the radical reform of current practices. There are significant similarities in the definition of 'the problem' and potential actions required in England, Wales and Northern Ireland[14] and in Scotland[15] and the attention that has been given

---

[14] In England and Wales: *Justice for Women* (Prison Reform Trust, 2000); *Lacking Conviction*, (Prison Reform Trust, 2004); Prisons and Probation Ombudsman Report into the series of deaths in HMP and YOI Styal (2003); Corston Report (2007) as well as reports by the Commission on Women and the Criminal Justice System (2009) and ongoing follow-up reports undertaken by the Fawcett Society. The New Economics Foundation (2008) set out an economic justification for the use of alternatives to prison for women. In Northern Ireland: *The Hurt Inside* (Scraton and Moore, 2005) and Convery (2009) *Addressing Offending by Women* for the Northern Ireland Office. Add to this, the series of reports by HM Inspector of Prisons; and a similar outpouring of reports and reviews internationally by organisations such as Amnesty International, Human Rights Watch, Inquest.

[15] In Scotland, Social Work Services and Prisons Inspectorates for Scotland (1998) and the Ministerial Group on Women's Offending (2002), Equal Opportunities Committee of the Scottish Parliament review on *Female Offenders in the Criminal Justice System* (2009) McIvor and Burman (2011), HM Inspector of Prisons for Scotland, Commission on Women Offenders (2012), Soroptomists (2014). The Scottish Prison Service (SPS) were proactive in the aftermath of the Commissions' Report, commissioning Reid Howie Associates (2012) to

to the imprisonment of women and application of criminal justice more broadly, has been considerable.

Prisons are filled with the most marginalised members of society, highlighting the underlying structural inequalities that characterise capitalism. Recognition of this inequity is reflected in many of the various enquiries and reports which have been produced. Perhaps inevitably, recommendations focus upon responding to women's 'needs' within the context of the criminal justice system, either through programmes and interventions in prison, or in specifically devised services for 'women offenders' in the community. There is ample evidence to illustrate that many women in the criminal justice system, and specifically those who end up in prison, have significant experiences of poverty, problematic drug and alcohol use, mental health problems, abuse, violence and bereavement (Carlen, 2008; Commission on Women Offenders, 2012; Malloch and McIvor, 2013; Malloch et al, 2014). Despite widespread acknowledgement of the significance of structural social problems (poverty and inequality) in relation to women's criminalisation, 'official' inquiries have consistently focused upon the penal context; even though most people involved recognise the limitations of addressing social justice issues via the criminal justice system (Carlen, 2008; Malloch et al, 2008). The circumstances of many women in prison highlight the inequity of attempts to obtain criminal 'justice' in a society characterised by inequality, poverty and marginalising structures. As Ruggiero (2010: 5) notes: 'There is nothing utopian in attempts to redress "remedial injustices"'.

There is general agreement that the ongoing increase in the number of women who are imprisoned in Scotland, can be attributed to the increasing criminalisation of experiences of distress (Malloch and McIvor, 2011), responded to by the increasing application of more punitive sentencing policies (McIvor and Burman, 2011). Piven and Cloward (1971) showed how the function of welfare was to 'regulate the poor', and more recently, Wacquant (2009) illustrated how welfare and penal interventions are increasingly merged. Gelsthorpe (2010) has pointed out that this merging is particularly pertinent to women, with a welfare system which both punishes and controls through what Wacquant (2009, 2012) calls the 'double regulation

---

chair a series of meetings across the country intended to consider the Commission Recommendations (specifically the six recommendations that were addressed to the prison). In 2015, the Scottish Prison Service held an international symposium which considered how to best move forward following the decision not to proceed with plans for HMP Inverclyde, producing a report, *From Vision to Reality: Transforming Scotland's Care of Women in Custody* (SPS, 2015).

of the poor'. Within the penal context, women's 'needs' are often reinterpreted as potential criminal 'risks' (Hannah-Moffat, 2001; 2008).

The disparity in visions between what is most 'needed', at a broader level, is resonant of Nancy Frasers' analysis of discursive power surrounding the struggle for the interpretation of 'legitimate social needs' as inherently political. She notes: 'Dominant groups need interpretations intended to exclude, defuse, and/or co-opt counter-interpretations' (Fraser, 2013: 59). These interpretations are themselves 'acts and interventions'.

With all major reviews into the female penal estate, and despite their broad vision for change, there has been ongoing selective endorsement of key recommendations, thereby limiting their overall potential for radical reform. A number of recommendations of specific relevance to the prison were set out by the Commission for Women Offenders (2012), including the reiteration of previous concerns about links between mental health programmes and interventions in prison and the community, use of remand, staff training and, significantly, a call to replace Cornton Vale with a smaller, specialist prison[16]. While proposals put forward for change may indeed be 'radical' within a context of current penal policy, they can hardly be described as such in the broader social, political and economic landscape. Indeed, proposed reforms have frequently been based on establishing the 'vulnerabilities' of women who encounter the criminal justice system, arguing in favour of compensatory programmes, therapeutic interventions (on an individualised basis) and improved relationships (multi-agency collaborations, individual and agency and often aimed at enabling women to improve their interpersonal skills when dealing with others) (Corston, 2007; Commission for Women Offenders, 2012; Scottish Prison Service, 2015).[17]

However, until attention is turned to diagnosis and critique **outside** the criminal justice system, the circumstances of the women who come **into** it, are unlikely to change. There have been attempts to address this through policies aimed at 'social inclusion', improved support to access benefits on release from prison, inclusion of welfare rights workers[18] in prisons and community-

[16] A call previously made by Carlen in 1982 on the basis that most women could be more appropriately dealt with by non-custodial measures; the minority of women who merited secure custody could be held in a small unit; and an open unit should be provided for long-term female prisoners.
[17] And practically all 'official' inquiries into women and the criminal justice system both in Scotland and internationally.
[18] Welfare rights workers, also known as welfare benefits advisers, provide free information, support and advice about welfare benefits and other areas such as housing, work and

based services for women, and mentoring aimed at linking women into mainstream services. However, the challenges of securing effective through-care provisions continue (Dryden and Souness, 2015). In essence, the bounded knowledge of criminal justice isolates a problem that is much more generic and explicitly linked to the structural organisation of capitalist society.

Penal versus non-penal 'alternatives'

> 'There can be few topics that have been so exhaustively researched, to such little practical effect, as the plight of women in the criminal justice system' (Corston, 2007:16).

Lack of significant progress has not been the result of disagreements about the need or desire to change things as they apply to women who encounter the criminal justice system; nor is it the result of lack of imagination. However, most 'official' attempts at reform, while they have much to offer, are limited by partial implementation, short-termism, and the deleterious effects of structural issues outside the criminal justice system itself. The 'realist' vision of simply reducing the female prison population runs into competing visions and this has a significant impact on the alternative practices that are presented. On the one hand, there has been an acknowledgement that advocates of the abolition of the prison system would do well to begin with women prisoners (Pate, 2013). Indeed, explicit blueprints have already been presented by Pat Carlen when, as far back as 1990, she provided clear arguments about the possibility of significantly reducing the female prison population and proposed practical steps regarding how to achieve this. Contrast this however with the visions of those with interests in retaining existing institutions, such as the Scottish Prison Service (SPS) and HM Prison Service. Their 'penal utopia' involves improving the penal estate, transforming 'imprisonment' for women within limited boundaries, and to be fair, with aspirations to deliver a useful and 'effective' service. SPS in particular, following the recommendations of the Commission for Women Offenders (2012), immediately began to develop plans for a new prison which would address the shortcomings of the existing system and which would provide an establishment that catered for those incarcerated within it, arguing that prison **can** provide interventions that address the 'needs' of women who come into conflict with the law. For abolitionists, and many penal reformers, this development was met with

money.

horror, highlighting existing concerns about the creation of the 'therapunitive' prison; a feature in the 'exponential growth in the international women-prisoners reintegration industry' (Carlen and Tombs, 2006: 339). The therapeutic language of intervention which has characterised provisions defined as 'gender-responsive' in relation to community punishments now features in the vocabulary of the gender-informed prison (Hannah-Moffat and Shaw, 2000; Hannah-Moffat, 2001).

While there is no doubt that prisons, where and when they exist, would serve society better as humane and purposeful institutions, experience has shown that when prisons are able to deliver services that are lacking in the community (i.e. drug treatment, trauma provision, education) then the likelihood of women being sent there in order to access such services increases. As a result, the many inquiries, reports and commissions which have been carried out have made recommendations which are wide-ranging and take account of the importance of 'service redesign' in the community (Community Justice Centres, multi-disciplinary teams and key workers, intensive mentoring, supported accommodation, appropriate and accessible mental health services, training for criminal justice professionals). The Commission on Women Offenders (2012) also made recommendations in relation to alternatives to prosecution (fiscal work orders, new powers for Procurators Fiscal in relation to composite diversion orders, new powers for police to divert women to community justice centres with conditional cautions); and alternatives to remand (bail supervision plus, further examination of electronic monitoring as a condition of bail, the need to ensure communication and awareness of alternatives to remand in custody). Other areas which the Commission considered and made recommendations on were sentencing and governance of community justice.

However, international evidence shows that attempts at penal reform are limited when proposals are partially implemented, particularly those which depend upon enhanced community provisions *and* a reduction in prison places. For example, a central recommendation from the Social Work Services and Prisons Inspectorate (2008) was that an expansion of community provisions should be accompanied by a cap on prison places. This was intended to ensure that community resources were used *in place of* custody, thus avoiding potential problems of 'net-widening' whereby increased numbers of women were drawn into the criminal justice system to access resources that were problematically absent in local areas. This cap was never introduced (see Tombs, 2004). Updates on the implementation of the

Transforming Rehabilitation agenda[19] in England and Wales have also noted concerns that more women may be drawn into the criminal justice system and kept there for longer (All Parliamentary Group, 2015).

The proposed closure of Cornton Vale and its replacement with smaller units across the country has noticeable parallels with Canada following the closure of Kingston Prison for Women (also deemed 'unfit for purpose') and its replacement with smaller institutions (Correctional Service Canada, 1990). Despite the involvement of campaign groups at the outset of this process, Hannah-Moffat and Shaw (2000) and Hannah-Moffat (2001 and 2008) highlight the ways in which policies aimed at enhancing the circumstances of women within the criminal justice system were highly vulnerable to distortion and manipulation in the process of implementation and practice (see also Malloch et al, 2008).

Although there has been significant investment in community provisions in Scotland, funding that is often provided in two-year cycles can cause considerable uncertainty for workers and service-users alike, allowing little time for services to continue beyond a set-up and pilot phase. Short-term interventions are generally unable to evidence longer-term impact (Loucks et al, 2006; Easton and Mathews, 2010 and 2011; Burgess et al, 2011, Hedderman et al, 2008; 2011; Dryden and Souness, 2015). 'Alternatives' which are suggested as significant innovations within the system are often absorbed into it in a way which softens them yet, at the same time, deflects the initial critiques within which they originated. This process can also impede the transformation from short- to long-term goals.

The search for 'alternatives' should not lead to provisions that are simply an 'alternative' to the prison. Community punishments, often presented as the antidote to custody, can themselves marginalise and stigmatise individuals and they are often upheld as solutions which fail to address the underpinning assumptions that characterise the justice system, often extending punishment into other time and space (Cohen, 1985; Christie, 2000). Problematically, debates too often become formed around resources for women as 'offenders' rather than directed towards reducing, or abolishing, the prison. Within this context, any call for closure of the women's prison is met with a 'taken-for-granted' claim that 'something needs to be done about criminal women'. The

---

[19] Transforming Rehabilitation is the name given to the government's programme for the management of criminal justice in England and Wales. The programme has involved the outsourcing to the private sector of a large portion of the probation service in England and Wales.

focus is retained on criminal justice solutions, or as Sim (2009: 155) has noted '(...) whenever a crisis has erupted, the prison has "always been offered as its own remedy" to its problems'.

Creating Change

In Scotland, the debates and activities surrounding the Scottish Referendum on independence in 2014 were characterised by grass-root activism which has had a number of broader effects. Women for Independence (WFI) emerged at this time, as an organisation for women but which looked more broadly (and critically) at Scottish society with a view to supporting an independent nation. One of their first campaigns was to highlight the proposed development of the new national prison for women and to campaign against it. Although joining a campaign that was already well-established (in the academy and reform organisations, but with little footing amongst the wider population), Women for Independence were able to make a significant contribution to the reversal of these proposals for the national prison which, although in line with calls from the Commission for Women Offenders (2012) for the closure of HMP Cornton Vale, did not fit with their recommendations for an alternative to it. Part of this campaign brought women who had been recipients of imprisonment and/or community disposals forward to share their experiences with a wider group of women, many of whom knew little about the administration of justice and how criminal justice is experienced. The outrage that many felt on hearing these experiences led to a broader campaign, Justice Watch, which is currently ongoing and where women (members of WFI) are encouraged (and supported) to sit in courts across the country and to observe the administration of 'justice' as it is applied in practice. Although in its early stages, this will potentially do much to highlight the nature of gendered justice and it will be interesting to see what broader impact it has on the collective imagination. WFI produced a manifesto which has two aims: (i) that Scotland has the most progressive justice system in Europe by the year 2020; (ii) to achieve social and economic justice for women through campaigning, informing and lobbying for change. Their aim is to establish a Women's Justice Service – not just for women who have been charged with an offence – but for all women in need of a service. And while the emphasis is on gender, this is underpinned by a recognition that society is characterised by inequality and poverty which is manifested in the administration of 'justice'. WFI aim to use their 'Justice Watch' campaign to inform the wider public about the process of justice as it is enacted in courts across Scotland; to inform the wider population about the economic sense of change; and to achieve cross party support for their proposals. Their hope is to remove prison as an option for remand or sentence for all minor offending; for the impact on any remand or sentence decision on the woman, her children and family and the wider community to be acknowledged and used to inform decisions; and to reinvest money that will be saved from custody in community solutions. Using this activist approach, and exploring common experiences of women inside and outside the prison, provides a space to unite around the reduction of the prison system, with an eye to the only context in which that is possible – political, social and economic change. Ultimately, change requires the reduction of poverty, inequality and social deprivation; addressing the process of criminalisation and reducing the social infliction of pain.

The 2014 Scottish Referendum was responsible for a rekindling of an 'optimism of the will' (an essential requirement for transformation according to Gramsci (1971 [1929]))[20] which also came about as the result of a desire to 'do politics differently'.[21] To make substantial change we need to imagine what is 'not yet possible'. Yet as Bammer (1991: 47) notes: '[ ]even as our radical theories and politics push to extend the boundaries of the possible and imaginable, we are always also bound by and to the very structures we are trying to escape'. In this respect, utopia is not 'no-place' but that place which is blocked from being so by the power of established society. Utopian thinking, like abolitionism, challenges orthodox views of what 'crime' is, particularly in relationship to property ownership and the law, and processes of criminalisation that arise from this relationship (Hulsman, 1991; Christie, 2000; Ruggiero, 2010). Both also require a reconceptualising of 'justice' and its position within the social structures of society.

Wright's 'real utopia' is a 'good place' that already exists. There are pockets of inspiration within the justice system, and positive practices within the community 'justice' setting. However, an abolitionist utopia for me involves de-centring the prison, looking beyond community punishments and instead developing the resources that are required to support healthy communities more broadly: a citizen's income; resourced health services; education and employment opportunities; safe places to live and work, where local

---

[20] Gramsci stated he was 'a pessimist because of intelligence but an optimist because of will' (1971[1929]).

[21] And although the 'Yes campaign' which led this charge was unsuccessful in achieving independence, the legacy of local activism was evident in 2015 when Scotland's voting patterns were transformed in the General Election.

communities are able to claim resources from the State and to have democratic control over how they are used. We have come some way in securing these resources – and certainly grass-roots movements like Women for Independence are prepared to stake their claims within society and will (hopefully) have an impact on how 'justice' is understood more broadly.

For me, the power of utopia is the opportunity it provides to examine 'traces' or 'impulses' of hope and move towards them without necessarily enacting a pre-mapped out programme of action. Perhaps reimagining justice for women first requires breaking existing illusions of the therapeutic prison or the 'penal community', rather than creating them; locating practical reforms within an emancipatory social theory. If we continue to think within existing paradigms, we will recreate the structures in which we are already located, so we need to imagine in entirely new ways.

References

All Party Parliamentary Group on Women in the Penal System (2011) *Women in the Penal System: Second Report on Women with Particular Vulnerabilities in the Criminal Justice System* London: Howard League

All Party Parliamentary Group on Women in the Penal System (2015) *Report on the Inquiry into Preventing Unnecessary Criminalisation of Women* London: Howard League

Bammer, A. (1991) *Partial Visions* Abingdon: Routledge

Beglan, M. (2013) 'The 218 Experience' in Malloch, M. and McIvor, G. (eds) *Women, Punishment and Social Justice* Abingdon: Routledge

Burgess, C., Malloch, M. and McIvor, G. (2011) *Women in Focus: An Evaluation* Irvine: South West Scotland Community Justice Authority

Carlen, P. (1982) *Policy Implications of Women's Imprisonment Denied: A Discussion Document,* unpublished paper University of Keele

Carlen, P. (1983) *Women's Imprisonment: A Study in Social Control* Abingdon: Routledge and Kegan Paul

Carlen, P. (1990) *Alternatives to Women's Imprisonment* Buckingham: Open University Press

Carlen, P. (2008) *Imaginary Penalities* Cullompton: Willan Publishing

Carlen, P. and Tombs, J. (2006) 'Reconfigurations of penality' in *Theoretical Criminology* Volume 10, No. 3 337-360

Chesney-Lind, M. (2006) 'Patriarchy, Crime and Justice', *Feminist Criminology*, 1 (6): 6-26

Christie, N. (2000) *Crime Control as Industry* Abingdon: Routledge

Cohen, S. (1985) *Visions of Social Control* Cambridge: Polity Press

Cohen, S. (1988) *Against Criminology* Cambridge: Polity Press

Commission on Women and the Criminal Justice System (2009) *Engendering Justice – from Policy to Practice* London: Fawcett Society

Commission on Women Offenders (2012) *Commission on Women Offenders: Final Report* Edinburgh: Scottish Government

Convery, U. (2009) *Addressing Offending by Women* Belfast: Northern Ireland Office

Correctional Services Canada (1990) *Creating Choices* Canada: CSC

Corston (2007) *The Corston Report: A report by Baroness Jean Corston of a review of women with particular vulnerabilities in the criminal justice system* London: Home Office

Easton, H. and Matthews, R. (2010) *Evaluation of the 218 Service* Edinburgh: Scottish Government Social Research

Easton, H. and Matthews, R. (2011) *Evaluation of the Inspire Women's Project* London: South Bank University

Equal Opportunities Committee (2009) *Female Offenders in the Criminal Justice System* Edinburgh: Scottish Parliament

Fraser, N. (2013) *Fortunes of Feminism: From Stage-Managed Capitalism to Neoliberal Crisis* London: Verso

Gelsthorpe, L. (2010) 'Women, Crime and Control' in *Criminology and Criminal Justice* Volume 10 pp 375-387

Gramsci, A. (1971[1929]) *Selections from the prison notebooks* London: Lawrence and Wishart

Hannah-Moffat, K. (2001) *Punishment in Disguise: Penal Governance and Federal Imprisonment of Women in Canada* Toronto: University of Toronto Press

Hannah-Moffat, K. (2008) 'Re-imagining Gendered Penalities' in Carlen, P. (ed) *Imaginary Penalities* Cullompton: Willan Publishing

Hannah-Moffat, K. and Shaw, M. (2000) *An Ideal Prison? Critical essays on women's imprisonment in Canada* Halifax: Fernwood Publishing Company

Hedderman, C., Palmer, E. and Hollin, C. (2008) *Implementing Services for Women Offenders and Those 'At Risk' of Offending* London: Ministry of Justice

Hedderman, C., Cunby, C., Shelton, N. (2011) 'What Women Want: The importance of qualitative approaches in evaluating work with women offenders' in *Criminology and Criminal Justice* Volume 11, No. 1, pp 3-20

HM Inspectorate of Prisons (1997) *Women in Prison: A thematic review* London: Home Office

HM Inspectorate of Prisons (2010) *Women in Prison: A short thematic review* London: Home Office

HM Inspectorate of Prisons for Scotland (2007) *HMP and YOI Cornton Vale Inspection: 19-20 March 2007* Edinburgh: Scottish Executive

HM Inspectorate of Prisons for Scotland (2009) *HMP and YOI Cornton Vale Inspection: 21-29 September 2009* Edinburgh: Scottish Executive

HM Inspectorate of Prisons for Scotland (2011) *HMP and YOI Cornton Vale Follow up Inspection: 1-4 February 2011* Edinburgh: Scottish Executive

Hulsman, L. (1991) 'The Abolitionist Case: Alternative crime policies' in *Israel Law Review* Volume 25, Nos. 3-4 pp 681-709

Jameson, F. (2005) *Archaeologies of the Future: The desire called utopia and other science fictions* London: Verso

Loader, I. (1998) 'Criminology and the Public Sphere: Arguments for Utopian Realism' in Walton, P. and Young, J. (eds) *The New Criminology Revisited* Hampshire: Palgrave

Loucks, N., Malloch, M., McIvor, G. and Gelsthorpe, L. (2006) *Evaluation of the 218 Centre* Edinburgh: Scottish Executive Social Research

Malloch, M. (2011) 'The Challenge of Developing and Sustaining a Recovery Group in Glasgow' in *Journal of Groups in Addiction and Recovery* Volume 6, Nos. 1-2 pp 117-131

Malloch, M. (2013a) 'A healing place? Okimaw Ohci and a Canadian approach to Aboriginal Women' in Malloch, M. and McIvor, G. (eds) *Women, Punishment and Social Justice,* Abingdon: Routledge

Malloch, M. (2013b) 'Crime, Critique and Utopian Alternatives' in Malloch, M. and Munro, B. (eds) *Crime, Critique and Utopia* Basingstoke: Palgrave Macmillan

Malloch, M. and McIvor, G. (2011) 'Women and Community Sentences' in *Criminology and Criminal Justice* Volume 11, No. 4 pp 325-344

Malloch, M. and McIvor, G. (eds) (2013) *Women, Punishment and Social Justice* Abingdon: Routledge

Malloch, M., McIvor, G. and Burgess, C. (2014) '"Holistic" Community Punishment and Criminal Justice Interventions for Women' in *Howard Journal of Criminal Justice* Volume 53, No. 4 pp 395-410

Malloch, M., McIvor, G., Loucks, N. (2008) 'Time Out for Women: Innovation in Scotland in a Context of Change' in *The Howard Journal* Volume 47, No. 4 pp 383-399

Malloch, M. and Munro, B. (2010) 'Crime, Critique and Utopia: Applying utopian principles in marginalised communities', *38th Conference of the European Group for the Study of Deviance and Social Control,* University of the Aegean, Lesbos, 1-5 September.

Malloch, M. and Munro, B. (2013) (eds) *Crime, Critique and Utopia* Basingstoke: Palgrave Macmillan

McIvor, G. and Burman, M. (2011) *The Drivers of Women's Imprisonment,* Stirling: Scottish Centre for Crime and Justice Research

Ministerial Group on Women's Offending (2002) *A Better Way* Edinburgh: Scottish Executive

New Economics Foundation (2008) *Unlocking Value* London: NEF

Pate, K. (2013) 'Women, Punishment and Social Justice': Why you should care' in Malloch, M. and McIvor, G. (eds) *Women, Punishment and Social Justice* Abingdon: Routledge

Piven, F. and Cloward, R. (1971) [1993] *Regulating the Poor* London: Vintage Books

Prison Reform Trust (2000) *Justice for Women: The need for reform* London: PRT

Prison Reform Trust (2004) *Lacking Conviction: The rise of the women's remand population* London: Prison Reform Trust

Prisons and Probation Ombudsman for England and Wales (2003) *The Death in Custody of a Woman and the Series of Deaths in HMP/YOI Styal August 2002-2003* London: Home Office

Reid Howie Associates (2012) *Women Offenders in Custody: Analysis of Consultation Findings* Edinburgh: Scottish Prison Service

Ruggiero, V. (1992) 'Realist Criminology: A Critique' in Young, J. and Matthews, R. (eds) *Rethinking Criminology: The Realist Debate* London: Sage

Ruggiero, V. (2010) *Penal Abolitionism* Oxford: Oxford University Press

Scottish Government (2015) 'New plans for women in custody announced', http://news.scotland.gov.uk/News/New-plans-for-women-in-custody-announced-1a61.aspx (consulted 13 May 2016)

Scottish Prison Service (2015), *From Vision to Reality* Edinburgh: SPS.

Scraton, P. and Moore, L. (2005) *The Hurt Inside* Belfast: Northern Ireland Human Rights Commission

Sim, J. (2009) *Punishment and Prisons* London: Sage Publications

Social Work Services and Prisons Inspectorates for Scotland (1998) *Women Offenders – A Safer Way* Edinburgh: Scottish Office

Soroptomists International and Prison Reform Trust (2014) *Transforming Lives: Reducing women's imprisonment* London: Prison Reform Trust

Tombs, J. (2004) 'From "A Safer to a Better Way": Transformations in penal policy for women' in McIvor, G. (ed) *Women who Offend: Research Highlights in Social Work 44* London: Jessica Kingsley

Wacquant, L. (2009) *Punishing the Poor* Durham NC: Duke University Press

Wacquant, L. (2012) 'Three Steps Towards an Anthropology of Actually Existing Neoliberalism' *Social Anthropology* Volume 19, No. 4 pp 66-79

Wright, E.O. (2010) *Envisioning Real Utopias* London: Verso.

Otherwise than Prisons, nor Prisons Otherwise: Therapeutic Communities as non-penal real utopias

David Scott and Helena Gosling[1]

Abstract

The aim of this paper is to critically engage with the idea that Therapeutic Communities (TCs) can be promoted in England and Wales as a radical alternative to prison for substance users who have broken the law. After grounding the discussion within the normative framework of an 'abolitionist real utopia' (Scott, 2013), the article explores the historical and theoretical underpinnings of TCs. Existing literature advocating TCs as a radical alternative to imprisonment is then reviewed, followed by a critical reflection of TCs' compatibility with the broader values and principles of an abolitionist real utopia. To conclude, the article suggests that although TCs could be a plausible and historically immanent non-penal real utopia for certain people in certain circumstances, we must not lose focus of wider social inequalities.

Introduction

Prisons are profoundly dehumanising institutions filled with socially disadvantaged people who have experienced multiple forms of social exclusion. Despite the best of intentions of those hoping to find some virtue in the current incarceration binge, the punitive rationale, which underscores prisons' very existence, inevitably undermines humanitarian attempts to bring about desired personal transformations or tackle social exclusion (Scott, 2008). What we urgently require is recognition that the prison as a place not only reflects, but perpetuates, social inequalities. At the same time, we need

[1] David Scott is senior lecturer in criminology at the Open University and his most recent book is *Emancipatory Politics and Praxis* (EG Press, 2016). He was coordinator of the European Group for the Study of Deviance and Social Control from 2009-2012. Contact: D.G.Scott@open.ac.uk. Helena Gosling is a senior lecturer in Criminal Justice at Liverpool John Moores University. In 2015 she completed her PhD entitled *An Invitation to Change? An Ethnographic study of a residential Therapeutic Community for substance use*. Helena has published articles in a number of leading journals, including *Criminology and Criminal Justice; Howard Journal of Criminal Justice* and the *International Journal of Crime, Justice and Social Democracy*. Contact: H.J.Gosling@ljmu.ac.uk.

plausible and historically immanent radical alternatives that can reach beyond hegemonic neo-liberal and penal logics currently informing policy, and offer a new way of responding to troubled individuals. Such radical alternatives must engender both the humanitarian impulse *to engage right now* with the tragedies of imprisonment and social injustice, but also be something that maintains fidelity with, and commitment to, the wider idealised aspirations of living in a world without prisons and the deep-seated social inequalities they mirror.

There are many difficulties when attempting to promote alternatives to prison, varying from net widening, where alternatives become add-ons to existing sentences, to falling through the net, where people are abandoned and neglected and nothing is done to help them. Radical alternatives must be able to incorporate both an engagement with the problems and possibilities of our historical moment, whilst simultaneously disrupting punitive and other ideologies which facilitate social inequalities. They must also be *genuine alternatives*, for only then, when coupled with policies promoting social inclusion and social justice, can they meet the criteria of an abolitionist non-penal real utopia (Scott, 2013).

In this article we consider whether Therapeutic Communities (TCs) can be promoted for substance-using lawbreakers as part of a wider abolitionist strategy aiming to reduce social harms and challenge social and economic inequalities. The article starts by outlining the normative framework of an abolitionist real utopia before moving on to critically explore the historical and theoretical contexts of TCs. The discussion then turns to the existing literature on TCs as an alternative to penal custody. At that point we evaluate whether TCs are compatible with the values and principles of an abolitionist real utopia. The article concludes that whilst there is no blanket alternative to prison, and no single answer to the way society responds to lawbreakers whose offending behaviour is influenced by substance use, TCs can be part of the solution, but they must be coupled with other interventions tackling structural inequalities grounded in the principles of social justice.

An Abolitionist Real Utopia

Prisons are inherently problematic institutions – they are places of interpersonal and institutional violence and legal, social and corporeal death – and these terrible outcomes are structured within the very fabric of penal institutions (Scott and Codd, 2010; Scott, 2015). It is possible that prisons can offer a place of reflection and refuge for a few people when all other options have failed but, given the deprivations, pains and iatrogenic harms that underscore daily prison regimes, these cases are the exceptions that prove the rule. Yet for penal abolitionists, critique is never enough. Abolitionists must be prepared to advocate constructive and radical alternatives to penal rationale. Such alternatives must be realistic and pragmatic, whilst at the same time being consistent with idealistic and utopian visions – a position which has been referred to as an 'abolitionist real utopia' (Scott, 2013).

In short, an abolitionist real utopia promotes visions of radical alternatives grounded in the following five normative principles that build upon continuities and possibilities in our historical conjuncture. A radical alternative must:

1.   Compete with a prison sentence.
Radical alternatives must implicitly or explicitly compete with, and contradict, current penal ideologies, discourses, policies and practices (Mathiesen, 1974). Alternatives must be competitive with the institutions of the criminal process by promoting interventions that are grounded in historically immanent potentialities, whilst simultaneously possessing an emancipatory logic that contradicts current practices of repression and pain infliction. Those in power must find it difficult to ignore or dismiss the proposed radical alternative but at the same time it must be impossible for them to re-appropriate the alternative within the logic of the penal rationale. The justification for a radical alternative must also be strong enough so that it can be considered a genuine alternative to a prison sentence.

2.   Be otherwise than prison.
To avoid net-widening, the radical alternative must directly replace a punitive sentence of the criminal courts. Interventions should not be considered 'add ons' or initiated alongside existing penal practices. They must be deployed in place of a prison sentence that would otherwise have been sanctioned against a given individual.

3.   Be a non-coerced intervention allowing meaningful participa-tion.
In conjunction with the above human rights standards, genuine radical alternatives must be non-coercive and demonstrate that they can be a productive and meaningful way of addressing problematic behaviours, conflicts and troublesome conduct. As such, radical alternatives must adhere

to democratically accountable values and principles requiring unhindered participation; recognition of the validity all voices; and facilitate a role in decision-making processes.

4.   *Safeguard human dignity and minimise human suffering.*
Radical alternatives must have a non-punitive ethos aiming to uphold, respect and protect the intrinsic worth and value of human beings. There must be no violations of human dignity, nor should the intervention create stigma, injury or harm. The radical alternative must therefore be *better* than prison, which is a place of pain, blame and death. These human rights standards place certain ethical boundaries upon interventions and help steer us towards alternatives that can reduce rather than create unnecessary human pain and suffering. To avoid an unintentional or hidden escalation of harms, radical alternatives must have sufficient transparency, procedural safeguards and be rooted in the principles of fairness, openness, equality and legal accountability. Care should therefore be taken to ensure that any proposed alternative intervention for handling conflicts does not become a form of punishment in disguise. Importantly, the alternative must be otherwise than prison, not a prison otherwise.

5.   *Promote (or at very least not inhibit) social justice.*
A radical alternative must look to facilitate, and not prevent, the promotion of social justice. An abolitionist real utopia is a form of emancipatory knowledge that challenges inequality, unfairness and injustice. This requires not only problematising the current application of the criminal label, which overwhelmingly punishes the poor, disadvantaged and vulnerable, but also actively promoting interventions which reduce social inequalities and aim to meet human need (Scott, 2013). Radical alternatives to prison must (at the very least) not impinge upon such interventions.

The following analysis explores whether TCs can be advocated as an abolitionist real utopia. In so doing, we appraise the reality and potential of the TC to meet the five normative values outlined above by considering the following key questions: Can TCs incorporate both an engagement with the problems and possibilities of our historical moment, and possess an emancipatory logic contradicting institutions and practices of penal repression? Are TCs genuine alternatives to penal custody? Do TCs adhere to values and principles safeguarding human dignity and reducing human suffering? And do TCs facilitate or hinder social justice? To answer these questions, we first explore the meanings, origins and theoretical priorities of TCs.

Origins of the TC

Generally speaking, each TC forms a miniature society in which staff and clients are expected to fulfil distinctive roles that are designed to support the transitional process individuals embark upon during their residency (Gosling, 2015). Although day-to-day activities vary depending on the population served and the setting of the programme, all TCs use a holistic approach based on principles of self-help and mutual aid.

The origins of the TC can be traced to two independent movements: the 'democratic' and the 'hierarchical'[2]. The democratic TC was developed at the Henderson Hospital, England during the 1960s, and specialised in supporting individuals with moderate to severe personality disorders, as well as those with complex emotional and interpersonal issues. Generally speaking, the democratic TC provides a psychosocial approach, which is intended to help troubled individuals understand and, as far as possible, lessen or overcome their psychological, social and/or emotional issues and difficulties (Stevens, 2013).

The hierarchical TC is derived from Synanon, San Francisco, which comprised a self-help community for substance users, established by Charles Dederich in 1958. The hierarchical TC is a psychosocial intervention which uses self-help and behaviour modification techniques to help individuals address underlying issues and difficulties that surround their substance use (Perfas, 2004). Given our focus on substance use, we explore only the priorities and values found in the hierarchical TC.

At first glance, the TC's historical origins do not look overly promising. Charles Dederich practiced a highly confrontational brand of therapy built on an autocratic, family surrogate model that required a high level of self-disclosure (Perfas, 2004). An individual's needs were met through total participation in Synanon, and individual roles and responsibilities evolved to serve the maintenance of the Synanon community. Clients were required to conform to rules, norms and expectations that detailed how to behave, and to

---

[2] Although it is becoming increasingly difficult to distinguish between the two traditions, the hierarchical TC typically provides a more 'hierarchical' and structured treatment environment, whereas the democratic tradition prioritises a more collective 'democratic' treatment approach.

uphold pre-determined values that applied to everyday life, from getting up in the morning to relaxing in the evening (Kennard, 1998).

A wide range of methods, such as reward and sanction systems, peer pressure and encounter groups were employed to introduce conformity and commitment to the rules and regulations. Rather problematically, in the late 1970s, completion of Synanon was abolished as Dederich redefined addiction as a terminal disease that could only be arrested by sustained participation in the community (White, 1998). This shift marked the beginning of the end of Synanon, as its earlier ethos gave way to the development of a community that introduced a greater degree of coercion and a series of loyalty tests which drove out all but the most committed residents (White, 1998). The authoritarian communitarian nature of Synanon and other early TCs has quite rightly evoked much criticism (Waldorf, 1971; Sugerman, 1986; Kooyman, 1986, 1993; White, 1998; Gosling, 2015). It is the alternative models which subsequently evolved in the TC movement that offer a firmer ground for inclusion within an abolitionist real utopia manifesto.

In 1968, Dr Ian Christie converted a ward of St. James Hospital, Portsmouth into Europe's first hospital-based TC for substance use. At around the same time, Professor Griffith Edwards of the Maudsley Hospital Addiction Unit established the Featherstone Lodge TC and Dr Bertram Mandelbrote created a TC in the Littlemore Hospital in Oxford. Hospital-based TCs were a result of a group of British psychiatrists who had been inspired by visits to Daytop Village and the Synanon-influenced Phoenix House in New York. Although essentially inspired by the American movement, European TCs went on to develop their own identity due to strong opposition to the harsh confrontation of residents and demoralising learning techniques that had taken place in Synanon. This dissatisfaction led to the development of a European TC that provided a more balanced and supportive dialogue between clients and staff (Broekaert, Vandevelde, Schuyten, Erauw and Bracke, 2004; Broekaert, 2006; Goethals et al, 2011; Vanderplasschen et al, 2014), and thus was much more in line with the normative framework of an abolitionist real utopia.

The residential TC identifies itself as an abstinence-based programme, providing a stark contrast to programmes available during the 1970s that sought to limit the harm that emerged from substance use[3]. During this time, heroin use, which was associated with American jazz music and Hollywood films, was at the centre of British public and political concern. It is perhaps unsurprising then that an American programme, such as the TC, was

---

[3] For example, substitute prescription programmes and needle exchange schemes.

integrated into the British alcohol and drug treatment system with relative ease, accounting for approximately half the 250 residential beds in Britain by the end of the 1970s (Yates, 1981, 2002, 2003).

When the hierarchical TC first emerged, the notion that a group of substance users could manage and control their own recovery was greeted with scepticism by mainstream alcohol and drug services (Yates, 2003; Broekaert et al, 2006; Yates, 2012). Despite initial and continuing scepticism from Europe's mainstream alcohol and drug treatment culture, the TC survived the test of time. The programme is a well-established self-help modality in countries such as Italy, Greece, Spain, Portugal, Lithuania, Hungary and Poland; with more than 1,200 TCs across Europe alone (Vanderplasschen et al, 2014).

Despite divergent origins, philosophies, clientele and settings, the democratic TC and hierarchical TC are considered to be vanguards of new and alternative therapies for individuals who have mental health or substance use issues (Rawlings and Yates, 2001). Since the inception of the TC there has been great debate about whether hierarchical TCs are similar to or significantly different from their democratic cousin (Glaser, 1983; Sugarman, 1984; Lipton, 1998; Lipton, 2010; Stevens, 2013). There is, however, a general agreement that TCs:

> .... share an encouragement of residents' active involvement in, and responsibility for, the day-to-day running of the TC; a respect for the social learning and behavioural reinforcement that occurs naturally in the course of communal living. (Stevens, 2013:14)

We now turn to a discussion of the TCs' theoretical and methodological priorities and their relationship to the normative framework of an abolitionist real utopia.

The theoretical priorities of the TC

For George DeLeon (2000), the first research director at Phoenix House New York and foremost evaluator of the TC for substance use, the theoretical priorities of the day-to-day workings of a TC can be separated into three distinct parts.

1.   View of the Disorder.

For DeLeon (2000), substance use is a disorder of the whole person affecting some, if not all, areas of functioning. Although substance users cite a variety of reasons and circumstances as to why they use substances, TCs emphasise that individuals must recognise how they have contributed to the problems that they are experiencing and develop coping strategies to manage potential future problems.

2.   *View of the Person.*

According to DeLeon (2000), substance users characteristically display a variety of cognitive deficits such as poor awareness, difficulty in decision-making and a lack of problem-solving skills. In addition to these cognitive characteristics, substance users commonly display difficulties in how they see themselves in relation to their personal self-worth and as members of society with self-regulation, as well as how they communicate and manage feelings. Although the origins of an individual's experienced and displayed trust issues are multifaceted, they typically reflect social and psychological influences such as histories of unsafe and abusive families, poor parental models of trust and negative socialisation. The problem is not only in an individual's inability to trust others, but the inability to trust themselves and their own feelings, thoughts and decisions (DeLeon, 2000).

3.   *View of Recovery and Right Living.*

Despite the various social and psychological backgrounds that substance users have, the fundamental goal of recovery in a TC remains the same: to learn or re-learn how to live without substances. According to the TC perspective, recovery is a gradual process of multidimensional learning involving behavioural, cognitive and emotional change (DeLeon, 2000). Behavioural change refers to the elimination of asocial and antisocial behaviour and the acquiring of positive social and interpersonal skills. Cognitive change refers to gaining new ways of thinking, decision-making and problem-solving skills; and emotional change refers to the development of skills necessary for managing and communicating feelings. Right living means abiding by community rules, remaining substance free, participating in daily groups, meetings, work and therapeutic interventions. According to the TC perspective, the daily practice of 'right living' not only provides a positive prototype that can be referred to after separation from the TC but, given time, will evolve into a change in lifestyle and identity (DeLeon, 2000).

The term 'community as method' refers to the self-help approach used within a TC where it is the community itself that brings about change (De Leon, 2000: 92). Community as method means encouraging residents to use their time constructively by teaching them how to learn about themselves and bring about personal change. These strategies and interventions place demands on the individual by expecting them to participate, behave appropriately and respect the rules of the programme. Being a member of a TC means that every individual is expected to monitor, observe and provide feedback on each other's behaviour, attitude and personal change. Residents are part of the programme 24 hours per day, 7 days a week, and are observed in everything that they do: work, leisure, peer interactions, group participation and so on. It is through these observations that a picture emerges of residents' behaviours and attitudes, which need to be challenged and developed. The fundamental assumption that underlies the community as method approach is that residents obtain maximum therapeutic and educational impact when they meet community expectations and use the peer community to change themselves (DeLeon, 2000).

TCs as a radical alternative to prison

We have explored the historical foundations and theoretical assumptions underscoring the TC. What is now required is some consideration of the evidence that TCs can be a plausible (effective) historically immanent alternative to custody. The first thing to note is the relative scarcity of research exploring the possibility of TCs as an alternative to prison for people with substance use issues. Below is a brief overview of the literature over the last few decades.

Exploring the importance of interventions other than prison, a longitudinal study by Bale et al (1980) compared the effectiveness of three residential TCs and an outpatient methadone maintenance programme for 585 male veterans addicted to heroin. The study's conclusions confirmed that therapeutic interventions could be much more progressive and appropriate than a prison sentence. In short, Bale et al (1980) discovered that when compared to those who received either no treatment or only limited forms of detoxification, those who had been in a TC or methadone treatment for over seven weeks were not only less likely to be convicted of a serious crime, use heroin or subsequently receive a prison sentence, but were also more likely to be in education or employment. A few years later, Wilson and Mandelbrote (1985) conducted a ten year follow-up study on Ley Community in Oxford (UK). Rather than using control groups, the authors compared the demography, criminal careers and substance usage of admissions from 1971 and 1973 with an analysis of the length of time people resided in the TC. On this basis, they found that programme involvement was the most significant factor in recidivism rates, arguing that residents who stayed for over six months had a reconviction rate of 15 per cent, whereas for those who stayed for under a month, the figure rose to 85 per cent. The most obvious and recurring problem with outcome measures such as (re)conviction and programme completion is the fact that such measures cannot provide definitive answers as to whether an individual has reverted back to substance use and/or participated in criminal activity.

In a similar vein, Nemes et al (1999) have examined the efficacy of providing Enhanced Abbreviated or Standard Inpatient and Outpatient treatment for substance users. The experiment randomly assigned 412 clients to two TCs, which differed primarily in planned duration. Findings suggest that a 12-month course of treatment, including at least 6 months in a TC followed by outpatient treatment, can produce marked reductions in substance use and 'crime' among persons who complete both phases. An additional study by Messina et al (2000) compared factors that predicted outcomes in men and women randomly assigned to two TCs differing primarily in length of inpatient and outpatient treatment. The results here showed that the predictors of outcome for men and women were the same regardless of gender. Results further suggested that longer residential programmes had a particularly beneficial impact on women. Furthermore, Farrall (2000) found that women participants of the CREST programme (n = 41) were statistically less likely to relapse on alcohol than the women in a work release programme or 'control group' (n = 37).[4] Of the women participating in the CREST programme, only 39 per cent relapsed. Taking specific drugs into account, women in CREST were significantly less likely to relapse on alcohol. Women in CREST were also more successful at forging some sort of social support system in the community.

Literature exploring the option of the TC in place of a prison sentence is very limited, particularly in the United Kingdom, but one such study was conducted by Lamb and Goertzel (1974) who undertook a detailed review of Ellsworth House rehabilitation programme in the US in the 1970s. Residents of Ellsworth House gained employment in the community whilst at the same time participating in a therapeutic programme. For the study, offenders already sentenced to a prison term of four months or more were randomly assigned either to Ellsworth House or to a comparison group which remained in prison.

---

[4]Although little insight is provided into the characteristics of the control group, it is important to recognise that the heterogeneity of the population served by a TC besides programme adaptation and modification means that establishing a true randomised control group is a complex, if not impossible, task.

Although the conclusions reached by Lamb and Goertzel (1974) were not decisively in favour of the TC over the prison (as recidivism rates were comparable for the two cohorts), the authors did find that the Ellsworth House group had a higher rate of employment upon release.

There is a little more literature examining whether referral to a TC is an option better than a prison sentence. For example, Dynia and Sung (2000) provided a detailed review of the Drug Treatment Alternative to Prison (DTAP) programme in Brooklyn, New York in the 1990s. The DTAP runs from 15–24 months and follows a traditional TC structure. The DTAP includes individual, group, and family counselling sessions, vocational and educational courses and relapse prevention. Residents are helped to find a job and accommodation before they leave. The aim of this TC is to divert non-violent drug users over the age of 18 away from prison and into residential services. The DTAP works on a 'sentence deferral system' so that, rather than being used as a replacement for a prison sentence, the accused must plead guilty before a referral is given. The guilty plea is conditional upon the offender completing the DTAP programme, for only then can it be withdrawn and the case dismissed. Belenko and colleagues (2004) also conducted longitudinal research on the DTAP in New York, finding that in comparison to the control group of prisoners, DATP residents were 56 per cent less likely to be re-arrested; 60 per cent less likely to be reconvicted; and 65 per cent less likely to receive a new prison sentence.

Additional research by Zarkin and colleagues (2005) focused on the financial benefits of the DTAP in comparison to a prison sentence. The authors argued that while the DTAP costs on average $40,718 per resident and $50,886 per resident for those who complete it, the financial outlays of the DTAP were much lower than the average $124,995 incurred in criminal justice costs. Zarkin et al (2005) argue that over a six year period, $7.13 million would have been saved if everyone in their comparison group had joined the DATP. It is also worthwhile mentioning here the study conducted by French et al (2002) which compared the economic benefits and costs of modified TC for homeless and 'mentally ill chemical abusers' (MICAs) relative to a comparison group. Data from the period 12 months pre-admission to the modified TC were compared to data from 12 months post-admission across three outcome categories: employment, criminal activity and utilisation of health care services. The economic costs of the average modified TC episode was $20,361. The economic benefit generated by the average modified TC client was $305,273 (French et al, 2002).

Despite the limited set of data available, there appears to be some evidence that TCs are cheaper, more humane and more effective in addressing substance use than prison. Whilst we acknowledge that such findings are provisional, they are promising and raise the question as to what findings might emerge if more substance users in England and elsewhere went to a TC rather than a prison. Yet we must caution against an overly optimistic appraisal. The vast majority of the problems facing substance-using lawbreakers are not due to personal inadequacies or failures of individual responsibility, but rather are structurally generated through the social and economic inequalities of neo-liberal capitalist societies. The divisions that really matter exist with regard to housing, health, transport, work, income and wealth. We must not be seduced into a medicalised illusion about the causes of distress, suffering and discontent which then obfuscates the broader structural contexts generating social harms (Illich, 1977; Scott and Codd, 2010; Rapey et al, 2011). Accordingly, the effectiveness of any therapeutic interventions, including the TC evaluation studies we have discussed above, must be contextualised within the hurt, trauma and injury generated by social inequalities and poverty; the notoriously weak and methodologically inconsistent scientific analysis of the treatment efficacy of therapy; and the fact there is much evidence which indicates that those who need help the most appear to benefit from therapy the least (Moloney, 2013). As Paul Moloney (2013: 93) pessimistically sums up:

> There is no consistent, good quality evidence that any type of therapy can outperform a well-designed placebo, that any approach is reliably superior to another, or that any given set of curative ingredients outdo their competitors. Only one observation is upheld: that confident and emotionally warm professionals are more appreciated by their clients, and get better results, a statement that applies equally to politicians, salespeople and prostitutes.[5]

---

[5] We would like to reiterate the point made above regarding the limitations of evaluations on therapeutic interventions. Critics have identified that evaluative studies of treatment efficacy, such as those regarding people who have sexually offended, have tied themselves in knots by trying to deploy positivistic methodologies (for a critical review of literature on the effectiveness of treatment programmes for prisoners from a number of different social backgrounds see Scott and Codd, 2010). Yet we would not wish to be overly pessimistic. We would draw attention to voluntary programmes in the community that have been adopted throughout Europe for people who sexually offend, such as the interventions by the late Ray Wyre at the Gracewell Clinic in Birmingham in the 1980s; the work of the Lucy Faithful

Can TCs be an abolitionist real utopia?

The commentary above has raised a number of questions which require further attention and deliberation. Of particular pertinence here is whether TCs can be promoted as part of a wider manifesto of an abolitionist real utopia? In other words, do TCs provide a historically immanent alternative that can move beyond the existing punitive-rationale and help to challenge social inequalities? Do they provide a genuinely different way of working alongside individuals who end up in the criminal process as a result of substance use? Are they better places in comparison to prison and can they protect human dignity and minimise human suffering? Can they respect and define clients as human beings who need to be consulted and whose voice is heard rather than merely entities that need to be managed and risk assessed? And do they facilitate or inhibit the requirements of social justice? Let us now reflect upon these questions in more depth.

1.   *TCs as a historically immanent challenge to the punitive rationale.*
TCs are predicated upon helping the individual rather than punishing them. It should be remembered that TCs developed during the 1960s when communal living and notions of peace making were advocated on a social level. In some ways, the TC is part of the legacy of the radical, emancipatory and utopian social movements of this time. In this sense, the TC has a similar historical counter-cultural foundation to that of penal abolitionism (and consequently the abolitionist real utopia). Importantly, the TC is an intervention which is deeply rooted in our historical conjuncture, and thus can provide a plausible and immanent alternative to imprisonment. Although there is some evidence (see below) that the TC can still be deployed in an oppressive and authoritarian manner, a genuine TC is rooted in compassion, mutual aid and the ethic of care. The TC draws upon a therapeutic rather than punitive-rationale, and whatever the limitations of therapy (Moloney, 2013), at its best this justification endeavours to alleviate, rather than inflict, pain. Undoubtedly, a genuine TC provides a progressive and contradictory space that undermines the logic of penalisation because its overriding philosophy is fundamentally grounded in humanitarian values such as empathy, respect for oneself and

---

Foundation in UK; and the Prevention Project Dunkelfeld (PPD) in Germany.

respect for others. Ultimately, the TC advocates individual and social forms of inclusion.

Government agendas focusing upon 'community values' and 'reintegration' ignore the harmful consequences of imprisonment post-release, notably the legacies of civil and social death and the further embedding of social inequalities. Evidence indicates that TCs can help reduce harms and may be more 'efficient, effective and economic' than penal custody. Therapeutic interventions can perhaps tap into official discourses around evidence-led policy and thus be attractive to Governments wishing to really break the links between substance use, criminalisation and penalisation. TCs could also fit into a localised agenda and even potentially have some resonance with populist governmental slogans such as the 'big society', albeit offering a very different form of intervention than that envisaged by Conservative politicians in England and Wales. There is also the argument which governments may find attractive regarding the TC as an intervention prior to incarceration. Imprisonment creates its own individual and social harms and can lead to prisonisation and de-habilitation. For those who genuinely wish to see a rehabilitation revolution, the TC is both revolutionary and grounded in rehabilitative and restorative principles. This all means that a case can be made for TCs to be considered a plausible and politically defensible option in a time of penal excess.

2.   *TCs can be a genuinely alternative way to work alongside substance users.*

TCs have an alternative conception of individuals who are deemed to be problematic which is much more positive than current dominant beliefs about substance users. TCs work with the person, not the socially constructed problems that surround them, such as criminal and deviant labels. TCs do not rely on, nor support, the use of diagnostic categories or proposals which suggest that substance users have a disease or some kind of faulty thinking that requires adaptation and modification. In theory, the ethos which underpins all day-to-day activities that take place in a TC is based upon recognising a person as an individual, not as a problem, number or risk. In practice, however, we have found that this is somewhat diluted as there is a reoccurring tension among staff and residents when it comes to the admission of individuals with a history of imprisonment. This illustrates the need to divert substance users away from the criminal process.

There then remains the very real possibility that a TC can operate in a similar way to that of the prison, or perhaps even inflict more pain. There is no guarantee that an intervention which calls itself a TC will automatically be *better than* prison (Scott and Gosling, 2015). In one large Italian TC we observed in November 2015, where members were compelled to reside for four years, the daily regime was rooted in exploitive labour practices. This 'TC' appeared to hide behind the claim that work is therapeutic and educational. From day one, residents were allocated to workshops producing goods for local, national and multinational capitalist corporations without recompense. This seems tantamount to a form of servitude. Community membership ranged from 14-25 year olds and, whilst selection criteria may have been based on the likelihood of desistance and malleability for change, at this age members are likely to be more flexible in developing skills to ensure that they are economically productive. The division of labour in these workshops was also profoundly masculinist with the role of men and women reflecting a gendered hierarchy of male and female work, ensuring the separation of men and women working in the community. An authoritarian communitarian ethos pertained – there was a rigid and dominating structure that was grounded in extensive supervision. Residents were supervised for their first year by a long-serving peer, which even included being observed and escorted to the bathroom (Scott and Gosling, 2015). Care must be taken therefore to ensure that any proposed alternative intervention does not become a form of 'punishment in disguise' (Hannah-Moffatt, 2001) or a 'prison without walls' (Cohen, 1980). We are calling for genuine alternatives and any proposed TC must not resemble 'semi-penal institutions' (Barton, 2005).

3.   *TCs facilitate meaningful participation and acknowledge residents' voices.*

Genuine TCs reject autonomy-sapping and power-abusing characteristics of total institutions in favour of supportive relationships between the service provider and client, described as evocative rather that didactic, as individuals can begin to understand themselves and their relationship with society through an ongoing interaction with their peer community, rather than some form of expert truth or knowledge about the situation that they may have found themselves in.

As we have identified, there can be a tension regarding the 'TC sentence' and the importance of voluntary engagement. This could perhaps in some cases be overcome, but the need for individuals to in some way choose the TC as an alternative sentence seems crucial. Inevitably, this concern places an increased burden on ensuring that democratic participation is at the heart of TC practices. Fitting the TC within the existing sentencing and criminal process can also result in problems of organisation, with tensions resulting from different working credos, orientations and assumptions (i.e. treatment, punishment or welfare logics).

There of course remains the question of what should happen if an individual chooses not to enter a TC and what would be the most appropriate responses under such conditions. We know that coercive therapeutic interventions are much less successful that their voluntary counterparts (Scott and Codd, 2010) and therefore the issue of voluntary participation remains paramount. We would suggest that alongside the TC there must also be spaces available, perhaps places which in the past have been called sanctuaries, where an individual could reflect upon the possible options available to them. Thus, alongside opportunities for substance users to carefully consider the right path at this moment in life, we would reiterate the point that the TC is only one of a raft of non-penal radical alternatives promoted in an abolitionist real utopia. If an individual was to refuse to voluntarily participate, then perhaps other non-penal interventions would be more appropriate in its place (for examples, see Scott, 2013).

4.   *TCs can protect human dignity and minimise human suffering.*
TCs are based on promoting human dignity, respect for all members of society and human liberation, rather than moral condemnation. In other words, they operate alongside individuals, enabling them to work through their problems and to challenge boundaries rather than constructing a neo-liberal 'responsibilised subject'. Instead of 'governing from a distance', TCs provoke questions of the self, but in so doing, also provide an 'invitation to change' (Gosling, 2015) which involves a safe and supportive environment in which longitudinal support, friendship and recognition of one and others' struggles and needs are embraced in the journey away from substance use and related harms.

To avoid an unintentional or hidden escalation of pain, the TC envisaged as an abolitionist real utopia must have sufficient transparency, respect procedural rights, and be rooted in the principles of fairness, equality and legal accountability. TCs can minimise harm on an individual and local community level, which is something of great significance, but we must recognise that they are unable to combat effectively the hurt, injury and suffering generated by structural inequalities and social injustices.

5.   TCs do not inhibit strategies of social justice.

The vast amount of people who are imprisoned in England and Wales are from socially marginalised and excluded backgrounds (Scott, 2008). In the focus groups we undertook with TC practitioners and clients, there was a general consensus that TCs can be used in place of a prison sentence for substance users who have committed a non-violent offence.[6] The emphasis here on 'non-violent' offenders is strategic. Focusing on such substance users in the TCs may be a good way to introduce the TC to a sceptical audience, but in the long term we would advocate the importance of challenging violence in all of its manifestations, including interpersonal violence. We do not have space to explore the issue of violence and related issues like 'community safety' in depth, but we recognise that not only may the TC be a non-violent means of responding to interpersonal violence, but that we must also promote policies which seek to challenge other forms of violence, most notably 'institutional violence' and 'structural violence' (Scott, 2015). Here we understand violence in its broadest sense as harmful outcomes damaging human potential through the organisational structures of an institution such as a prison and the structured inequalities of advanced capitalist societies. We have argued throughout this paper that the TC cannot adequately address such harms and injuries, nor can it sufficiently provide 'community safety'. Community safety and reductions in violence can only be achieved by challenging hierarchies of domination and inequitable structures of power and promoting policies grounded in social justice.

We have noted elsewhere that in the focus groups we found there was often caution surrounding 'how many prisoners' a programme could accept before 'they had an impact' on day-to-day therapeutic interventions (Scott and Gosling, 2015). Although this provides a stark contrast to the TC ethos we briefly touched upon earlier, it provides a perfect illustration as to how a substance user's involvement with the criminal process simply adds further pressures and strains when it comes to accessing help and support. With this in mind, we suggest that using TCs alongside the criminal process is ineffective

---

[6] Focus groups took place between August and November 2014 and were carried out in 5 residential TCs for substance use in England, France, Denmark, Italy and Australia. Further focus groups were organised in 2015 across a number of countries in Europe. The number of participants to date is 60.

as the context of the intervention compounds inequalities that lead people to prison in the first instance: dehumanising rather than humanising people.

More broadly, we need to locate the focus on the TC as a solution within consideration of broader socio-economic and political contexts, shaping both the application of the criminal label and the focus of the criminal process on impoverished and marginalised communities, which may reinforce individual pathological explanations of 'crime'. An over-emphasis on TCs as a solution may mystify the structural contexts and so must not be separated from a wider commitment to promote other radical alternatives and wider emancipatory changes regarding how we deal with wrongdoers and social injustice.

Conclusions

Voluntary engagement remains vital and the need for individuals to in some way choose the TC as an alternative sentence seems crucial. Inevitably, this concern places an increased burden on ensuring that democratic participation is at the heart of TC practices. Fitting together the TC within the sentencing and criminal process can also result in problems of organisations, with tensions emerging from different working credos, orientations and assumptions that may prove difficult to overcome. We also remain concerned that through individualising problems, attention may be distracted from how the individual troubles and social problems are generated in the first instance. An over-emphasis on TCs as a solution may obscure the material constraints shaping individual choices. We must never lose our focus on challenging economic and social inequalities. As Moloney (2013:208) argues, if problems:

> ... are caused by material things happening to material bodies: on one side, traumatic abuse and persecution; and on the other, soul-deadening labour, squalid impoverishment, the boredom of joblessness, the moralising sermons of the privileged ... then it seems sensible ... to change the world [through] a concerted effort to take the plight of the poor and marginalised seriously, to redistribute wealth [and] to give them more say over their own future ...

Yet despite the fear that the TC may only be able to provide a 'plaster for a broken leg', this intervention remains a politically plausible option in the UK where talk of rehabilitation continues to have resonance with public opinion and a radical alternative to the prison sentence, albeit one that cannot hope to fully address all of the problems which its clients face in a structurally unequal society.

A TC is something that exists right now and could be implemented immediately in place of a prison sentence in England and Wales. The TC is an alternative that would not be automatically ruled out of the debate – it is a radical alternative for substance-use lawbreakers that can compete with the punitive logics of our time. Its logic of support is the antithesis of the punitive trajectory and so long as deployed *beyond* the criminal process, should be able also to avoid co-option, although as we highlighted earlier, this is something that must be closely monitored.

There are a number of existing examples from across Europe where TCs are currently being utilised as alternatives to prison, albeit this option is still, in the main, relatively under-used. There is (some) evidence that TCs are more likely to be effective interventions in terms of preventing recidivism for substance use law breakers, but importantly, the principles and practices of genuine TCs also allow us to focus upon human need and human growth as a rationale for their promotion. The evidence suggests the TC is *better* than the prison and, though this may not be the best of all possible solutions (as David Small (2011) has argued, we require a political approach challenging existing material power relations rather than therapy) the TC may yet offer a non-penal real utopian alternative to the current incarceration binge (Scott, 2013; Scott and Gosling, 2015). The TC, when promoted as part of wider strategy to tackle social inequalities and social injustice, may be an intervention that can help ameliorate, rather than exacerbate, some of the worst harms, pains and injuries generated in advanced capitalist societies. On these grounds, TCs can be promoted as a non-penal abolitionist real utopia.

Authors' note
A version of this article has been published in the *International Journal for Crime, Justice and Social Democracy*. Full reference: Scott, D. and Gosling, H. (2015) 'Before Prison, Instead of Prison, Better than Prison: Therapeutic Communities as an abolitionist real utopia'. *International Journal of Crime, Justice and Social Democracy*. 5 (1).

References
Bale, R. Van Stone, W. Kuldau, J. Engelsing, T. Elashoff, R. and Zarcone, V. (1980) 'Therapeutic Communities versus Methadone Maintenance: A prospective controlled study of narcotic addiction treatment, Design and

one-year follow-up' in *Archives of General Psychiatry* Volume 37, No. 2 pp 179-193

Barton, A. (2005) *Fragile Moralities, Dangerous Sexualities* Aldershot: Ashgate

Belenko, S. Foltz, C. Lang, M. Hung-En, S. (2004) 'Recidivism Among High-Risk Drug Felons: A longitudinal analysis following residential treatment' in *Journal of Offender Rehabilitation* Volume 40, No. 112 pp 105-321

Broekaert, E., Vandevelde, S., Schuyten, G., Erauw, K. and Bracke, R. (2004) 'Evolution of Encounter Group Methods for Substance Abusers' in *Addictive Behaviours* Volume 29 pp 231-244

Broekaert, E., Vandevelde, S., Soyez, V., Yates, R., and Slater, A. (2006) 'The Third Generation of Therapeutic Communities: The early development of the TC for addictions in Europe' in *European Addiction Research* Volume 12 pp 1-11

Cohen, S. (1980) 'Preface' in Dronfield, L. *Outside Chance* London: Null

DeLeon, G. (2000) *The Therapeutic Community: Theory, model and method* New York: Springer

Dyna, P. and Sung, H. (2000) 'The Safety and Effectiveness of Diverting Felony Drug Offenders to Residential Treatment as Measured by Recidivism' in *Criminal Justice Policy Review* Volume 11, No. 4 pp 299-311

French, M. McCollister, K., Sacks, S. McKendrick, K., DeLeon, G. (2002) 'Benefit-cost analysis of a modified Therapeutic Community for Mentally Ill Chemical Abusers' in *Evaluation and Programme Planning* Volume 21, No. 2, pp. 137-198

Glaser, A. (1983) 'Therapeutic Communities and Therapeutic Communities: A personal perspective' in *International Journal of Therapeutic Communities* Volume 4, No. 2 pp 150-162

Goethals, I., Soyez, V., Melnick, G., DeLeon, G. and Broekaert, E. (2011) 'Essential Elements of Treatment: A comparative study between European and American therapeutic communities for addiction' in *Substance Use and Misuse* Volume 46 pp. 1023–1031

Gosling, H. (2015) *An Invitation to Change? An ethnographic study of a Therapeutic Community for substance use* Unpublished PhD Thesis: Liverpool John Moores University

Hannah-Moffatt, K. (2001) *Punishment in Disguise* Toronto: University of Toronto Press

Farrall, A. (2000) 'Testing the Effect of Therapeutic Communities' in *Women and Criminal Justice* Volume 11, No. 1 pp 21-48

Illich, I. (1977) *Limits to Medicine: Medical Nemesis – the expropriation of health* Harmondsworth: Penguin Books

Kennard, D. (1998) *An Introduction to Therapeutic Communities* London: Jessica Kingsley Publishers

Kooyman, M. (1986) 'The Psychodynamics of Therapeutic Communities for treatment of heroin addicts' in DeLeon, G. and Ziegenfuss, J. *Therapeutic Communities for Addictions: Readings in theory, research and practice* USA: Springfield

Kooyman, M. (1993) *Therapeutic Communities for Addicts: Intimacy, parent involvement and treatment outcome* The Netherlands: Swets and Zeitlinger

Lamb, H.R. and Goertzes, V. (1974) 'Ellsworth House: A community alternative to jail' in *American Journal of Psychiatry* Volume 131 pp 64-68

Lipton, D. (1998). 'Therapeutic Community Treatment Programming in Correction' in *Psychology, Crime and Law* Volume 4, No. 3 pp 213-263

Lipton, D. (2010) 'A Therapeutic Distinction with a Difference: Comparing American concept-based therapeutic communities and British democratic therapeutic community treatment for prison inmates' in Shuker, R. and Sullivan, E. (eds) *Grendon and the Emergence of Forensic Therapeutic Communities: Development in Research and Practice* Chichester: Wiley-Blackwell

Mathiesen, T. (1974) *The Politics of Abolition* Oxford: Martin Robertson

Messina, N. Buldon, W. Hagopian, G. and Prendergast, M. (2000) 'Predictors of Prison-based Treatment Outcomes: A comparison of men and women participants' in *American Journal of Drug and Alcohol Abuse* Volume 32, No. 1 pp 7-22

Moloney, P. (2013) *The Therapy Industry* London: Pluto Press

Nemes, S. Wish, E. Messina, N. (1999) 'Comparing the Impact of Standard and Abbreviated Treatment in a Therapeutic Community: Findings from the district of Columbia treatment initiative experiment' in *Journal of Substance Abuse Treatment* Volume 17, No. 4 pp 339-347

Perfas, F. (2004) *Therapeutic Community: Social Systems Perspective* Lincoln: iUniverse, Inc.

Rapley, M., Moncrieff, J. and Dillon, J. (2011) 'Carving Nature at its Joints' in Rapley, M., Moncrieff, J. and Dillon, J. (eds) (2011) *De-Medicalising Misery* London: Palgrave

Rawlings, B. and Yates, R. (2001). *Therapeutic Communities for the Treatment of Drug Users* London: Jessica Kingsley

Scott, D. (2008) *Penology* London: Sage

Scott, D. (2013) 'Visualising an Abolitionist Real Utopia: Principles, policy and practice' in Malloch, M. and Munro, B. (eds) (2013) *Crime, Critique and Utopia* London: Palgrave

Scott, D. (2015) 'Eating your Insides Out: Interpersonal, cultural and institutionally-structured violence in the prison place' in *Prison Service Journal* September, 2015

Scott, D. and Codd, H. (2010) *Controversial Issues in Prison* Buckingham: Open University Press

Scott, D. and Gosling, H. (2015) 'Counterblast: Thinking Beyond the Punitive Rationale – promoting TCs as a radical alternative to prison?' in *Howard Journal of Criminal Justice* September, 2015

Small, D. (2011) 'Psychotherapy: Illusion with no future' in Rapley, M., Moncrieff, J. and Dillon, J. (eds) (2011) *De-Medicalising Misery* London: Palgrave

Stevens, A. (2013) *Offender Rehabilitation and Therapeutic Communities: Enabling change the TC way* Oxon: Routledge.

Sugarman, B. (1984) 'Towards a New, Common Model of the Therapeutic Community: Structural components, learning processes and outcomes' in *International Journal of Therapeutic Communities* Volume 5, No. 2 pp 77-98.

Sugerman, B. (1986) 'Structure, Variations and Context: A sociological view of the therapeutic community' in DeLeon, G. and Ziegenfuss, J. (1986) *Therapeutic Communities for Addictions: Readings in theory, research and practice* USA: Springfield.

Vanderplasschen, W. ,Vandevelde, S. and Broekaert, E. (2014) *Therapeutic Communities for Treating Addictions in Europe: Evidence, current practices and future challenges* European Monitoring Centre for Drugs and Drug Addictions, http://www.emcdda.europa.eu/attachements.cfm/att_226003_EN_TDXD1 4015ENN_final.pdf (consulted 10 October 2014)

Waldorf, D. (1971) 'Social Control in Therapeutic Communities for the treatment of Drug Addicts' in *The International Journal of the Addictions* Volume 6, No. 1 pp 29-43.

White, W. (1998) *Slaying the Dragon: The history of addiction treatment and recovery in America* Bloomington: Lighthouse Institute

Wilson, S. and Mandelbrote, B. (1985) 'Reconviction Rates of Drug Dependent Patients Treated in a Residential Therapeutic Community: 10-year follow-up' in *British Medical Journal* Volume 291 p 105

Yates, R. (1981) *Out from the Shadow* London: NACRO

Yates, R. (2002). *A Brief History of British Drug Policy: 1950–2001. Scottish Drugs Training Project.* University of Stirling, https://dspace.stir.ac.uk/bitstream/1893/1135/1/1950-2001.pdf (consulted 22 January 2014)

Yates, R. (2003) 'A Brief Moment of Glory: The impact of the therapeutic community movement on drug treatment systems in the UK' in *International Journal of Social Welfare* Volume 12: 239–243

Yates, R. (2012) 'In It For The Long Haul: Recovery capital, addiction theory and the inter-generational transmission of addictive behaviour' in Adan, A. and Vilanou, C. *Substance Abuse Treatment: Generalities and Specificities* Barcelona: Marge-Medica Books

Zarkin, G. Dunlap, L. Belenko, S. and Dyna, R. (2005) 'A Benefit-Cost Analysis of the Kings County District Attorney's Office Drug Treatment Alterative to Prison (DTAP) Program' in *Justice, Research and Policy* Volume 7, No 1 pp 1-24.

What to do with the Harmful Corporation? The case for a non-penal real utopia

Steve Tombs[1]

Abstract

The central concern of this paper is how to respond to health and safety harms caused by corporations. I confine my considerations to health and safety harms, and focus on corporations, not individuals. Once one begins to try to identify ways of effectively 'punishing' the corporation, one is led to think about undermining the very basis of the corporation – that is, one is forced into envisioning real utopias. And it is an area in desperate need of 'real utopian' thinking, given the scale of harm at issue. The paper begins by indicating the scale and nature of this harm. Then, I critically discuss the use of the fine as the common response to corporate crime in this sphere, before going on to consider more effective responses to corporate crime and harms, and the extent to which they may further the task of abolishing the corporation.

Introduction

Media reports of corporate crime and punishment seem to be an almost daily occurrence – even if the word 'crime' is often notable for its absence. Central to such tales of corporate offending are financial services companies – not least, 'the banks'. In fact, in July 2015, a calculation by the *Financial Times* claimed that 'global banks have paid $162.2bn in fines and legal settlements with US regulators since the financial crisis' (Stabe and Stanley, 2015), while a month later it was estimated that 'Britain's big four banks [have] rack[ed] up £50bn in fines since the financial crisis with HSBC set to pay £500m in US for rigging foreign exchange markets' (Salmon, 2015). Such headlines, of course, tell us virtually nothing about the scale and level of corporate crime or harm.

These are figures of unimaginable proportions, and raise some important questions: how are such fines calculated; who pays them; how do they affect

---

[1] Steve Tombs is Professor of Criminology at the Open University. He has a long-standing interest in the incidence, nature and regulation of corporate crime and harm. His most recent publication is *Social Protection After the Crisis: Regulation without enforcement*, Bristol: Policy Press. He works closely with the Hazards movement in the UK, and is a Trustee and Board member of Inquest.

individuals who might have benefited from the crimes of the banks so punished; and, how effective are such fines? These questions are even more problematic in the context of a form of corporate harm where there is far less popular, political and criminal justice scrutiny – namely occupational health and safety. In fact, this sphere of corporate harm tends to hit the headlines for quite different reasons to banking harms: the former is widely derided, synonymous with red tape, petty rules and regulations, where stories circulate about hanging baskets and kids playing conkers being banned by an over-zealous health and safety police (Almond, 2009).

This article considers penal and real utopian non-penal alternatives to responding to health and safety harms caused by corporations. More specifically, my concern is what to do with the harmful corporation? In these considerations, I should make it clear that I confine my focus to health and safety harms arising out of or connected to the activity of work and focus on corporations, not individuals. It should be noted that individuals can be prosecuted and punished for health and safety crimes, and that this can lead to imprisonment, albeit that this is very rare indeed. Interestingly, employees are almost as likely as employers (whether directors or senior managers) to be prosecuted for such offences. Thus, typically, 95 per cent of prosecutions by the UK Health and Safety Executive (HSE) are against organisations, 3 per cent against directors, and 2 per cent against employees (Tombs and Whyte, 2015b).

What is particularly of interest here, is that once one starts to try to identify any way of thinking about 'punishing' the corporation that is vaguely effective, one is led to think about undermining the very basis of the corporation – that is, one is forced into envisioning a *real utopian* response to the issue, that is, one which takes seriously concrete and specific redesign of the corporate form. Also of interest is that the issue of corporate harms in the form of health and safety violations is not one where we can detect punitiveness, 'a punitive turn' (Pratt et al, 2007; Bell, 2011), 'a culture of control' (Garland, 2001), and nor, then, is it one which has attracted the focus of those arguing for abolitionism, de-carceration, and so on. But it is an area in desperate need of 'real utopian' thinking, given the scale of harm at issue. It is to the latter issue which I now turn. Then, I critically discuss the use of the fine as the common response to corporate crime in this sphere, before going on to consider more effective responses to corporate crime and harms.

Socialising Harm with Impunity

Each year, HSE press releases the numbers of 'fatal injuries' to workers as the trail to its annual statistical publication. Often referred to by HSE as fatal *accidents*, this headline figure of somewhere around 150 deaths omits vast swathes of fatal injuries as well as deaths from occupational exposures which it in fact records. HSE's *Health and Safety Statistics 2014-15* reveals: 'Around 13,000 deaths each year from occupational lung disease and cancer are estimated to have been caused by past exposure, primarily to chemicals and dust at work' (Health and Safety Executive, 2015: 2). This data still remains a gross underestimate. For example, in 2009, researchers from the European Agency for Safety and Health at Work calculated 21,000 deaths per year in the UK from work-related fatal diseases, though noted that such data 'might still be an under-estimation' and that deaths from work-related diseases are 'increasing' (Hämäläinen et al, 2009: 127). Another UK study estimated that up to 40,000 annual deaths in Britain are caused by work-related cancers alone. And long-term research by the Hazards movement[2], drawing on a range of studies of occupational and environmental cancers, the number of heart-disease deaths with a work-related cause, as well as estimates of other diseases to which work can be a contributory cause, showed a lower-end estimate of 50,000 deaths from work-related illness in the UK each year. This figure ranks highly in comparison with virtually all other recorded causes of premature death in the UK (see Tombs, 2014).

This is a significant toll of physical harm, produced on an annual basis, and does not even begin to incorporate the non-fatal injuries and illnesses caused by work each year – which even on recorded data runs into the hundreds of thousands, and on the basis of HSE's collection of self-reported data is counted in seven figures (see next section). These data, for all their limitations, are enough to allow us to reach one indisputable conclusion: work is a major source of physical harm. If 'capitalist class relations perpetuate eliminable forms of human suffering', (Wright, 2010: 37) such data are a stark illustration of this observation.

Further, the harm is not simply physical – these physical harms are associated with a wider series of harms generated by each death, injury or illness. These include various emotional and psychological harms, many of which may be short-lived, others of which may endure over long periods.

---

[2] Independent organisation campaigning for justice and safety at work. See http://www.hazardscampaign.org.uk/

These in turn have knock-on harmful effects in terms of family, dependants, friends, and so on, and again may incur costs upon the State. In effect, each form of physical harm is, albeit differentially, likely to be associated with ripples of harms.

There are also significant financial costs entailed here, in the form of a loss of income or additional costs incurred by the injured person or the families of those bereaved. But there are also wider, economic costs, in the sense that all of these harms entail various layers of costs for the State, ultimately borne by taxpayers and with knock-on effects for the provision of other state goods and services; such costs range from those associated with health-care, welfare and sickness payments, lost income and production, legal and administrative costs, as well as regulatory resources, and so on. Where the harms are generated in profit-making settings, these costs are socialised, while profits remain privatised – so there are clear, harmful wealth-distribution effects, also.

HSE intermittently calculates the overall financial costs of injuries and ill-health, its most recent such calculation being for the year 2013/14. In that year, injuries and new cases of ill-health 'cost society an estimated £14.3 billion' (Health and Safety Executive (2015b: 2). Further, it notes that 'The majority of costs fall on individuals, while employers and government/taxpayers bear a similar proportion of the costs of workplace injury and ill health' (*ibid*). More specifically, the distribution of costs is estimated as follows: £8.2b borne by individuals, £2.8b by employers and £3.4b by government/taxpayers; thus employers bear some 20 per cent of the costs, the smallest absolute and relative figure (ibid).

This is quite typical. Corporations are generally not required to pay the costs of the most damaging effects of their activities. This is due to the system used in accounting practice that privileges some costs and benefits over others. In general, corporate balance sheets only reflect particular costs. The costs that typically *are* counted are the standard inputs of commercial or productive activity: the costs of raw materials, of processing these through energy and using technologies, the costs of building or renting and maintaining premises or the costs of labour power. However, industrial injuries and diseases, alongside harms such as environmental pollution and food poisoning, involve major social costs that are not included: these are what economists call 'externalities'. It is the cost-accounting mechanisms used in standard accounting practice which reduces the value of death, injury and illness to mere externalities; that is, peripheral side-effects of corporate activity, which remain absent from the balance sheets of costs and benefits of such activity.

Quite simply, some costs of doing business are counted and other costs are not. It is this principle that enables corporations, to use Bakan's (2004: 60) term, to act as 'externalising machines'.

Responding to the Harmful Corporation

How, then, does the State respond to such a grotesque scale of routine, consistent harm? Formally, the State's approach is to seek to regulate the corporation with respect to health and safety law – and to be clear, this is regulation *not* policing. The term 'regulated' immediately indicates that those crimes are not policed in the usual sense of the word: corporate crimes are normally dealt with by different types of enforcement authorities ('regulatory agencies') and often with different types of ('administrative' or 'regulatory') law. But these are more than administrative distinctions, of course.

There now exists a mass of studies – mostly nationally based, though with some useful cross-national comparative studies also – regarding the practices of a whole range of regulatory bodies (see Clarke, 2000: 136-161). Several broad generalisations can thus be made about the practices and effects of regulatory enforcement agencies: non-enforcement is the most frequently found characteristic; enforcement activity tends to focus upon the smallest and weakest individuals and organisations; and sanctions following regulatory activity are light (Snider, 1993: 120-124)[3]. Prosecutions for corporate crime are relatively rare (compared with 'conventional crime').

The increasingly dominant strand of studies around regulatory enforcement focuses on specific business sectors and discrete areas of legislation, documenting the extent to which the compliance-oriented approach is the predominant one amongst regulatory bodies. Indeed, some have argued that there is a generalised convergence across enforcement bodies, jurisdictions, bodies of law, and so on, towards such an enforcement approach (see Tombs, 2015). On the basis of such a strategy, regulators enforce through persuasion – they advise, educate, and bargain, negotiate and reach compromise with the regulated. As a result, business offences typically remain outside the ambit of mainstream criminal legal procedure. If they do become subject to law enforcement, they tend to be separated from the criminal law (and processed using administrative or informal disposals rather than prosecution). Even if

---

[3] These are, of course, generalisations: there are important national differences in enforcement strategies (Pearce and Tombs, 1998: 229-45) and important differences in enforcement strategies across different spheres of regulatory activity (Snider, 1991).

they are subject to the formal processes of criminal law, corporate crimes are rarely viewed as equivalent to 'real' crimes (ibid).

Relatedly, then, what we know in terms of the sentencing and punishment of corporate offenders is that: smaller corporations are more likely to be prosecuted than larger counterparts; offenders are likely to be treated more leniently at sentencing stage than those successfully prosecuted for 'conventional' crimes; and overwhelmingly the most common sanction imposed on a company convicted of any criminal offence is a monetary fine, on which more below.

To illustrate the significance of these processes – effectively, processes of non- or de-criminalisation – let us return to recorded injury and illness data, extending our analysis beyond the sub-set of occupational fatalities. According to HSE's most recent data, in 2014/15, there were: an estimated 2.0 million people suffering from an illness (long-standing as well as new cases) believed to be caused or made worse by their current or past work; 76,000 reported injuries to employees; a total of 611,000 injuries which occurred at work, of which 152,000 led to over 7 days absence (Health and Safety Executive, 2015a: 1-4).

Yet the companies which cause these deaths, injuries and illnesses are subjected to virtually no regulatory oversight. Between them, the Health and Safety Executive and Local Authority Environmental Health Officers are responsible for enforcing health and safety law in over 2.5 million workplaces. In 2013/2014, inspectors from these two sets of regulatory agencies made just 130,000 inspections, with an 'average' of one in 20 workplaces receiving an inspection, and a total number of inspections that continues to be in long term decline (Tombs, 2016: 155). Moreover, it is not simply that inspections are low, and declining, so too are investigations: only a very limited sub-set of the deaths recorded by HSE – the 150 or so which constitute HSE's headline figure – are subject to investigation, while less than one in 20 major injuries are subject to regulatory scrutiny. On the basis of such state inactivity, then, it is unsurprising that prosecutions are few and far between.

Moreover, in 2014/15, there were 1047 separate offences successfully prosecuted by HSE and local authorities across Britain, the average penalty being just under £18,500.[4] Thus, the chances of a death, injury or illness resulting in a successful prosecution are infinitesimal, while the sentence attached to any such conviction is, on any criterion, low.

Somewhat differently, in the case of a limited sub-set of deaths, companies may be charged with corporate manslaughter, on the basis of a new law

---

[4] Source: http://www.hse.gov.uk/statistics/prosecutions.htm

introduced in 2007, the Corporate Manslaughter and Corporate Homicide Act (CMCH Act), designed to facilitate the prosecution of large, complex organisations for death or deaths. However, at the time of writing[5], with the law in force for almost eight years, there have been just 14 successful prosecutions under the new Act. Further, only two had attracted a sentence which reached the putative minimum figure of £500,000: CAV Aerospace Ltd. was fined £600,000, while Sterecycle [Rotherham] Ltd was fined £500,000 – albeit, by the time the trial had begun, the company was in administration.

Sentencing guidelines for health and safety offences – under both CMCH Act and the Health and Safety at Work Act 1974 (HSW Act) – have recently been subject to revision. From February 2016, organisations which are convicted of breaches under the HSW Act should be fined in the range of £50-£10 million, while successful prosecutions under the CMCH Act should generate fines in the range of £180,000 fine-£20 million (Sentencing Council, 2015: 3, 21). Given the limited use of either body of law, and the fact that levels of fines under the previous guidelines failed to reach minimal suggested levels, it is tempting to view these guidelines as purely symbolic. In fact, what we have here is a sphere of activity which produces significant harm but which is effectively non- or de-criminalised – in distinction to many much lower-level incivilities which, many have convincingly argued, are increasingly subject to punitive (and counter-productive) levels of state responses.

The Problem of Corporate Sanctions

Several objections are often noted about the efficacy of the use of fines – and these apply specifically in the context of responding to health and safety offences, even though they are usually made more generally – and it is worth rehearsing these briefly here.

First, fines are not proportionate to the offence committed or the harms caused, as is demonstrated by above data about actual levels of fines in respect to health and safety crimes and harms.

Second, even if fines were to be significantly increased, this still begs the question of whether heavy fines are an appropriate way to deal with corporate wrong? In relation to corporate crime it might be thought that the fine is a perfect disposal because, unlike individuals whose offending is often committed whilst the person is affected by alcohol or drugs, corporations strive, generally, to behave rationally. They conduct business through decision-making processes that

---

[5] March 2016

are susceptible to rationally predictable outcomes like profits and fines. Businesses use cost-benefit analysis as a routine procedure. The problem is that such calculations are as much based on the likelihood of *being caught* as they are upon the level of fine if caught and convicted. Thus, many companies decide to take the risk of unsafe systems as there is a very low chance of being inspected or, indeed, if inspected and detected, of actually being prosecuted for the offence. Thus, the very factors which make the use of fines superficially attractive – that the corporation is a rational, calculative entity – also render them problematic. This is exacerbated by the fact that even high fines and the possibility of detection and their being imposed might be deemed as a calculable, rational risk to take as a cost of doing business – witness the classic Ford Pinto case, for example (Dowie, 1987).

Third, fines at whatever level do not aid rehabilitation – and, indeed, the higher they are set, they may actually hinder more effective systems of health and safety being developed in the aftermath of a conviction since they impose costs on the company.

Fourth, however, such costs may not at all be borne by the offending company itself – many argue that the costs of fines tend to be counter-productive since they are dispersed to the 'innocent'. Thus it has been argued that the burden of such fines is inappropriately borne by employees, through worsening working conditions, cuts to, or deferred increases in, wages, or even potential redundancy; or by consumers, through higher prices; or both. In other words, if the corporation is indeed an externalising machine, then it is difficult to see any rational response to large fines other than attempting to externalise these.

Fifth, the very use of fines is partly an effect of the fact that the overwhelming object of prosecution is the corporation and not its directors or other senior managers. In this approach, the criminal justice system acts upon, but at the same time continually reproduces, what is known as the 'corporate veil', an effect of corporate personhood and limited liability.

The combination in law of the principle of limited liability (limiting the liabilities of investors in a company to the sum invested) and the creation of the corporation as a legal subject (a legal person), recognised as having a single identity or 'personhood' that is separate and distinct from the human persons that make up the corporation (its owners, directors, managers, employees and so on), are the two key legal principles which constitute the corporate veil – and are the basis for the corporation as a structure of irresponsibility. The veil protects those who own, control and benefit from the corporate entity, as the corporate entity is the object of responsibility and accountability for 'its' actions or omissions. Note here a double-movement: the emergence in law of the corporate person was accompanied by a process of *depersonalising* the corporation, that is, setting it free from, independent of, and indeed structurally separate to, the actions and decisions of its senior managers, directors and shareholders.

The idea of the anthropomorphic corporation – the metaphorical person-writ-large which thinks, decides, acts, innovates, and so on – is one which holds considerable sway on the popular and legal consciousness. But it is clear that in reality the corporation is not, and can neither think nor act as a person, while legal personhood is historically and contemporaneously deployed in ways which generally allow corporate entities to evade legal accountability. But it is the separation of the various human elements of the corporation that is crucial in permitting what the company actually does – what it produces, the services it provides, its investment activities and so on – to become abstracted from the human actions that occur within the corporation itself.

Beyond Monetary Fines

I return to the issue of the corporate veil, and corporate personhood in particular, below. For now, it is worth noting that there are a range of other responses to corporate offending which have been proposed or attempted, if not in the UK and if not necessarily nor solely in the context of health and safety offences (see, for example, Braithwaite and Geis, 1982; Croall, 2005; Etzioni, 1993; Punch, 1996; Slapper and Tombs, 1999). That said, many of these responses have been considered in two recent UK consultations on sentencing corporate offenders – the Macrory Review (Macrory, 2006) which was held very much as part of the Hampton-Better Regulation initiative (Tombs, 2016) – and an HSE consultation in 2012. The latter, for example, sought views on restorative justice, conditional cautioning, enforceable undertakings, remedial orders, probation (for companies and directors) and adverse publicity orders.[6] Both remedial and publicity orders are available as sanctions under the CMCH Act.

Amongst these, arguments for corporate probation are particularly worth exploring. The starting point for this is that if rehabilitation has generally failed as a doctrine for the control of traditional crime, it can perhaps better succeed with corporate crime (Braithwaite and Geis, 1982). That is, many corporate crimes, but

---

[6] HSE, Alternative penalties for health and safety offences,
http://www.hse.gov.uk/consult/condocs/penalties.htm#alternative

one might argue health and safety crimes in particular, arise from defective control systems, insufficient checks and balances within the organisation, and poor communication systems (Braithwaite, 1985). These failings are sometimes deliberate, and made by the corporation to reduce costs, and sometimes the failings are inadvertent. Either way, it is possible for legal orders to force corporations to correct criminogenic policies and practices. Thus:

> Rehabilitation is a more workable strategy with corporate crime than with traditional crime because criminogenic organizational structures are more malleable than are criminogenic human personalities. A new internal compliance group can be put in place much more readily than a new superego. (Braithwaite and Geis, 1982: 310; see also Etzioni, 1993: 155)

Moore argues that this alternative strategy of 'rehabilitation' could be achieved by putting the offending corporation on supervised probation with the stipulation that it must implement stated reforms (Moore, 1987). Failure to comply could warrant other, more severe sanctions (such as incapacitation, below) to be applied. The object of internal reform, he concludes, is a preferable alternative to a deterrence strategy based on increased sanctions to control corporate wrongdoing through punitive means. This does not, however, address the potentially enormous resource requirements necessary to effectively monitor such reform for hundreds of corporate convicts – any forms of remedial orders or corporate probation currently in use require oversight, a point I return to in the following section.

Braithwaite and Geis (1982: 307) have argued for sentences which would limit the charter of a company by preventing it from continuing those aspects of its operations where it had seriously failed to respect the law. Following Braithwaite and Geis, Moore (1987:395-396) suggests a form of corporate incapacitation, whereby a corporation may be limited in the type of economic activity or regions in which it could legitimately operate. This is logically related to contract compliance, whereby the buyer of corporate goods and services imposes conditions upon the way in which those goods and services are delivered. Such contract compliance is used ubiquitously where central or local government – major customers of the private sector – are the purchaser, and there is absolutely no reason why these contractual terms cannot include those preventing health and safety harms. Failure to deliver on the conditions of such a contract means that the corporation is prevented from bidding for future tenders.

Relatedly, Braithwaite and Geis (1982: 307) argue for sentences which would limit the charter of a company by preventing it from continuing those aspects of its operations where it had seriously failed to respect the law. They also consider 'capital punishment for the corporation'. This would entail the imposition of a 'death penalty' which could be accomplished through absolute revocation of a corporation's charter, nationalisation, or being put into the hands of a receiver. Moreover, to preserve jobs as well as the goods and services provided by the firm, the assets of the offending company could be sold or otherwise transferred to a new parent company or companies with an established record of compliance with the law.

Disrupting the Corporation

The preceding section leads us to the view that in responding to corporate harm, a key aim must be to disrupt the corporation, both in terms of *how* and *where* it operates. Either approach entails challenging the power of the corporation to operate as freely as it would otherwise prefer. Thus, this principle of disruption opens up other possibilities for responding to, and preventing further, corporate crime and harm.

In this context, I can return to the issues of fines and, specifically, to Coffee's (1981) argument for a system of 'equity' fines against owners of corporations on conviction – a reform which, *inter alia*, is designed precisely to undermine the integrity of the corporate veil. This proposal for 'equity fines' entails offending companies being ordered by a court or regulatory authority to issue a set number of new shares in the firm. The shares would then be controlled by a state-controlled compensation fund. More radically, these could be handed over to a victims' or campaigning organisation, or a (relevant) trades union. This process, which effectively dilutes the value of shares held by the owners of the company, prevents the corporation from simply passing on the costs of a sanction to customers through price increases or to workers through job or wage cuts, since the funds for investment would not be depleted, merely reallocated from existing shareholders to the compensation fund. Such proposals were debated – though rejected – by the Scottish Parliament in 2010.[7]

There are further, logically related demands, to be pursued through other bodies of law, and these can be activated as a response to corporate crime and

---

[7] The Criminal Sentencing (Equity Fines) (Scotland) Bill (SB 10-54) was introduced and debated at the committee stages of the Scottish Parliament on the 1st June 2010.

harm. Numerous proposals exist for reform of company law, not least those which enable a diverse range of stakeholders to be increasingly empowered; these range from weak reforms to corporate governance, to rights of and protections for whistle-blowers (however limited and individualising such forms of challenge may be, they can have some minor progressive effects – see Pemberton et al, 2012), through to legally facilitating the strength of collective organisation and corporate oversight from within companies.

A key example here, crucial in the context of health and safety regulation in the UK, is that of legally protected rights inside companies. Thus, firms with legally-protected, effective trade union safety representatives and safety committees have half as many recorded injuries as those where these countervailing sources of power do not exist (James and Walters, 2002; Reilly et al, 2005; Walters et al, 2005). Legally-protected workers' rights at best place inspectorial oversight within workplaces, on a daily basis, by those who know the details of a job and workplace most intimately. Violations of law can be immediately responded to, as workers stop-the-job or impose Provisional Improvement Notices (PINs) on their managements, requiring improvements to plant or process by a certain date with the threat of work then being stopped. Roving safety representatives, moving across different workplaces, can play similar roles where workplaces are not organised. All of these rights exist in certain jurisdictions. It is important to emphasise the level of disruption at issue here: such workers' rights impinge upon capital's tendency towards maximising profitability, allowing organised workers to challenge management's expropriated rights to manage, and hence generate a surplus as freely as they wish.

It is no coincidence, then, that the central demand of 'The Hazards Campaign Charter'[8] is about extending safety representatives' rights, thus:

> Hazards Campaign demand: Full recognition and enforcement of existing safety reps' rights and the establishment of additional rights, including the right to be Roving Reps, serve Provisional Improvement Notices (PINS)[9], refuse dangerous work by stopping

[8] As noted above, the Hazards campaign is a UK-wide network of resource centres and campaigners established in 1987 to improve health and safety at work; its Campaign Charter sets out its key demands on Government.

[9] PINs have long been argued for by the Hazards and trades union movement. It was in Victoria, Australia, where safety reps were first given the legal power to impose a Provisional Improvement Notice. This is a notice whereby workers' representatives have the power to stop the job when there is an imminent danger. PINs thus represent a legal challenge to managements' 'rights' to manage and grant power to those who best know the

the job, and to fully participate in all aspects of health and safety in the workplace.[10]

In this context, Snider's (1991) analysis of the emergence and level of regulation is useful, and revolves around two central sets of claims. She argues, first, that regulation must be understood dialectically, via a dynamic complexity of 'specific mechanisms' which affect 'the balance of power between the regulated firm and the regulatory agency' (Snider, 1991: 210). Second, these relationships need to be set in the context of a similarly dynamic set of relations between the State and capital, and between the State 'and the broad electorate, as represented by relevant pressure groups' (ibid). Through this at once simple yet sensitive schema, Snider analyses four areas of regulation, including 'occupational health and safety laws'.

On occupational health and safety, she notes that crucial considerations are that: occupational health and safety is not viewed as necessary for capitalist survival; enforcement in this context may be antithetical to capitalist interests (in terms of a direct attack on profitability; see Szasz, 1984); states are most likely only to make symbolic efforts to regulate. But the key observation here is that pro-regulatory forces are potentially strong since they are most likely to originate in organised labour, making opposition to corporate freedoms here more viable and achievable in this context than many others, thus altering what Wright calls the balance of possibilities for transformation (Wright, 2010: 1-29). Moreover, there is political traction here, since the imagery of victimisation is powerful in this context. To this it might be added that the key problem for employers are injuries – since these are immediate, visible, perhaps attract wider public sympathy, and are easily associated with a specific employer and, perhaps, working conditions or practices. This is in contrast to ill-health, which often has such long incubation periods and causal chains that any company evades virtually all responsibility for these.

Quite differently, in the realm of criminal law, we can still identify reforms which have the potential to be transformative – that is, which maintain the potential for more radical reform, rather than ultimately bolstering the power of capital through a limited instrumentalism, a mere symbolism, or indeed both. Key contemporary examples of legal reforms which might radically undermine the legal protections which corporations currently enjoy are those

---

risks of any job.
[10] The Hazards Campaign Charter, at
http://www.hazardscampaign.org.uk/charter/newcharter.htm

which seek to pierce the corporate veil – that ideological and material, legal construction through which the corporate form exists as if independent of those who own and control it, guaranteeing a compartmentalisation of legal (and moral) liability. A key instance of this was the possibility, during the tortuous passage of the CMCH Act, that *positive* duties as regards health and safety might be placed upon directors; thus an early Home Office consultation document on the law proposed that, alongside a corporation being convicted for manslaughter, company directors should be able to be disqualified if it is found that their conduct has 'contributed' to the company committing the offence, while the Government also stated that it 'would welcome comments' on whether company directors should be able to be prosecuted for such conduct (Home Office, 2000). Ultimately, organised lobbying from employers organisations, and notably the Institute of Directors[11], saw the potential criminalisation of Directors removed from the law. Yet, this debate represented a sustained period in which there was a genuine possibility to pierce the corporate veil. Similar proposals continue to circulate in the context of legal liability for workplace killings that precisely establish a clear legal relationship between such deaths, the corporate form, and the senior officers and shareholders of that corporation. These are potentially radical, and are on various political agendas (Tombs and Whyte, 2015a: 173-5).

Thus, the key task must be to attack the legal basis upon which corporate power and irresponsibility is constituted – legal personhood, from which follow so many of the features of the corporate form. It is no coincidence, then, that ending legal personhood was one of the original demands of Occupy Wall Street.[12] Although those proposals are hardly likely to be adopted in any meaningful form, they are visible on mainstream political agendas and they are beginning to be visible in some academic work that has engaged politically with the possibility of reforming or abolishing limited liability protections (Plesch and Blankenburg, 2008; Blankenburg et al, 2010). The debate on the privileges afforded by the legal construction of corporations as 'persons' also reached the US Congress when Bernie Sanders, Senator for Vermont, introduced a Bill to abolish the recognition of corporate persons in the US constitution in December 2011.[13] The Bill sought to overturn a decision made

---

[11] The key UK body which represents individual directors, senior managers and 'entrepreneurs'.

[12] See DETAILED LIST OF DEMANDS and OVERVIEW OF TACTICS FOR DC PROTEST, at http://occupywallst.org/forum/detailed-list-of-demands-overview-of-tactics-for-d/

[13] A series of cases dating back to 1819 have asserted that corporate persons have the same rights as real persons. Those rights have been most famously asserted under the Fourteenth

by the US Supreme Court in January 2010. In this case, *Citizens United v. Federal Election Commission*, the Court ruled that corporations are persons, entitled by the U.S. Constitution to fund parties standing in elections. Although the Bill fell, similar Bills have been supported in several state legislatures.[14] The Bill also gave impetus to a wider movement based around the umbrella organisation 'Move to Amend' that has developed a popular basis for the campaign against corporate personhood.[15]

Beyond the Archetypal Capitalist Corporation

Such proposals and considerations, however radical they may appear, can only at the moment be an interim demand and tactic in the abolition of the corporate form *per se*. But this transformative goal is furthered through the kinds of intermediate demands indicated because each has the effect of disrupting, disturbing and undermining the legal bases upon which the corporation is structured.

Thus there are wider challenges to be faced than legal reform. We should be continually demanding that a range of services should be (re-)nationalised and taken out of the for-profit sector, as the latter demonstrates its inability to deliver these according to its own promise, and as the State consistently demonstrates its inabilities to hold consistent corporate failure to account. Thus we must also challenge corporate claims of efficiency, of freedom, of choice, of autonomy from (and superiority over) government, claims which are disproven for all of us on a daily basis, perhaps so obviously that we almost become anaesthetised to the supporting rhetorics of corporate power. At the same time, we must seek out, document and evaluate experiments in alternative forms of delivering goods and services – they have long existed and continue to exist all across the globe. There are a whole plethora of ways in which the production, distribution and sale of goods and services can be organised in ways which depart from archetypal capitalist models (Wright,

---

Amendment to the US Constitution which was introduced after the abolition of slavery to give all persons equal rights before the law. In a key judgement, the US Supreme Court in *Pembina Consolidated Silver Mining Co. v. Pennsylvania* (125 U.S. 181; 1888) decided: 'Under the designation of "person" there is no doubt that a private corporation is included [in the Fourteenth Amendment]. Those rights have been invoked by corporations to claim the right as "citizen" to participate in the funding of political parties and to use the courts to challenge state regulatory laws and rules'.

[14] Sourcewatch provides a guide to those states:
http://www.sourcewatch.org/index.php/Move_To_Amend
[15] See https://movetoamend.org/

2010: 191-269), including a variety of social and employee-owned enterprises, community-based public offerings and co-operatives. Each of these deserve our interest and evaluation, and might offer the basis for real, utopian inspiration.

The struggle for safer and healthier workplaces is, as has been intimated above, essentially a struggle over the level of exploitation – it impinges upon 'the most minute details of production', making safety and health at work 'antagonistic to the logic of firms within a capitalist economy' (Szasz, 1984: 114), so that 'safety' and 'profits' are, ultimately, contradictory (Nichols and Armstrong, 1973). In this context, worker self management – 'essentially the idea that those who produce value should control their workplaces, making decisions on what is produced, how it is produced, and how the organisation is structured' (Corporate Reform Collective, 2014: 155) – is of potential significance. The traditional model of worker self management is via the co-operative model, heralded by Marx as 'a major achievement of the working class' (cited in Wright, 2010: 235), not socialist *per se* but a key element of a strategy for building alternatives to capitalism and the dominant forms of organising production within it (ibid); as such, the co-operative form can be pre-figurative of a new form of economic organisation. By far the most celebrated example of such an organisational form is the Mondragon Co-operative. The Mondragon co-ops had their origins in the Basque country in 1956, eventually reaching their present form at the Mondragon Congress of Co-ops in 1991. By 2008, the end of the last decade, 120 Mondragon co-ops employed over 100,000 people across industrial, financial, consumer goods, agricultural, educational, research and welfare services. By this time, there were 69 production plants across many countries. Representation in all Co-ops includes a health and safety Committee (Hitchman, 2008).

The Mondragon principles are ten-fold, and include the following:

- Democratic Organisation. A basic equality of worker-members in a democratically organised company based on the sovereignty of the General Assembly, electing governing bodies and collaborating with managerial bodies.
- Sovereignty of Labour. A recognition that labour is the main factor for transforming nature, society and human beings themselves, with full sovereignty so that wealth created is distributed in terms of the labour provided.

- The instrumental and subordinate nature of capital. Capital is an instrument subordinate to labour, necessary for business development.

- Participatory management. The steady development of self-management and, consequently, of member participation in company management which, in turn, requires the development of adequate mechanisms for participation, transparent information, consultation and negotiation and training.

- Social Transformation. A process that helps towards all peoples' economic and social reconstruction and the construction of a freer, fairer and more caring Basque society.

- Universality.   Solidarity with all those who work for economic democracy and share the objectives of Peace, Justice and Development which are inherent to the International Co-operative Movement.
  (http://www.mondragon-corporation.com/eng/co-operative-experience/our-principles/)

For Schnall and Wigger (2013), what is 'most profound' about these are their

> focus on the sustainable relationship of mutual benefit between worker and company. In contrast to most capitalist companies, whereby the measure of a successful company is almost always based on maximum profitability, the cooperative model offers an alternative approach that supports democracy in the workplace through an egalitarian voting system, while at the same time promoting job security for worker-members, social justice and community responsibility.

Thus, it is claimed, both its structure and values allow Mondragon to 'vouchsafe' the health and safety of its workers (Schnall and Wigger, 2013).

Such initiatives are not without their critics. Kasmir (1996), for example, has argued that most social scientists who have commented upon the Mondragon cooperatives have idealised them as a form of alternative capitalist organisation, claiming that these do not resolve but merely transform and/or displace worker-management conflicts. The idea that Mondragon is a superior form of organisation is, for her, a myth. More specifically, others have argued that any business enterprises with high levels of worker control are not necessarily *safer* places to work: in employee-owned firms in the wood-processing sector, for example, Grunberg et al (1996), conclude that such forms might actually 'be hazardous for worker morale and worker safety' due to the 'precarious economic conditions these employee-owned firms find themselves in'. Others have responded to this claim by warning that we should be careful about equating employee ownership with high levels of worker participation (Kardas, 1997) – it is the latter which is likely to protect against business harms, not the former. As one Mondragon employee noted, then, the co-operative business has 'all sorts of problems': 'We are not some paradise, but rather a family of co-operative enterprises struggling to build a different kind of life around a different way of working.' (cited in Wolff, 2012)

Mondragon is not, of course, the only model of a co-operative organisational form. One recent commentary noted that, 'In England in 2010 there were 4,784 co-ops with a turnover of £29.7billion' (Corporate Reform Collective, 2014: 157). The International Co-operative Alliance claims that co-ops employ 250 million people worldwide, generating 2.2 trillion USD in turnover (http://ica.coop/en/facts-and-figures). Equally obvious is the fact that existing co-ops will range from the more to less efficient and indeed from the more to less exploitative and harmful. The point is, however, that alternatives to traditional business models are a-plenty and ubiquitous, so that there are 'many different institutional designs that in one way or another embody the idea that producers should 'own' their means of production' (Wright, 2010: 237).

Conclusion: Thinking beyond the corporation

This article has highlighted a heterogeneous set of considerations, from the reformist to the utopian. But there is no necessary contradiction here: the idea that there is a mutual exclusivity between 'reform' and 'revolution' or 'practical' and 'utopian' is not the concrete experience of many counter-hegemonic organisations. And there is a lesson here for academics, since neither utopianism nor radical imagination can emanate from an atomised realm of 'mere' thought. As Haiven has put it,

> imagination is not a thing that we, as individuals, 'have'. It's a shared landscape or a commons of possibility that we share as communities. The imagination doesn't exist purely in the individual mind; it also exists between people as a result of their attempts to work out how to live and work together. The imagination can, therefore, be extremely dangerous... The radical

imagination is a matter of acting otherwise, together. (Haiven, 2014: 218)

The first thing we have to do is reject the idea that being idealistic can never be pragmatic or useful in winning concessions or influencing policy. Second, and following this, a reformist discourse and agenda can, under some circumstances, bolster more radical movements for fundamental social change. Third, it is possible to remain outside the ideological terrain of the State and at the same time to engage on the terrain of the policy world or with the current political system. In fact, there are a number of counter-hegemonic groups that stand firmly and unapologetically in opposition to the State's regulatory agenda but still remain engaged with government in consultations, lobbying and policy work. Those groups, which in the context of UK health and safety campaigns include the Hazards Campaign and its network of Hazards centres, Families Against Corporate Killers, the Blacklist Support Group, the Construction Safety Campaign, and Asbestos Victims Support Groups, have shown us that idealism does not necessarily constrain the effectiveness or political impact of counter-hegemonic struggle. Therefore, the question remains: how best we might develop a pragmatic idealism that revolves around making connections between, and interventions across, state, economy, politics, history and 'culture', and which stands in direct opposition to 'principled pluralism' with its 'tendencies towards fragmentary problems and scattered causation' (Mills, 1970: 104).

I need to emphasise that avoiding these tendencies is dependent upon us retaining an element of utopianism – our demands and our actions must be achievable yet at the same time unashamedly utopian (Wright, 2010). And, following Jacoby, we would argue that these should be utopian in an 'iconoclastic' rather than 'blueprint' sense (Jacoby, 2005). Further, not least if we are to avoid political immobilisation likely to be induced by a perceived need to set out a blueprint which lays down an image of a future utopia in detail, we should, as one commentator has recently put it, 'learn to think about capitalism coming to an end without assuming responsibility for answering the question of what one proposes to put in its place' (Streeck, 2014: 46). This radical imagination means abandoning the acceptance that things cannot change much, an acceptance which ever-narrows hope and possibility:

The current conjuncture's dominant liberal culture has redefined idealism and pragmatism to realign the usual opposition between them. Now, those who adopt the 'pragmatic' position of slightly modifying the existing system's socioeconomic framework are redefined as the idealists. Conversely, in this current period of economic crisis and rapidly approaching environmental change to believe that the current order can continue indefinitely should be defined as idealistic – even insanely so – but, instead, it is defined as pragmatic as we seek individual solutions tailored to the systems 'problems' as they crop up. To adopt such a position means turning away from a reality judged too traumatic to be faced head-on, and falling victim to the belief that any attempt to change it will only succeed in making things worse. (Winlow and Hall, 2013: 167)

Thinking about what dealing with the harmful corporation might actually mean, and how it can be achieved, requires a utopianism 'essential to any effort to escape the spell of the quotidian. That effort is the *sine qua non* of any serious thinking about the future – the prerequisite of any thinking' (Jacoby, 2005: Preface). Utopian thinking is not the opposite of seeking reform. And, indeed, a real utopianism, one which identifies alternative forms of institutions and practices which are at once desirable, viable and achievable, not least by their very existence, is a key illustration of how reforms can both co-exist with and be sustained by utopian thinking. Indeed, reforms without a utopian spirit are likely to lapse into reform*ism*, not just with relatively few positive effects, but indeed are likely to be counter-productive, bolstering the corporation as it seems to have been somewhat tamed. If we cannot even imagine a world without corporations, then we will never inhabit a world without them – and the devastation that the corporate form wreaks on human life, with state, legal and regulatory acquiescence will remain but a fact of life.

References

Almond, P. (2009) 'The Dangers of Hanging Baskets: "Regulatory myths" and media representations of health and safety regulation' in *Journal of Law and Society* Volume 36, No. 3 pp 352–75

Bakan, J (2004) *The Corporation: The pathological pursuit of profit and power*, Toronto: Viking Canada

Bell, E. (2011) *Criminal Justice and Neoliberalism* Basingstoke: Palgrave

Blankenburg, S, Plesch D and Wilkinson, F (2010) 'Limited Liability and the Modern Corporation in Theory and in Practice' in *Cambridge Journal of Economics* Volume 34 pp 821–836

Braithwaite, J. (1985) *To Punish or Persuade: Enforcement of coal-mine safety* Albany: State University of New York Press.

Braithwaite, J. and Geis, G. (1982) 'On Theory and Action for Corporate Crime Control' *Crime and Delinquency* Volume 28, No. 2 pp 292-314

Clarke, M. (2000) *Regulation: The social control of business between law and politics* London: Macmillan.

Coffee, J. (1981) '"No Soul to Damn, no Body to Kick": An unscandalised essay on the problem of corporate punishment' in *Michigan Law Review* Volume 79, No 3 pp. 386-459

Corporate Reform Collective (2014) *Fighting Corporate Abuse: Beyond predatory capitalism* London: Pluto

Croall, H. (2005) *Penalties for Corporate Homicide*, Paper prepared for the Scottish Executive Expert Group on Corporate Homicide August 17, http://www.scotland.gov.uk/Publications/2005/11/14133559/36003 (consulted 13 May 2016)

Dowie, M., (1987) 'Pinto Madness' in Hills, S. (ed) *Corporate Violence: Injury and death for profit* New Jersey: Rowman and Littlefield

Etzioni, A. (1993) 'The US Sentencing Commission on Corporate Crime: A critique', in Geis, G. and Jesliow, P. (eds) *The Annals of the American Academy of Political and Social Science: White-Collar Crime* Volume 525 pp 147-156

Garland, D. (2001) *The Culture of Control: Crime and social order in contemporary society* Oxford: Oxford University Press

Grunberg, L., Moore, S. and Greenberg, EW. (1996) 'The Relationship of Employee Ownership and Participation to Workplace Safety' in *Economic and Industrial Democracy* Volume 17, No. 2 pp 221-241

Haiven, M. (2014) *Crises of Imagination, Crises of Power: Capitalism, creativity and the commons* London: Zed Books

Hämäläinen, P., Saarela, K. and Takala, J. (2009) 'Global Trend According to Estimated Number of Occupational Accidents and Fatal Work-Related Diseases at Region and Country Level' in *Journal of Safety Research* Volume 40 pp 125–39

Health and Safety Executive (2015a) *Health and Safety Statistics, Annual Report for Great Britain 2014-15* London: Health and Safety Executive

Health and Safety Executive (2015b) *Costs of Workplace Fatalities and Self-Reported Injuries and Ill Health, 2013/14,* http://www.hse.gov.uk/statistics/pdf/cost-to-britain.pdf (consulted 13 May 2016)

Hitchman, J. (2008) *Mondragon Cooperative Corporation. A critical analysis of the strengths, weaknesses and potentialities of the model,* http://base.d-p-h.info/es/fiches/dph/fiche-dph-7693.html (consulted 13 May 2016)

Home Office (2000) *Reforming the Law on Involuntary Manslaughter: the government's proposals* London: Home Office Communication Directorate

Jacoby, R. (2005) *Picture Imperfect: Utopian Thought for an Anti-Utopian Age* New York: Columbia University Press

James, P. and Walters, D. (2002) 'Worker Representation in Health and Safety: Pptions for regulatory reform' in *Industrial Relations Journal* Volume 33, No. 2 pp 141-156

Kardas, P. (1997) 'Employee Ownership, Participation and Workplace Safety: A Response to Grunberg, Moore and Greenberg' in *Economic and Industrial Democracy* Volume 18 pp 621-633

Kasmir, S. (1996) *The Myth of Mondragon: Cooperatives, politics, and working class life in a Basque town* Albany: SUNY Press

Macrory, R. (2006) *Regulatory Justice: Making sanctions effective. Final Report* London: Better Regulation Executive

Mills, C.W. (1970) *The Sociological Imagination* Harmondsworth: Penguin

Moore, C.A. (1987) 'Taming the Giant Corporation? Some cautionary remarks on the deterrability of corporate crime' in *Crime and Delinquency* Volume 33, No 2 pp 379-402

Nichols, T. and Armstrong, P. (1973) *Safety or Profit: Industrial accidents and the conventional wisdom* Bristol: Falling Wall Press

Pearce, F., and Tombs, S. (1998) *Toxic Capitalism: Corporate crime and the chemical industry* Aldershot: Ashgate

Pemberton, S. and Tombs, S., with Chan, M. and Seal, L. (2012) 'Whistleblowing, Organisational Harm and the Self-Regulating Organisation' in *Policy and Politics* Volume 40, No. 2 pp 263-279

Plesch, D. and Blankenburg, S. (2008) *How to Make Corporations Accountable* Liverpool: Institute of Employment Rights

Pratt, J., Brown, D., Brown, M., Hallsworth, S., Morrison, W. (eds) (2005) *The New Punitiveness: Trends, theories and perpectives* Cullompton: Willan

Punch, M. (1996) *Dirty Business: Explaining corporate ùisconduct* London: Sage

Reilly, B., Pace, P. and Hall, P. (1995) 'Unions, Safety Committees and Workplace Injuries' in *British Journal of Industrial Relations* Volume 33, No. 2 pp 273-88

Salmon, J. (2015) 'Britain's big four banks rack up £50bn in fines since the financial crisis with HSBC set to pay £500m in US for rigging foreign exchange markets' in *This is Money* 3 August, http://www.thisismoney.co.uk/money/news/article-3184282/Britain-s-big-four-banks-rack-50bn-fines-financial-crisis-HSBC-set-pay-500m-rigging-foreign-exchange-markets.html#ixzz3xyodsWI1 (consulted 13 May 2016)

Schnall, P. and Wigger, E. (2012) *The Mondragon Corporation: structure/model*, 17 December, http://unhealthyworkblog.blogspot.co.uk/2012/12/the-mondragon-corporation-alternative.html (consulted 13 May 2016)

Schnall, P. and Wigger, E. (2013) *The Mondragon Corporation: criticisms*, 22 January, http://unhealthyworkblog.blogspot.co.uk/2013/01/the-mondragon-corporation-criticisms.html (consulted 13 May 2016)

Sentencing Council (2015) *Health and Safety Offences, Corporate Manslaughter and Food Safety and Hygiene Offences. Definitive Guideline* London: Sentencing Council

Slapper, G. and Tombs, S. (1999) *Corporate Crime* London: Longman

Snider, L. (1991) 'The Regulatory Dance: Understanding reform processes in corporate crime' in *International Journal of the Sociology of Law* Volume 19 pp 206-36

Snider, L. (1993) *Bad Business: Corporate Crime in Canada* Toronto: Nelson

Stabe, M. and Stanley, A. (2015) 'Bank Fines: Get the data', *Financial Times*, 22 July, http://blogs.ft.com/ftdata/2015/07/22/bank-fines-data/ (consulted 13 May 2016)

Streeck, W. (2014) 'How Will Capitalism End?' in *New Left Review* Volume 87 pp 35-64

Szasz, A. (1984) 'Industrial Resistance to Occupational Safety and Health Legislation, 1971-1981' in *Social Problems* Volume 32, No. 2 pp 103-116

Tombs, S. (2016) *Social Protection After the Crisis: Regulation without enforcement?* Bristol: Policy Press.

Tombs, S. (2015) 'Crisis, What Crisis? Regulation and the academic orthodoxy' in *Special Issue of The Howard Journal of Criminal Justice* Volume 54, No. 1 pp 57-72

Tombs, S. (2014) 'Hard Evidence: Are work-related deaths in decline?', *The Conversation*, 29 October, https://theconversation.com/hard-evidence-are-work-related-deaths-in-decline-33553 (consulted 13 May 2016)

Tombs, S. and Whyte, D. (2015a) *The Corporate Criminal: Why corporations must be abolished* Abingdon: Routledge

Tombs, S. and Whyte, D. (2015b) *Corporate Crime and Ruling Class Impunity in the UK: Social divisions, surveillance and the security state*, Paper presented to 43rd Annual Conference of the European Group for the Study of Deviance and Social Control, 26th-29th August, Tallinn.

Walters, D., Nichols, T., Conner, J., Tasiran, A. and Cam, S. (2005) *The Role and Effectiveness of Safety Representatives in Influencing Workplace Health and Safety. HSE Research Report 363* London: HSE Books

Winlow, S. and Hall, S. (2013) *Rethinking Social Exclusion: The end of the social?* London: Sage

Wolff, R. (2012) 'Yes, there is an alternative to capitalism: Mondragon shows the way', *The Guardian*, 24 June, http://www.theguardian.com/commentisfree/2012/jun/24/alternative-capitalism-mondragon (consulted 13 May 2016)

Wright, E.O. (2010) *Envisioning Real Utopias* London: Verso

Utopia in the Midst of Dystopia? The Peace Community of San José de Apartadó, Colombia

Thomas MacManus and Tony Ward[1]

Abstract

The Peace Community of San José de Apartadó is a self-governing community of peasant farmers ('campesinos') in Urabá, one of the regions of Colombia where violence by the State, leftist guerrillas and right-wing paramilitaries has been most intense. It is based on a rejection of all violence and on autonomy from, and neutrality between, the State, paramilitaries and guerrillas. Drawing on interviews with community members by the first author, this paper considers how far the Peace Community has succeeded in establishing a radical alternative to the State legal and penal systems in pursuit of what could be called a 'real utopia' (Wright 2010).[2]

Introduction

Colombia is a society associated more with 'magical realism' than with 'real utopias', and the war-torn region of Urabá seems a singularly unpromising setting for a utopian project. We argue, however, that significant elements of a 'real utopia' can be found in the *Comunidad de Paz de San José de Apartadó* (the 'Peace Community'), a grouping of rural settlements that refuses to take sides in the armed conflict that has raged in the country for over half a century. With no end to the violence in sight, the Peace Community decided to

---

[1] Thomas MacManus is a Leverhulme Early Career Fellow at the International State Crime Initiative and is based at Queen Mary University of London's School of Law. His current research focusses on the public relations industry and state crime denial. Thomas is Associate Editor of *State Crime* journal and Joint Editor of *Amicus Journal*. Tony Ward is a Director of the International State Crime Initiative and is based at the University of Northumbria in Newcastle. He is co-author with Penny Green of *State Crime: Governments, Violence and Corruption* (Pluto, 2004) and with Gerry Johnstone of *Law and Crime* (Sage, 2010).
[2] We thank David Rodriguez Goyes for his comments on a draft of this article.

run its affairs independently of a repressive state and its brutal paramilitary allies, and of the violent opposing guerrillas. In taking the Peace Community as an example of a 'real utopia', we do not mean to suggest that it is by any means an ideal society, but rather that its creation of a peaceful, self-governing enclave in the midst of armed conflict is both a successful pragmatic strategy for survival and one that is guided by a utopian vision. If by a 'real utopia' we understand not a perfect realisation of an ideal society, but rather a vision of the ideal that provides real guidance under very imperfect circumstances (Wright 2010), then the Peace Community has a fair claim to embody a utopian vision.

This article does not attempt to provide a complete analysis of this unique social experiment. Our research on the Peace Community was part of a larger project on the resistance of civil society in Colombia and five other countries to the crimes of the State and of paramilitary organisations, so we were interested primarily in that aspect of the community's work and only incidentally in its social organisation, its economy, and what we would characterise as its autonomous, informal legal system (see also MacManus and Ward 2015; Ward and Green 2015). Our interviews with members and supporters of the Peace Community do, however, provide the basis for the following brief account of its history and of its informal legal system.

Colombian society is marked by over 100 years of multiple conflicts. The Colombian state has rarely exercised an effective monopoly of the organised use of force within its territory since colonial times (Palacios 2006), but peasant farmers have not been able to evade state interference to the extent that James C. Scott (2009) celebrates in his study of Southeast Asian uplands.

La Violencia, the complex and brutal civil conflict of the late 1940s and early 1950s, began a period of internal warfare that has lasted almost continuously until the present time, with portions of Colombian territory being controlled by guerrilla forces opposed to the State. In much of its territory, the State has never been an effective arbiter of land ownership disputes (Richani 2013), which further contributes to disorder. Nor has the Colombian state been able to maintain a criminal justice, social control presence. Expanding the reach of its challenged monopoly, the delivery of organised violence has been partially delegated to state-validated paramilitary forces, sometimes referred to as the *paraestado,* or para-state. The *paraestado* metes out its own vicious form of justice in the areas that the paramilitaries control, or seek to control. Consultoría para los Derechos Humanos y el Desplazamiento (CODHES) (2011) estimates that over 5,200,000 people were forcibly displaced in Colombia between 1985 and 2011. Paramilitary groups are the 'primary force responsible for displacement' (García-Godos and Lid 2010: 491), which usually takes place in areas with fertile land or valuable natural resources (Hristov 2009: 76).

In response to the constant violence, communities have developed resistance in the form of a separation, or 'rupture', from all armed actors – including the State and its agents – which is inspired by, yet goes beyond, forms of neutrality recognised by international humanitarian law (Romero Ramirez 2013). The community has adopted and adapted familiar concepts of international law in extraordinary ways and has earned recognition of the Inter-American Court of Human Rights via protection orders[3].

This paper charts the rise of the Peace Community and its principal tormentors – the State and its paramilitary agents – and discusses the emergence of a radical alternative to the State's legal apparatus.

Origins of the Peace Community

'They cut him up like a pig', the elderly man announced as the first author stood beside him in San Josésito (a small plot of land down the road from San José, from where the community have been displaced). He pointed to a picture of Santiago Tuberquia Muñoz, who was about 18 months old when he was killed by a joint military-paramilitary operation on Monday, 21st February 2005. The aftermath of this 'Operation Phoenix' compounded years of violence perpetrated against these *campesinos* and led to the establishment of the Peace Community:

> In 1997, we began suffering violence … we saw massacres, we saw a lot of torture, we saw kids being chopped up, we saw the rape of our women, we saw indiscriminate bombings, and this all was carried out against *campesinos*. After seeing all these consequences of violence, we came to San José. The town was all alone … there are only two old people living there. So the farmers occupied the houses, we were 370 families, and that's when the first massacre occurred … the 17th Brigade committed the first massacre with the paramilitaries, three people were killed.

---

[3] See The Order of the President of the Inter-American Court of Human Rights of 9th October 2000; and see also the Orders of the Inter-American Court of November 24, 2000; June 18, 2002; November 17, 2004; March 15, 2005 and February 2, 2006, which have repeatedly called upon the Colombian state to maintain the measures.

People were extremely fearful and lots of people left. They went to Medellin, or they went I don't know where. And then there was another massacre [2005]. Five [in fact, eight, five men and three children] people were killed by the 17th Brigade and the paramilitaries, and even more people fled. That's when we, the people who decided to stay, met, and we started organising. Of course we were afraid, but I dunno, it's pride, we are going to resist. They are not going to take away our lands. So you can kill us but we're going to stay here … we decided to sign an agreement that says we wouldn't participate with any of the armed actors, neither directly, nor indirectly. To be able to be outside of the conflict, and that's how the Peace Community was created. (Interview, Sebastián)[4]

Separating from the parties to the conflict necessarily disconnects the community from the apparatuses of the State. But in a region of developmental neglect in a country where a state government struggles to maintain order, government services are not missed as much as one would expect. As to whether they were interested in receiving health, education, and other services that are normally provided by the State, a member remarked: 'it doesn't really matter, because they've never fulfilled them anyway' (Interview, Enrique).

A refusal to cooperate with any of the competing systems of violence constitutes a challenge to sovereignty over the area. The community has suffered enormously at the hands of armed actors, and it reports that over 200 members have been murdered (interview, Sofia). In February 2005, eight people 'were killed by the paramilitaries and the army', including a 6-year-old girl and an 18-month-old boy (Interview, Agustín). In 2008, the Attorney General's Office investigated 69 soldiers for the killing. An army captain was arrested for his role in the massacre (Amnesty International 2008), and in 2010 he was sentenced to 20 years' imprisonment (González Arango 2010). However, the Peace Community is still under threat from the military-paramilitary complex[5]. On 21 July 2014, a government soldier reportedly stated that 'the time has arrived for that son-of-a-bitch Peace Community, we

---

[4] The names of Peace Community members are fictitious. All quotations cited by first name only are from interviews with Peace Community members conducted by Thomas MacManus in November 2013, translated into English by a local (anonymous) interpreter.
[5] Collusion between paramilitaries and state security forces is a well-documented feature of the Colombian situation (see, for example, Hristov 2009).

are coordinating with the paramilitaries for the extermination of that son-of-a-bitch Peace Community' (Amnesty International 2014: 1).

The community leaders feel that the paramilitaries have filled a vacuum left by the State in their territory: 'there's a [paramilitary] control of the social, economic and political contexts here in the region' (interview, Enrique). In the absence of the State, the Peace Community has taken on the day-to-day running of their community based on newly conceptualised fundamental principles:

> The principles that the peace community at San Jose Apartadó have are of great importance. These principles were created in 1997 and we saw that if we were with the army, or the paramilitaries or the guerrillas, that the others would kill us. If we were with the army, the guerrillas would come in, if we were with the guerrillas, the paramilitaries or the army would come in. (Interview, Enrique)

The principal 'law' of the Community is contained in two instruments adopted in 1997, the *Declaratoria* and the *Reglamento Interno*[6]. The *Reglamento* (Regulations or Code of Conduct) sets out (in numbered Articles and Paragraphs) some of the basic rules in force today, including a ban on alcohol, and the disciplinary process which interviewees described: a first breach of the rules results in a hearing 'to resolve the problem', a repetition of the offence leads to a second hearing and a final warning, and a third to expulsion from the community. The idea of expulsion echoes the principles of formal legal processes and may limit claims to a genuine utopian alternative. Furthermore, there are serious questions surrounding the efficacy of 'due process' in proceedings which result in such expulsions. Going beyond merely internal matters, the *Reglamento* also demands respect for the rights of the Community from the State and other armed groups. The Internal Council of the community has the duty to 'regulate [*regular*], represent [*representar*] and demand [*exigir*] the rights of the Peace Community before the competent authorities or before any armed actors' (*Art.* 9d) and to 'monitor respect for the Declaration of the Peace Community on the part of armed actors; in the case of a violation, a public denunciation shall be issued at national and international level' (Art. 9g); and the whole community is to respond to a violation of the rights of any of its members by any of the armed actors (Art. 10).

---

[6] Available on the Community's website: cdpsanjose.org

Commandeering international legal norms

Recognising that the persistence of the Colombian conflict is fuelled by issues surrounding land, and to discourage interference from the State, the Peace Community created a self-styled neutral zone which, Fr Alberto Franco (of the Comisión Intereclesial de Justicia y Paz, an NGO that supports the various peace communities and similar initiatives) argues, is 'a small place that is identified, and has signs to label it, using the international humanitarian law principle of distinction of civilians in war'.

While their neutral status does not enjoy formal legal protection, a kind of recognition is extended to them in practice. Members and supporters of the Peace Community interpret a series of decisions by the Inter-American Court of Human Rights as recognising the humanitarian zones as an expression of international humanitarian law (Interview, Fr Alberto Franco, November 22, 2013). In fact, these orders do not accord the Peace Community as a body any formal recognition, but require the State to protect 'a plurality of persons' who are identified by their membership of the Community (IACHR 2002, para. 8). The community is nevertheless able to use these judgments as a source of legitimacy, and has won a degree of informal acceptance of its autonomy from the Colombian state. Even under the presidency of Álvaro Uribe Velez (2002-10), who was openly hostile to the peace communities, Mason observed:

> Although the government is emphatic that it never formally agreed to the rules of the Peace Communities, informal practices by public officials in fact constitute de facto approval of their autonomy and independent authority. (Mason 2010: 21)

For example, local officials would ask for permission to enter community land. Other peace communities have received some formal recognition under Law 70 of 1993, which provides for collective ownership of land by Afro-Colombian communities; this in turn has been used by the Inter-American Commission of Human Rights to persuade the Inter-American Court to make protection orders in their favour (IACHR 2003).

Communities across Colombia have emulated the peace community model (e.g. in Curvaradó) or have adapted alternative versions to suit their own distinct circumstances. CAVIDA (Comunidad de Auto-determinación, Vida y Dignidad) established a 'humanitarian zone' in 2001, making creative use of international humanitarian law—it is based on the principle of distinction between combatants and civilians, a key theoretical tenet of international humanitarian law, which aims to protect civilians in conflict zones from becoming casualties of war. The idea is to demarcate a space designated solely for the civilian population—similar to the Red Cross sign on a hospital. (Burnyeat 2013: 439)

A similar model is adopted by the 'zones of refuge' of the Naga river communities:

... a place inside the community that has signs and is identified as a place where they can all go in a time of conflict ... and it will be respected and that helps avoid possible displacement. And it also helps them make visible their commitment to being civil society in the middle of a conflict. (Interview, Fr Alberto Franco, November 22, 2013)

Some indigenous communities have adopted similar versions that are sensitive to their own cosmovision, called 'humanitarian reserves' or 'areas of autonomous coming together'. Other communities had developed 'areas of biodiversity' to protect land: '... So even though they don't have formal legal protection, there's a kind of recognition that happens in practice ...' (Interview, Fr Alberto Franco, November 22, 2013).

The Peace Community's project is more radical than that of these various zones because of its 'rupture' with the State:

This 'rupture' is part of a profound, grassroots, all-or-nothing ethical stance, for the Peace Community is not just about civilian protection in the midst of a war zone. It has become the expression of an alternative life project, a refusal to participate in the capitalist system which contributes to the violence in Colombia. (Burnyeat 2013: 442)

There is, then, a distinctly utopian element in the Peace Community's project:

So this is why our community has been formed, we believe that where death has occurred, life should flourish, we believe that amongst all the assassinations, the killings that have occurred, all the blood that has been spilled, that we should come together, we should construct a community that supports life. That we can flourish amongst all of the violence that has occurred and we can be an example for the entire world, of how life should move forward, in the face of all of the violence. (Interview, Agustín)

Although this ethical stance is not directly inspired by international humanitarian law in the way the more modest goals of CAVIDA appear to be, it has made equally creative use of international law as a source of legitimacy and protection.

International solidarity and 'accompaniment'

To help maintain their bold experiment, the Peace Community enjoys 'accompaniment' from international organisations – for example, Peace Brigades International (PBI), Fellowship of Reconciliation (FOR), and Palomas de Paz (or Operazione Colomba) – whose physical presence in the villages significantly increases the political cost of any attack. The community also has sister cities around the world, including Maddison, Wisconsin (USA), three cities in Spain, and one each in Portugal, Italy, Luxembourg and Belgium:

Both national and international level sister cities have had huge advantages for us. They've allowed us to really sustain ourselves as a community and they've given us support that we're not alone, and we think without these sister cities it would have been much easier for the government, together with the paramilitaries, to wipe us out, to destroy us. (Interview, Enrique)

... that's what solidarity is all about, it's joining together to defend people's rights. We don't feel alone ... we have an accompaniment to fight for our territory. The paramilitaries, the government, when there's problems there, everyone goes to support the member of the community that's been affected, and so if something happens we all go and we can be there for that person. We also have international accompaniment, and so when things get really hard, when there is a hard public order situation in the region, we have that confidence that we are going to be supported and we are not by ourselves, that we have that solidarity. And the people who aren't part of the community, when something happens they tend to just get out of town. (Interview, Daniel)

The government of the Netherlands donated the money to buy the land that San Josésito, the hub settlement, stands on (Interview, Isabella); the private ownership of the property provides further legal protection from State intervention.

As a result of this non-violent 'preservation' of international laws, the formal state has been all but excluded from their affairs and the Peace Community have to manage traditional, 'street crime' internally.

Internal law, state law and autonomy

When asked about the presence of crime within the community, a resident replied:

> Internally we are extremely autonomous, we have our own laws and we have our own internal structure, so if someone from the community commits a mistake regarding our process, we look at how to deal with that, but crimes? Crimes, no. Maybe differences regarding land lines or something like that, but crimes, like abuse or accidents… no, I don't think so. I guess maybe at the beginning, when the community was just formed, when there was still the consumption of alcohol, but we have the principle that says that we don't consume alcohol within the community; that helps. No, I don't think so. I think in this aspect we're doing fairly well, the people are pretty conscientious, aware, a farmer population and we're able to look more at the impacts of the conflicts, of the conflicts in our region. And crimes? No, I don't think so. (Interview, Enrique)

Another member was somewhat less sanguine:

> No, it's not always easy, there are some people who follow the rules and there are some people who don't. The youth want to go out and have a little party, or go and have something to drink and have alcohol and… it's not easy, and in the community we try to teach them that these are the rules and whatnot, but that doesn't mean that there aren't people who might go to San Jose for the afternoon and have some alcohol. (Interview, Sofia)

Drinking alcohol might be thought of as wrong but not as a 'crime'. It may be that Enrique's reply meant simply that nothing came to his mind that he would call a 'crime', even if some incidents – like one that was mentioned in conversation of a woman beating her child with a hose – would be crimes according to the Penal Code. Crime, as Louk Hulsman (1986) famously argued, has no 'ontological reality' – but a beating does have ontological reality, and whether the Community had an effective way of responding to such incidents, we do not know.

What is the origin of the Community's principles? Where do they come from? What happens if they are breached? It may seem that we have already answered these questions: the principles come from the Declaration and Internal Code of Conduct of 1997. In terms of positivist legal theory the Community's acceptance of the validity of these documents as sources of binding norms could be called the *Grundnorm* of its autonomous legal order (Kelsen 1949). However, the documents so prominently displayed (for outside consumption) on the Community's website were mentioned only twice in interviews with community members. The only interviewee who gave them more than a passing mention, Ximena, began by using an organic metaphor to describe the role of the principles in community life:

> The principles, to us, can be related to the roots of the tree. It's allowed us to create ideals for our struggle and the principles are the roots that allow us to survive amidst the conflict and so many problems that we see. We've seen pressures from all parts of society, but the roots of our principles are to maintain our activities and to move forward as a community.

Only in response to further probing did she mention a written document:

> *Thomas*: But where do the actual principles come from?
> *Ximena:* Where did they come from? They didn't come from the president, or the armed actors, or government institutions, they came from us [....] One by one we developed these different principles through a series of meetings and assemblies and then everyone agreed to them. Everyone sat down and signed the agreement, we've all signed that we're in agreement that these ideas came from us.

Boaventura de Sousa Santos, a leading scholar of unofficial legal systems, points out 'the meaning that Western culture attributes to *writing* as a ceremony and to the *written product* as expression of commitment' (Santos 2002: 107). The act of signature (stipulated by Article 1 of the *Reglamento*) exemplifies this use of ceremonial writing. The danger of such written acts of commitment, Santos writes, is that the signed document becomes an 'impersonal fetish' alienated from the individual who signed it. In community members' rhetoric, however, the emphasis is not on written or spoken commitment to the rules but on the importance of the principles to the survival and daily life of the community. As another member expressed it:

> These are the fundamental rules of our community, they help to keep us together, they help to hold us together as a community, many communities have been created on a national level, but without the principles that held us together. And they've been broken down or torn apart by the guerrillas, or by the paramilitaries, or by the government. (Interview, Enrique)

Nicolás explained that the ban on alcohol was introduced a few months after the Community was founded, after one member killed another in a drunken fight at a party.

> *Nicolás*: So this has been an issue for us from the beginning and it continues to be an issue, that there's no alcohol in the community, that there are people like ___, who from time to time drink and so we need to figure out how to deal with that. If there's some sort of sanction, or if it's something that's ongoing, if it's a repeated case, then the assembly needs to decide in the face of this grave situation how we're going to react as a community.
> *Thomas*: What kind of sanctions can you apply?
> *Nicolás*: It's mostly work. A day's work, two days' work, of doing hopefully community work, something that benefits the community. Something pretty simple.

For more serious cases, the disciplinary procedure was described in a way consistent with the *Reglamento*:

> The person is talked to ... three times, and if in that three times the person isn't willing to make a commitment to not continue that activity then they're removed from the community. Only one person has left the community, because of illicit crops ... we had to tell the person to leave, that they couldn't be a part of the community anymore ... illicit crops have brought us too many problems, the government was using that as a way of taking away

people's land, taking away community land and it's not just something that we can accept. (Interview, Mateo)

In talking about their 'rupture' with the State Community members took pride in their autonomy but also criticised the State for failing to fulfil its obligations:

Regardless of the rupture, the breakdown we have with the State, regarding the services that they provide, we have alternative education, the internal processes that we have work, to collect the garbage, and if you think about it, this is the same thing we've done since the beginning. The mayor here we've asked for education, for health care, for improvements on the roads, for garbage pickup. We've been asking the government, regionally, nationally, for so long to fulfil their obligations with the civil population, but it doesn't really matter if we're in rupture or not, because they've never fulfilled their obligations to begin with. And so for us being autonomous works pretty well, everyone makes it function. (Interview, Enrique)

This ambivalence also extends to state criminal justice: 'We don't really believe in the justice system. We're not against the State – there's a difference. What we're asking is that they fulfil the Constitution' (Interview, Agustín). The hoped-for constitutional rule includes a prospect of retributive justice against criminals such as the former president of Colombia, Álvaro Uribe Velez:

Sebastián: Some people talk about forgiveness, but I don't agree with that. Someone who's done so much, how are we supposed to forgive them? We live just over here and then there are 290 sets of remains, sets of bones. Bones that were sometimes thrown in a hole, sometimes thrown wherever. Who did this? Uribe did this.
Thomas: What should happen to Uribe?
Sebastián: He should be stuck in jail. (Interview, Sebastián)

Another member, Matías, hoped 'that they stick [Uribe] in jail until he dies'. The rejection of reparations in their current form[7] was seen as an important matter of principle:

---

[7] Under the Colombian Victims and Land Restitution Law (Ley de Victimas y de Restitución de Tierra, Law 1448, June 2011), individual victims are entitled both to material and to moral reparations. The law also establishes the Commission for Reparation and Reconciliation to ensure the right of victims to collective reparations.

> ... the money that they receive is a [pittance] compared to maybe what they could deserve and there's often conditions that are attached, that you can't talk about it again, or you can't make for the demands on it. There are other ways that reparation can occur, but that's not acceptable. (Interview, Nicolás)

The participant continued to outline that reparations are not enough in any case, and that there is a truth seeking element in the refusal to be 'paid off':

> ... we looked for a more integral approach to reparations, that we know who committed the crime, who was responsible for that kind of crime to be committed. On a higher level, why was the crime committed, and that there's a trial, that the people are said to be guilty, that there's a legal process that says that they're guilty and it's not just economic. (Interview, Nicolás)

Here we see a reliance on the state legal apparatus, again suggesting the temporary nature of the current rupture. The Community also fear that reparations have been used as a means to undermine their solidarity:

> I think the government's attempts to destabilise, they're ready to wipe out the community, the government has used different tactics to divide people. Some people might get a house, some people might get some food, some people might get some money. (Interview, Nicolás)

Despite claims of autonomy, it appears that the Peace Community are operating under two normative regimes, the formal legal structure of the State, and the informal internal principles. They are at pains to cut the State out of everyday life; for example, independent contractors installed the electricity infrastructure for the Community so that they wouldn't have to depend on unreliable state services (Interview, Enrique). They resist the building of roads:

> The construction of roads would generate like an infiltration, a way to really penetrate the zone, that we don't feel is positive, that it would damage the *campesinos*' culture, our

> way of life, as well as helping the other interests that would destroy the lifestyle that we have. No, we don't want roads that would be very negative for the *campesinos'* lifestyle. (Interview, Enrique)

The Community needs an income to offset the lack of state welfare provision. Part of this comes from charitable funding for infrastructure projects but another important source of revenue is the sale of cacao to the British cosmetics firm Lush Ltd. In 2011, Lush Ltd. took their 'risky' first shipment, 25 tonnes for £50,000, and the 10th shipment was contracted late 2015 (Interview, Lush Ltd., 2015). To export cacao to the UK, the community has to engage with the state legal system to the extent of applying for an export licence (facilitated by Empresa Cooperativa del Sur del Cauca or COSURCA, a cooperative that exports fair-trade products). They also have to make contracts that will, in the event of a dispute, be recognised as binding by the courts.

There are also instances when the Community's values and the State's laws are congruent, but are still considered to be at odds. A good example of this is state and Community attitudes to military service:

> Luckily we're able to generate our own laws and so community members don't have the obligation of doing their military service, of using weapons, because we know, we know what a weapon is for, you don't pick up a weapon to defend someone, you pick up a weapon to kill someone. Weapons are used to kill and we're very clear about that, that's why many of us have declared ourselves as conscientious objectors. When I was 18 [in 2000] I was picked up twice and they tried to force me to do my military service and both times I said 'no', no I'm not going to give them my time, I'm a displaced person and I'm not going to give my time to the State to do that. I'm a conscientious objector and I know weapons are used to kill … If you want to be a guerrilla member, a paramilitary, or in the army, that's your decision, but you need to leave the Peace Community. We have very clear internal principles on that. (Interview, Enrique)

Knowingly or otherwise, Enrique relied on the spirit of Article 18 of the 1991 Colombian Constitution guaranteeing freedom of conscience, which the Constitutional Court has interpreted as implying a right to conscientious objection (Corte Constitucional 2009). The state relied on part of Article 216,

'All Colombian citizens are obliged to take up arms when public need mandates it in order to defend national independence and the public institutions'. Some years after the attempt to recruit Enrique, the Constitutional Court came down in favour of his position: Article 18 will trump 216 if the objections are considered 'deep, fixed, and sincere' (ibid, headnote and para. 5.2.6).

Discussion

When Peace Community members talk of a 'rupture' between the Community and the Colombian state, they are not adopting a strategy of 'ruptural transformation' in Wright's (2009, 2010) sense of an overt attack on the State led by class-based parties. Such a strategy is closer to that of the leftist FARC guerrillas, whose path the Peace Community rejects as emphatically as it does the State. (At the time of writing, however, the FARC and the government have reached a deal that will require approval by referendum.)

Rather than aspiring to 'ruptural transformation' the Peace Community is, in Wright's terms, an example of 'interstitial transformation'. Within the 'interstices' of the State and the capitalist economy, the Community has created new social relations that embody significant features of Wright's 'real utopias,' subordinating state power to a civil society which democratically controls the means of production (Wright 2009: 268-9). Rather than confronting the State head-on, the Community seeks to ignore it as far as possible.

Ximena's use of an organic metaphor, that of a tree whose roots enable it to survive in a harsh environment (see above) chimes with Wright's use of ecological metaphors to describe 'interstitial transformation'. Successful interstitial transformation resembles 'a complex ecological system in which one kind of organism gains a foothold initially in a niche and eventually out-competes rivals for food sources and comes to dominate the environment' (Wright 2009: 213). Wright is, however, quite sceptical about the prospect of interstitial alternatives out-competing the State or the capitalist system – and rightly so. To extend the ecological metaphor, we might think of small mammals in a world dominated by dinosaurs. If some catastrophe wipes out the dinosaurs, the mammals will inherit the earth; but while the environment remains as it is, the best the mammals can realistically expect is to flourish in their own little niches. Similarly, the Peace Community members thought that their values and principles – the 'roots' of the community – would enable their way of life to survive, we heard nothing to suggest that they thought they were paving the way for a comprehensive transformation of society.

The third model of transformation described by Wright is a 'symbiotic' one, which reflects the idea that 'bottom-up social empowerment within a capitalist society will be most stable and defendable when such social empowerment also helps solve certain real problems faced by capitalists and other elites' (Wright 2009: 240). Although Wright says very little about any 'other elites' besides capitalists, we would suggest that the Peace Community shows a degree of 'symbiosis', not with the Colombian state or the capitalist system but with international law and the transnational institutions, particularly the Inter-American Court of Human Rights, that aspire to enforce it. The Peace Community and its allies help to solve the problem of the impotence of international law in the face of paramilitary violence. Through the system of 'accompaniment' it provides a kind of 'bottom up' policing that formal transnational organisations cannot provide. At the same time, it confers on international law a legitimacy that it arguably does not deserve, particularly given the Inter-American Court's unwillingness to recognise the Community as anything more than an aggregate of individuals.

In this appeal to legal principles (a feature of many of the civil society organizations in our larger study) we can see another kind of utopianism, which consists simply of taking legal ideals seriously. A state which fully and impartially meets its obligations to its citizens, and imprisons its former Presidents for their crimes, is a kind of utopia, though not perhaps one that will appeal to penal abolitionists. The cause of human rights arguably represents a kind of utopia, filling the gap left by the apparent failure of other internationalist utopian visions (Moyn 2010).

The Peace Community, united against a common set of enemies, report low levels of crime internally but may have a narrow definitional boundary for crime and focus on the breaches of the Regalamento. Internally, the Community reject state interference, and specifically the Colombian criminal justice system, in favour of informal sanctions such as 'community labour' or even – in extremis – exile. These non-penal forms of the Community's sanctions system may be seen as purely pragmatic, in that the Community do not have the capacity to incarcerate, and do not support the view that the Community is against imprisonment per se; neither do their calls for the imprisonment of their oppressors. But, as a principle-driven community, its informal sanctions are designed to benefit the community through contribution to the work load or by the removal of members that make the settlements a military target (such as the expulsion of growers of drugs crops): it is not punishment of the individual that is the focus but the smooth working of the Community as an entity. Should there be a serious crime committed in the community, it is unlikely that they will be able to deal with it internally and likely that the State would step in.

The ultimate goal of the Peace Community is not to remain in a permanent state of autarky but to enjoy the benefits of a legitimate state. That is a very modest kind of utopia, and as Colombia inches its way towards peace, we can only hope that it is not entirely devoid of realism.

References

Amnesty International (2008) Annual Report 2008, www.amnesty.org/en/region/colombia/report-2008 (consulted July 2014)

Amnesty International (2014) Armed Forces Threaten Peace Community, Urgent Action Document – Colombia, UA: Amnesty International Index Number: AMR 23/027/2014, 24th July.

Burnyeat, G. (2010) 'On a Peak in Darien: Community Peace Initiatives in Urabá, Colombia' in *Journal of Human Rights Practice* Volume 5, No. 3 pp 435-445

Corte Constitucional (2009) *Sentencia C 728-09*, http://www.corteconstitucional.gov.co/relatoria/2009/C-728-09.HTM (consulted January 2016)

CODHES (2011) 'De la seguridad a la prosperidad democrática en medio del conflicto' Documento 23 Bogotá: CODHES

García-Godos, J. and Lid, K.A.O. (2010) 'Transitional Justice and Victims' Rights Before the End of a Conflict: The unusual case of Colombia' in *Journal of Latin American Studies* Volume 42, No. 3 pp 487-516

González Arango, G. (2010) 'Condenan a 20 años de cárcel a capitán Gordillo, por masacre de San José de Apartadó' in *El Espectador,* 28 July 2010.

Hristov, J. (2009) *Blood and Capital: The Paramilitarization of Colombia* Athens: Ohio University Press

Hulsman, L.H.C. (1986) 'Critical Criminology and the Concept of Crime' in *Crime Law and Social Change* Volume 10, No. 1 pp 63-80

IACHR (2002) *Peace Community of San José de Apartadó Case,* Order of the Court, 18 June, http://www1.umn.edu/humanrts/iachr/E/apartado6-18-02.html (consulted July 2015)

IACHR (2003) *Case of the Communities of the Jiguamiando and the Curbarado,* Order of the Court, 6 March, http://www1.umn.edu/humanrts/iachr/E/curbarado3-6-03.html (consulted July 2015)

Kelsen, H. (1949) *General Theory of Law and the State* Cambridge, MA: Harvard University Press

MacManus, T. and Ward, T. (2015) 'Para-state Crime and Plural Legalities in Colombia' in Barak, G. (ed) *The Routledge International Handbook of the Crimes of the Powerful* New York: Routledge

Mason, A.C. (2010) 'Constructing Authority Alternatives on the Periphery: Vignettes from Colombia', in González Arana, R. and Mason, A. C. (eds) *Colombia y el hemisferio frente al nuevo orden global* Barranquilla: Ediciones Uninorte

Moyn, S. (2010) *The Last Utopia: Human Rights in History* Cambridge, MA: Belknap Press

Palacios, M. (2006) *Between Legitimacy and Violence: A history of Colombia, 1875-2002* Durham, NC: Duke University Press

Richani, N. (2013) *Systems of Violence: The political economy of war and peace in Colombia* (2nd edition) Albany: SUNY Press

Romero Ramirez, L. (2013) *Análisis de la incidencia del principio de neutralidad en la conformación de las redes transnacionales de defensa de las Zonas Humanitarias y de Biodiversidad de Curvaradó y Jiguamiandó (1997- 2003). Internacionalista* dissertation. Universidad Colegio Mayor de Nuestra Señora del Rosario, Bogotá

Santos, B. de S. (2002) *Toward a New Legal Common Sense* London: Butterworths

Scott, J.C. (2009) *The Art of Not Being Governed: An anarchist history of Upland southeast Asia* New Haven: Yale University Press

Wright, E.O. (2009) *Envisioning Real Utopias* Manuscript, http://citeseerx.ist.psu.edu/viewdoc/download?doi=10.1.1.152.6099andrep=rep1andtype=pdf (consulted 13 May 2016)

Wright, E.O. (2010) *Envisioning Real Utopias.* London: Verso

Apartheid in Modernity[1]

Nils Christie[2]

Abstract

This article explores ways of breaking down the social and cultural barriers that lead people to place others in closed categories rather than regarding them as individuals. Christie begins by briefly describing his own experience of living in a 'ghetto' before moving on to discuss the role of institutionalisation, notably of children, in the creation of 'apartheid'. He deplores the erection of walls between children and adults, the middle and working classes. Christie sees an important role for criminologists in the breaking down of barriers. He argues that, rather than being the servants of the State, they ought to work as 'translators', giving meaning to the actions of those who seek to resist the conditions of apartheid. Finally, he advocates deinstitutionalisation and the return of children to society as a means of moving beyond apartheid.

Life in a ghetto

I once lived in one. It was a good life in a good ghetto. Close to 200 persons lived there. A sort of village. No walls, but apart from neighbours by distance and culture. No public transport, no television. No salaries, income shared according to needs. Some families with children, but most single and a bit different from the majority of Norwegians. Outsiders might have used terms such as 'dumb', 'insane', 'illiterates' etc. to refer to these people. My preference was to call them 'extraordinary'. In addition, there were some more ordinary people there who liked the ideas behind these ghettoes. The daily interactions made us to persons, not categories. I wrote a book about the

---

[1] This text was given as a lecture in June 10, 2013 at Max-Planck-Institut für ausländisches und Internationalen Strafrecht, Freiburg, Germany. Together with David Rodriguez Goyes and Per Jørgen Ystehede, I (Hedda Giertsen) have added information in some of the footnotes, proofread the text, made a few edits and completed the references. I know it would have been a great pleasure for Nils to know that this text now is published.

[2] Nils Christie was a sociologist and criminologist, Professor of Criminology at the Faculty of Law, Oslo from 1966 until his death in May 2015.

place. In English: *Beyond Loneliness and Institutions* (1989). My preference had been to call the book *In Defence of Ghettoes*. There are bad ghettoes, the enforced ones; memories of their horrors come easily to the mind. But there are also good ghettoes, those selected for their qualities: apartheid by choice.

Life in this ghetto brought me to the core of what has been my personal as well as scientific interest throughout my life: the question of conditions for, and consequences of coming close to others.

One of my first studies in criminology was a comparative study of killers versus non-killers among Norwegian guards in a concentration camp in the north of Norway in 1942 and 1943 (Christie 1952, 1972). The prisoners had been deported from Yugoslavia to Norway. The non-killers described the prisoners as suffering human beings, 'who behaved as we would have done in such a situation', while the killers described them as 'wild animals from the Balkan area'. A later book of mine had the title *How Tightly Knit a Society?* (1982). Again the central question: how to create social systems where we are able to see each other, systems where we are coming so close to the other, through life or art, that it becomes possible to recognise elements of common humanity in all sorts of people.

The man behind the atrocities in Norway on July 22nd 2011[3] seems to have been an especially lonely person, one standing outside social life, a man forcing himself to remain an outsider, not seeing the others. A man blinded by his mission. The challenge ahead will be to see him as one of us. Hopefully, this might be helpful to him, if he ever is released. But more importantly, also helpful to us as Norwegians; if the man behind the atrocities is seen as one of us, what is it with us and our culture that made these acts possible for him?

In all simplicity, it is my supposition that the more we are brought to positions that enable us to see each other as full human beings, not only stereotypes as evil, criminal, insane, the more we are influenced by that knowledge. We might recognise similarities with ourselves, and are then sensitised to the whole set of norms ingrained in us throughout life on how to behave towards people of all sorts, from babies to old folks. To see the other is to be captured in the web of norms that makes us human. The closer we in this way come to another person, the more inhibitions are also created against

---

[3] On this date the 32 year-old Norwegian detonated a homemade bomb on the government buildings, killing eight persons. Shortly after, he left for a small island southwest of Oslo where AUF, the Labour Party Youth, had their yearly summer camp. Bringing with him machine-guns, he shot and killed 69 people and injured 66, most of them young people.

handling that person in ways usually seen as unacceptable within the culture we belong to.

But, and as already touched upon, the ghetto must be for all sorts of people. Secluded, but with internal variation. Not only insane, not only blacks, not only Nobel Prize winners, not only persons with Down syndrome, not only... . I could go on forever. The point is to give attention to *manageable variation*, one where human beings can get to see each other as individuals, not only as categories.

When kids were useful

Then to a man I got to know some fifty years ago. He was rather old when we first met, and still living in the house where he was born. It was a house close to the shore in a little inlet on the North Sea. His father had been a fisherman. As was usual for most children of this place and time, he and the other kids were out in the boat with the father when needed. Often they were.

One of his stories was about what once happened late in the autumn. They had been on the fjord most of the day, catching fish and crabs. It had become dark. They rowed homeward, rounded the point where they could see the house, and cheers erupted from the kids. There was light from *two* windows! This meant they had guests in the house. And that meant there would be no more work that evening.

Like this it was, all over the country. For survival, all hands were needed. He got to know that as an itinerant teacher arriving somewhere along the coast in 1870. Edmund Edvardsen (1989) describes him in a book he called *Den gjenstridige almue* (*The Obstinate Commoners*). These ambulant teachers walked from district to district, used farms and kitchens as classrooms. They came to teach the children rudimentary reading and writing. The children were obliged to come and the parents might be punished if they did not. Yet, sometimes the kitchens remained empty. In a letter to his employer, the local bishop, one of these teachers complained bitterly; the children had not arrived, and he himself was made to sleep in the pigsty.

But he had arrived at the peak of the cod-season. Children were needed to clean tools and hang fish for drying; they could not be expected to attend school at such a time. The pigsty was chosen as a means to get him to move on all the more quickly to the next school district.

The emerging teachers

But then it changed. Gradually teachers came to be among the most respected in their local communities – maybe lousy at fishing, but good at reading and fast talk. Schools of various sorts were built all over the country.

There were several reasons for this. Some of them obvious; bigger boats were built, engines installed in boats and everywhere, soon we lived in an industrialised society. Production moved out from homes to factories. So did much of the care for the sick and feeble. Abstractions became important and slowly there developed a special class of people; the academics. Children were in this process converted from producers of necessary services to consumers of learning.

And there were additional reasons to keep them in institutions described as educational. Where else should they be? The useless child represents a hindrance for adult life in general. Far back in time, I wrote a book with the title *If the School Did not Exist?* (1971). Parents maybe bought the book to motivate theIR kids for school. But my main answer was a simple one: If the school did not exist, that would be bad for the life of their parents. The home is empty during daytime and the streets are dangerous.

The last stage in the development of apartheid in modernity did not fully arrive until quite recently. The majority of small children down to the age of one have now been institutionalised. At present nearly 90 percent of preschool children in Norway go to some form of daycare or kindergarten (SSB 2015). Well, to say that they go, in the meaning of walking, is a bit of a misnomer. Many of the youngest are not yet able to walk and many of the older ones are not allowed to; they are driven or pushed in strollers – we are all short of time in the morning.

And they don't stay for just a few hours. A new kind of kindergarten is in the process of being established: the extended-hours kinder-garten. One of them reports (Bakken 2011) that 'here the children are given a bath and put to bed just as they would be at home. Then they are carried, soundly asleep, out to the car when their parents come to pick them up...'. This kindergarten is open from five in the morning until eleven at night – and there is increasing demand for even longer opening hours. 85 percent of kindergarten-aged children are attending them for more than 40 hours a week. We are told that private daycare centres and kindergartens with extended opening hours have a competitive advantage.

As a next step, the nearly inevitable occurs: Kindergartens are transformed into preschools. In one week-plan I came across, the children start every day with 'Good Morning', sung in English. Later they continue with various pedagogical topics, including training in good manners at the dining table. I quote from the plan: 'At mealtime we pretend that we are at a fancy restaurant. We eat at tables set with candles and inspire the children to engage in conversation.' This is for four-year olds. It is good for socialisation and development, it is said. And for some, it is probably fine. I would have died.

The Danish filmmaker Lise Roos (1984) portrays a preschool that shifted course. From having shepherded the children through one organised activity after the other, the staff held back for a period, intervening only in crisis-situations. Otherwise they allowed the children to do whatever they wanted. Much happened. The noise level sank dramatically as the children no longer had to compete for new positions in the constant stream of new activities. Moreover, now they got to decide when they were finished with their tasks. The main character in this film was a little slow. In the first part of the film, whenever a staff member clapped her hands to indicate that it was time for everyone to begin with something else, this boy had seldom managed to get started with his first task. But then, when the grown-ups had retreated from directing the children, this boy stood for most of the time out in the washroom with large scissors. A thick, even stream of water ran from a faucet, and he was cutting the stream. Cutting and cutting until, finally satisfied, he put down the scissors. It *was* possible to cut the stream of water. I found myself quite at home with his situation.

But kids need other kids! They find each other more easily in these 'gardens for children'. True enough. But they also need to be on their own. Manage things without the help of others, discover imaginary friends, do something for hours on end. Endless hours. Maybe it's OK if kids get bored? I like little kids who, left to themselves, become engrossed in their own doings. Cutting water, for example.

Apartheid, modern times

Apartheid has to do with keeping people apart. Some in privileged positions – gated communities – others in deprived positions as we remember from South Africa. My concern is about the situation of children and young people in modernity. From age 1 to 19, most of them, in our types of countries, are stowed away in educational institutions. They are kept outside of the most important arena for adult life; work for money. That is apartheid in modernity. And even more; it is an internally class-divided apartheid.

An important part of kitchen equipment on old farms was a hand-driven separator. Milk poured in at the top, out on one side came a stream of thick cream, on the other skimmed milk. I watched in awe. The educational system has a similar centrifugal power, separating the cream of youth from the rest, but then, as a refinement, continuing by dividing the remaining youth in thin layers based on supposed abilities, until point zero: those good for nothing. No wonder that there are strong incentives to convert kindergartens into pre-schools.

In a way, it sounds good. Justice at last. A move from ascribed status to the achieved one. The best out at the top, measured through objective scales of examinations. Maybe the best was the daughter of a poor illiterate immigrant, while the son of the bank-director dropped out at an early stage. Justice, at last! The road is open for all. From being born at the bottom, personal achievement can bring all sorts of youngsters to the top. For societies with emphasis on egalitarian values, it is a beautiful story.

This occurs, sometimes. But as we know, it is not the usual result. Those born at the top tend to remain there. They have the correct cultural background; books on the shelves, a language suited for the educational system, and their surroundings ensure that they keep up with the demands from the school. The kids succeed, but now in harmony with egalitarian values.

Last month (*Aftenposten*, May 28, 2013)[4], there was a report from a district in Oslo called Tøyen. It is the district where the museum for Edvard Munch, the painter, was built. This was and still is a working class area, filled with immigrants. The school has 250 pupils. Two of them have Norwegian as their mother tongue. It is what I would say is a damaging type of ghetto. The immigrant-parents complain bitterly, 'No Norwegian classmates or friends. Our kids will fall behind.' The Norwegian parents feel guilty, but nonetheless move themselves or at least their children to another district where the children will meet their equals; children suited for school. As expressed by parents; 'We have to think of the future for our child.' Like this it is, throughout the educational system. As usual, class trumps.

To counteract this type of injustice, a popular slogan has been used.[5] It is: '*Nobody shall be left behind!*'

---

[4] http://www.aftenposten.no/meninger/kommentarer/Den-hvite-flukten-fra-Toyen-7213488.html

And the slogan is taken seriously. Much is done to help as many as possible to pass. But the slogan is also a dangerous one. It has two major defects.

First; *if* you fail, after receiving so much help, the fault is yours. So much is done to help you, that if you do not make it, it is somehow you, as a person that is not good enough. For a person from a working class background, it might in many ways have been less damaging to experience defeat in school 50 years ago. Back in time, a young person with a safe identity as a worker might have climbed the barricades with demand for social and economic justice. Today, in an educational system seemingly designed for all, defeat is easily experienced as a personal defeat. It is not the system, but you as a person who are not good enough.

Unemployment may lead to anger transformed to personal shame, to resignation, – or sometimes – to spontaneous rage. This may more easily happen in Scandinavia where there appear to be more opportunities and more social welfare offers, compared to most other European countries.

Here, in my view, we are facing an important element in the youth turmoil which hit Sweden some months ago,[6] and probably soon also Norway and other welfare states. It is an anger directed against an undefined enemy. Something is wrong. You have been given all opportunities, all sorts of help, but were not able. Not able enough. You take to the streets, your own streets, yell, smash what you find, set cars on fire, they belong probably to someone more able than you who has made it in life. You fight a system that is supposed to be just, but not for you. Rage of this sort is not easy to convert into political activism. Police power becomes the answer. Cameron in London and Reinfeldt in Stockholm agree on this point.

The slogan, 'Nobody shall be left behind', contains also another message: 'To be left behind' – that sounds like a terrible destiny; most probably unemployment or to become an ordinary worker of some sort.

---

[5] This slogan was used by The Labour Party (*Arbeiderpartiet*) before the election to Parliament in 2013,
http://arbeiderpartiet.no/file/download/6510/79501/file/utdanning_hefte.pdf
[6] On May 19 2013 there were riots in Stockholm, in a part of the city inhabited mostly by immigrants. Several hundred people took part, and the riot lasted for five nights and spread to other cities in Sweden. *Megafonen*, a youth organisation, made a statement that the reason for the riots was that an armed 69 year-old man had been shot dead by the police. A Swedish criminologist, Sarnecki, says that the background for the riots is a general disapproval caused by social problems like lack of jobs, education, and of problems with the police. http://www.theaustralian.com.au/news/world/sweden-riots-revive-immigration-debate/story-e6frg6so-1226648963077

My thoughts go to craftsmen I have met. They are maybe not always so good in explaining why they do what they do, but good at doing it. I was in a repair-shop for bikes the other day. It was a very old-fashioned one. Happily, my bike was not ready yet, so I had time to hang around. The master was continuously in the middle of it all, giving small hints to some four or five younger workers. There was a spirit of inventiveness, and also joy and accomplishment in the room. If necessary, they kept on to midnight, they said. My bike was already perfect by nine o'clock.

A case of theft

What I say here can also be given a different focus. The story can be seen as a grave case of theft. It is a case where the upper and middle classes stole the knowledge base of workers, abstracted the principles, put them in books and claimed that no work of value could be done by persons who had not first proved that they could master these abstractions. But the thieves did not succeed with Stradivarius.

As recounted by Sennet (2008) in his book on craftsmen and craftswomen, nobody was ever able to describe how Stradivarius and his co-workers in his craft-shop were able to create these masterpieces of violins. As other able workers, Stradivarius had probably much of his knowledge in his body, in his fingertips, in his way of moving around in his workshop to encourage, inspire or correct his assistants. All good craftswomen and men have such a body knowledge, writers also. Much thinking takes place in fingers.

Observers were not able to watch Stradivarius carefully, study all his moves in minute detail, write it down, convert it to productive machines, and make the recipe parts of the obligatory curriculum in high schools for violin-makers. It has been easier to tap into the carpenter's experience, and convert it to curriculum in schools of architecture, or use social work practice or nursing practice in the same way. And to reproduce it in textbooks presented in courses available to those who have not dropped out of school.

Destruction of the neighbourhood academies
Schools, universities, academies – they form a blossoming industry. When I think of it, I can only find one type of important academy that has been destroyed in my lifetime. That is the neighbourhood academy – that created by ordinary people living close to each other, reflecting on and reacting to matters of common interest. From living glued to local neighbourhoods and

dependence on those living there – to global citizens. They are killed by opportunities and possibilities for geographical and social mobility.

It is as we act according to a prescription on how to dissolve community ties. Neighbours become less and less important. We don't see them, we don't know them, and we don't think we need them. We have lost the knowledge base for evaluation of what happens. And we know what then follows: when mutual knowledge moves out of a neighbourhood, experts move in. They are supposed to know, and often they do. Under these conditions, it is obvious that many among us feel incompetent when things go wrong. Better to hide in front of the television and let the children and youth live their own lives.

Working class kids in this situation are double losers in many ways. They lose in a school system built by and for an academic background they don't have. They are, by lack of formal academic qualifications, barred from access to what for many would be 'real life.' And, as the rest of us, they have lost access to the neighbourhood academies.

What to do? Some answers seem obvious. First:

Abolish youth

We have created a sort of apartheid in modernity. It is a wall between children and youth on the one side of the divide, and the adults on the other. Since children are seen as being of no practical use in the type of society we have created, we place them in institutions called kindergartens and schools. A reform of importance would therefore be to reduce the number of years young persons are compelled to spend in institutions called schools. It is ten years now in my country. A good first step would be to reduce the compulsory stay to seven or eight.

At the same time, we ought to *open* the walls around these schools, so that the kids can be released for other than purely academic tasks. My life has recently led me to many visits in nursing homes. In the entrance hall, or where the lifts end, I find flocks of elderly people; in wheel chairs, ordinary chairs or just standing. Why there? Because, just there, at the entrance points, it is a hope that someone might appear, someone to say hello to, someone with a sign of life from the external world. What a blessing for such places if they on a regular basis could be invaded by hordes of children, to disturb those old people, but maybe also to be told stories from life passed. Teachers might get fascinating new challenges as coordinators in such situations. Kindergartens are other possible arenas for segregated kids. What a blessing if kindergartens, on a regular basis, were invaded by older kids. Or children might be let free from school one or two days a week to do 'real work' and receive salaries for it. There exists in many countries a powerful organisation called 'Save the children', or in my country 'Redd Barna'. I would like to give them as a central task to rescue youth from state and school regulations intended to prevent them from engaging in adult tasks at an early stage in life.

Impossible, says the establishment. We would fall behind in development. OECD, the *Organisation for Economic Cooperation and Development*[7] says the same. Based on standardised exams, they claim that Norwegian school children are *not* among the best among 56 countries in language and mathematics. It is in the so-called PISA-study that they find this.[8] The result created a panic in Norway – a completely unfounded one in my view. The major goal for our compulsory school, decided by the Parliament, is that the basic school ought to help to shape what in old-fashioned Norwegian is called *'gagns menneske'*: these are persons with valuable human qualities; cooperative, kind to others, and stable and good at work – qualities once welcomed among decent people.[9] These qualities are not, and cannot be, measured by tests in language or mathematics.

Philippe Ariès (1960) pointed to historical periods where children, as a social category, did not exist. I don't think he is right, and would not in any case go that far. But I believe it would be a good thing to considerably shorten the period of childhood. And in the same line of thinking, we ought to change social conditions to undermine, preferably abolish the social category called 'youth'. We might rescue them, and us, from the grip of apartheid based on age and instead convert them to young adults from a much earlier age.

Another point on reform:

Restore the neighbourhood academies
It is obvious: Mobility kills neighbourhoods. If we want to restore the neighbourhood academies, we must create types of social organisation where ordinary people get to know each other. I have said so much about this in my book on *A Suitable Amount of Crime* (2004) that I will not go further into it here.

---

[7]   http://www.keepeek.com/Digital-Asset-Management/oecd/education/pisa-2012-results-skills-for-life-volume-v_9789264208070-en#page1
[8] http://www.oecd.org/pisa/keyfindings/PISA-2012-results-norway.pdf
[9] LOV 1998-07-17 nr. 61. § 1-1.

Criminologists – interpreters or servants?

I am not unaware of the amount of vested interests I am confronting here. But what I am talking about is large-scale crime prevention. Not of that type that is so easily embraced by everybody, the one that focuses on increased street lighting and more uniformed police in certain districts. I am back to basics:

If we create a society where the most important rewards are supposed to be available to all, but this is a fake, then that society will face trouble. If we make these rewards for those few more and more valuable, and visible, then the system is in even more trouble. If we create a society without responsible tasks for many of those living there, chances are great that relatively many among those without responsibility will answer with irresponsible behaviour.

But this ordering of life is in the interest of large parts of the population. Apartheid is useful. Adults could not function as they now do in their daily work if not. As things are, female interests in waged labour would be particularly threatened. But with this ordering of life, accepted by powerful segments, it is also clear what becomes the expectation placed on criminologists: help us to defend our system, 'our common system'. 'Help' means upholding the system. 'Upholding' means assistance to keep children and youth under control in their segregated quarters or enmeshed in their youth culture.

Criminologists are in this situation strongly encouraged to take on the role as servants to power. Children that protest might need treatment, or maybe to be met by more severe sanctions as deportation to other schools or in severe cases forms of penal sanctions. Maybe drop-outs ought to be seen as a new form of youth delinquency and their parents punished due to their lack of control. The school-fires have already given surveillance experts a profitable new market. Cameras are installed and cover the schools day and night. In Swedish schools thermo-censors are installed. They register heat from anybody approaching the schools, and a patrol from a security company will immediately appear. Schools must be helped in their roles as containers.

But there is an alternative path open, one I am fond of. This is one that sees the schools on fire as part of a language. Acts are words; a major role for criminologists ought to be to work as translators from acts to words and thereby give meaning to what happened! The fires have a message, a message important both to understand and to answer.[10]

* * *

I feel a sort of melancholy watching this development. In much of my life I have been striving to come close to other people, see them as whole persons, and being seen by them as such a person myself. I am deeply convinced that closeness to others is one of the factors that makes civilised interaction possible. This is about to evaporate. This is a fundamental threat against what is often called *Scandinavian exceptionalism* in penal policy (Pratt 2008). Why should we, the rich, well-fed people from Scandinavia, handle those that threaten our wealth, welfare and security – such as bewildered drop-outs from schools, or immigrants, or drug users – in any other way than what is usual in other rich countries? We are even rich enough to build new prisons, beautiful prisons: single rooms with a bath and television for all, the last of these prisons in Norway was inaugurated by the King himself in 2010.

Academics as dangerous people

Have I then no respect for the culture and values and knowledge we are carrying as intellectuals?

I have. I love my work as an academic. And I am happy if I receive respect for my work, as a craftsman. I think this work is important. But academics are at the same time dangerous people. Particularly, there is no guarantee that people of our sort are the best to protect fundamental values. Our more recent history has an endless amount of examples on what experts have been allowed to do according to theories on what is best for other people, or for their countries.

The committee in Wannsee who accepted the 'final solution' to the Jewish question in January 1942 had among their members quite an extraordinary number of academic people. Dr. Norbert Kampe (no date), director of the *House of the Wannsee Conference* had this to say:

> The 15 participants at the conference were among the elite of the National Socialist regime. Their biographies show that many had completed an academic education and had brilliant careers.

---

[10] Bourdieu and colleagues (1999) exemplify this approach from France. In my country, Høigård (2002) gives a revealing interpretation of graffiti as a language, while Larsen (1992) and Giertsen (2000) do the same with forms of serious violence. Such studies help us to make acts intelligible and dialogue possible.

Eight held doctorates. Most were from 'good middleclass' homes. Some were staunch National Socialists but others had joined the party for opportunistic reasons. Their average age was just 43.

In Norway, civil servants with law-degrees obediently registered all Jews in the country (Johansen 1984) and were also organisers when the registers were used for arresting and later deportations of all Jews that could be found, as well as confiscation of their property. Those arrested ended in Auschwitz. Law degrees were no guarantee.

Law degrees were no guarantee. Nor were medical degrees. The extermination of whole unwanted folk-groups was often seen in analogy with medical treatment of the body. The unwanted had to be removed from the national body, just as an infected appendix from the individual body. So also with the selection at the ramp when trains arrived in Auschwitz. Selections between those who were to die immediately in the gas chambers and those who got a respite by being evaluated as able to work for a while; this evaluation was always done by medical personnel. If no doctor was available, a dentist might do. Seen as a medical operation, it all became easier (Lifton 1986).

In contrast to this, we have moving stories from all over Europe about how ordinary people rescued refugees that knocked on their doors. They saw it as a self-evident thing to do, even under threat of execution, nothing to brag about after the war (2002). Or in a formulation by Rochat (in Hagtvet 2012): they expressed 'the ordinariness of goodness' – a picture opposite to 'the banality of evil'.[11]

But then, again, we have the contrast to the contrasts; ordinary people phoning the police in Norway, informing the authorities that the neighbour probably was a Jew (Johansen 1984), or villagers in Poland, hunting the Jews in the village, forcing them into one big barn, and then setting it on fire.[12] Or

---

[11] Hannah Ahrendt used this concept in her book on Adolf Eichman (*cf.* Hagtvedt 2012). Thanks to Bernt Hagtvedt who gave another reference on 'the ordinariness of goodness', which took place in the French village Chambot where approximately 1000 Jews were hidden, or transported, to Switzerland during the war of 1939-1945 (Halle 1979). This was done by ordinary citizens lead by Huguenot priests who had received a simple 'yes' from the ordinary citizens when asked to help Jews (Hagtvedt e-mail, September 6 2015). According to Hagtvedt (2012) it is common that ordinary people intervene and help others, even if they risk heavy sanctions.
[12] This is known as the Jedwabne pogrom, July 1941 in Poland, *cf.* https://en.wikipedia.org/wiki/Jedwabne_pogrom for further references.

Bosnia, where attempts to create national identities led to 'killing in broad daylight, with the murderers known by face and name to their victims and the victims being the murderers' kith and kin, acquaintances and next door neighbours' (Bauman 2009:105).

There are no guarantees, except the old one: attempt to create social systems without great social distance between people, distance in class, ethnicity, geography – and education. But experts represent here a particular danger. They have the armour of professionalism. They are difficult to control. To get them back to the ordinary, they ought to be made vulnerable.

My particular experience in life is with experts on social matters. Let me therefore exemplify from that area when it comes to the de-armouring of a profession:

Professionals like to flock, in offices, in whole buildings, – preferably all for themselves. It gives access to a pool of knowledge, they claim. I want to make them lonely. Social workers, one or two in small offices close to the streets, visible to the local people, forced to know their clients from encounters in local shops or the post office, if that still exists. Social workers will gain knowledge from these encounters, but they will also be seen, evaluated and controlled by those in the neighbourhood. Slowly, those living around might regain trust in their own sense and understanding.

I also have another suggestion about how to make highly educated people vulnerable. I want to take much of their language away. So much of it is just status language, words to express their high-ranking positions. Some years ago I published a little book, well hidden in Norwegian, with the title *Small Words for Big Questions* (2009).[13] It is an attempt to make academics as ordinary as they ought to be.

I want academic people, university people included, made highly ordinary, in rank and pay and language. But if education were no ladder to particular status and income, then would motivation for higher education go down? Fine. We would be left with those particularly interested in that type of craft. But then, it would be because of the craft, not the money.

But this might hamper our material and economic development. Again fine, both for us and for the Globe. With the breakdown of the UN Climate Summit 2009 in Copenhagen in mind, it is close to obvious that continued material

---

[13] By 2015 this book is published also in Danish and Russian. In 2016, it will be published in Spanish (*cf.* reference list).

growth is not the right course. I am not much in doubt that our material level in Scandinavia is much too high, and also that the race towards the top has damaging consequences. We could live well at a much lower level. Soon we might be forced to do so. But we do not need a system where craftsmen and craftswomen as an obvious fact are to be seen as losers, 'too dumb' to reach our level, the level all obviously would like to be at, and only more so the more we are rewarded also materially.

Maybe the future is somewhere in the past?

In January 1949 Harry Truman was installed as president in the US. In his program-talk on the occasion he said: '...we must embark on a bold new program for making the benefits of our scientific advances and industrial progress available for the improvements and growth of underdeveloped areas' (Truman in Esteva 1992:6).

This was the point when underdevelopment was invented, was the dry comment from Gustavo Esteva (ibid). And he continued: 'On that day, two billion people became underdeveloped. In a real sense, from that time on, they ceased being what they were, in all their diversity, and were transmogrified into an inverted mirror of others' reality: a mirror that belittles them and sends them off to the end of the queue. ...' (p. 7.). Or, from the perspective of Ivan Illich (1992:90) in the same volume: 'The human being was transformed from Homo sapiens (the wise and tasteful human) into Homo Miserabilis'.

On the caretaking of social systems

The Scandinavian states are generally seen and also called 'welfare states'. An alternative term is sometimes found in Sweden. *Folkhemmet* it is called, or in English 'the people's home'. It is an extraordinary designation for a state. It entails some unpleasant aspects; the State might be intrusive, become too much of an authoritarian caretaker. But at the same time, it is a system where ideas of common welfare, solidarity and unity remain central.

All the Scandinavian countries are Welfare States. As a general principle, it is not a debated form. On the contrary, this form is by and large a matter of pride, a form of social organisation we to a large extent take for granted. And so it still is, but nowadays as a threatened form, one of those rare species in danger of extinction. The fundamental ideas in the Welfare States are under siege from ideas of market-liberalism with its emphasis on individuals in contrast to community, the acceptance of huge differences in rank, income and standards of living, the adherence to the idea that the best takes all: these are thoughts in grave contrast to much of the welfare thinking that up to now has ruled in Scandinavia.

If we want to keep the welfare model, I think it is essential to shift attention from material growth to caretaking of the social system. It is not money and houses and new commodities we need. It is the Welfare States that are in need of care, not our material system.

To me, the burning schools indicate that the institution of education has been allowed to embrace too much of essential life-activities in society. In contrast, activities outside that institution have lost both meaning and respect. One answer to this seems to me obvious:

Return the stolen property

If we really want to prevent the degradations and drop out situation for working class kids in school, we ought to move as much as possible of what needs to be known for performing the jobs out of schools and theory and into places of concrete work. Much instruction can be transferred from teachers in school to workers on jobs. If impossible to arrange, some teachers might leave their castles, the school buildings, and join as instructors at their places of work. Foreign languages might be easier to learn in the workshop than in the classroom. The best training of social workers, nurses and all sorts of helpers might also come out of instructions from those that work, those that can, and not from those that teach. It would make the instruction directly relevant, and also upgrade the instructors. It would not be necessary for nurses to leave the patient to gain teachers status. One could remain at the bedside as a nurse, and as an instructor. Some courses or seminars might be necessary in addition to what could be explained in the ordinary work processes.

Nothing new in this. It is the ancient way, the young person close to mother and father, learning their ways. Or maybe it was a master somewhere, a master in the old system of apprenticeship. To move education for work out of schools and back into places for work would be to restore respect for the work-process and for the master workers. That knowledge has to be respected wherever found, as among carpenters or plumbers, or bakers, mothers or writers. Some of the old masons wore full evening dress at work, just as conductors in music halls today. A reminiscence of this can be found in the black top hat still used by some chimneysweepers. They knew something of importance, demanded respect, and got it.

Of course, I know the reactions to sayings like this: the utmost of naiveté. Workers need, as all of us, a solid basic education. And several tests show that Norwegian children fall behind many nations on international comparative tests of the PISA-type. Particularly when it comes to mathematics, we are far behind. The need for upgrading seemed obvious, according to the minister of education, and she promised to make that possible.

What I am advocating here is an upgrading of workers' knowledge and workers' culture (a theme I have touched upon above). To be a worker ought not to be something to be educated out of, and with terrible consequences if you fail. To be a worker, a craftswoman or craftsman, ought to be given such conditions that it again becomes a position of pride and status.

* * *

It was on a train home from Germany, early in the 1950s. At the bench just across from me a young Norwegian threw himself down. He had been abroad half a year as a sailor. Now he was on his way home to mother somewhere on the coast, but only for a short vacation, until the next boat out. Maybe he was 15. Age limits protecting young workers from entering the labour marked were not so strict at that time. Today, he would have been a pupil somewhere, maybe, with his activity level, in danger of being diagnosed with ADHD – Attention Deficit Hyperactive Disorder. Sometimes I wonder how they in the old days had managed to get youngsters to climb the mast and reef the topsails in stormy weather with crews where the hyperactive were screened out and calmed down with drugs before they left harbor.

References

Ariès, P. (1960) *Centuries of Childhood: A social history of family life* London: Random House

Bakken, A. (2011) 'Pusser tenner og sover i barenhagen' [Brush teeth and sleep in the kindergarten] in *Aftenposten* January 7

Bauman, Z. (2008) *Does Ethics Have a Chance in a World of Consumers?* Cambridge, MA: Harvard University Press

Bourdieu, P. et al (1999) *The Weight of the World: Social suffering in contemporary society* Stanford: Stanford University Press

Christie, N. (1952) *Fangevoktere i konsentrasjonsleire: En sosiologisk undersøkelse* [Prison officers in Concentration Camps. A sociological study] Oslo: Departement of Sociology

Reprinted (1972). *Fangevoktere i konsentrasjonsleire: En sosiologisk undersøkelse av norske fangevoktere i 'serberleirene' i Nord-Norge i 1942-43.* [Prison officers in Concentration Camps. A sociological study of Norwegian prison officers in 'Serb Camps' in the north of Norway 1942-43] Oslo: Pax

Christie, N. (1971) *Hvis skolen ikke fantes?* [If the school did not exist?] Oslo/København: Universitetsforlaget/Christian Ejlers' Forlag

In German: (1974). *Wenn es die Schule nicht gäbe? Ketzerisches zur Schulreform* München: Paul List

Christie, N. (1982): *Hvor tett et samfunn?* [How tightly knit a society?] Oslo: Universitetsforlaget

Christie, N. (1989): *Beyond loneliness and Institutions: Communes for extraordinary people* Oslo: Scandinavian University Press

In German: (1992): *Jenseits von Einsamkeit und Entrfemdung: Gemeinschaften für aussergewöhnliche Menschen* Stuttgart: Verlag Freies Geistesleben

Christie, N. (2004) *A Suitable Amount of Crime* Oslo: Universitetsforlaget

In Spanish (2004) *Una sensata cantidad de delito* Buenos Aires: Editores del Puerto.

Christie, N. (2009): *Små ord for store spørsmål* [Small words for big questions] Oslo: Universitetsforlaget

To be published in Spanish in 2016. *Pequeñas parlabras para grandes preguntas* Bogotá: Fondo Editorial Universidad Antonio Nariño

Edvardsen, E. (1989) *Den gjenstridige allmue. Skole og levebrød i et nordnorsk kystsamfunn ca 1850-1900.* [The obstinate Commoner. Schools and work in a coastal society North in Norway, ca. 1850-1900] Oslo: Solum forlag

Esteva, G. (1992) 'Development' in Sachs, W. (ed) *The Development Dictionary: A guide to knowledge as power* London: Zed Books

Giertsen, H. (2000) *K og måter å forstå drap på* [K – and ways to understand murders] Oslo: Universitetsforlaget

[Hagvtvedt, Bernt] 2012. Interview. Alminnelige helter [Ordinary heroes]. In: *Morgenbladet*, February 2 2012.
http://morgenbladet.no/samfunn/2012/alminnelige_helter

Halle, P. (1979). *Lest Innocent Blood be Shed: The story of the village of Le Chambon and how goodness happened there* New York: Harper Collins

Høigård, C. (2002) *Gategallerier* [Street gallery] Oslo: Pax

Illich, I. (1992) 'Needs' in Sachs, W. (ed) *The Development Dictionary. A guide to knowledge as power* London: Zed Books

Johansen, P.O. (1984). *Oss selv nærmest – Norge og jødene 1914-1943* [Ourselves first – Norway and the Jews 1914-1943] Oslo: Gyldendal norsk forlag

Kampe, N. (no date) *House of the Wannsee Conference: The participants at the conference.* http://archive-de-2014.com/de/g/2014-01-24_3584087_14/House-of-the-Wannsee-Conference-nbsp-E-newsletter-in-German/ (consulted 13 May 2016)

Larsen, Guri (1992) *Brødre. Æreskamp og hjemløshet blant innvandringens ungdom* [Brothers. Fight on honour and homelessness among the youth of immigration] Oslo: Pax

LOV 1998.07-17 nr. 61. Opplæringslova [Law on education]. Lovdata: http://www.lovdata.no/all/tl-19980717-061-001.html (consulted 13 May 2016)

Lifton, R. J. (1986) *The Nazi Doctors: Medical killing and the psychology of genocide* New York: Harper Collins

Pratt, J. (2008) 'Scandinavian Exceptionalism in an Era of Penal Excess' *British Journal of Criminology* Volume 48, No. 1 pp 119-137 and No. 2 pp 275-292

Roos, L. (1984) *Kan man klippe i vand?* [Can you cut water?] Film, documentary. Denmark.

Sennet, R. (2009) *The Craftsman* London: Penguin Books

SSB (Statistisk sentralbyrå) Norwegian statitsics (2015) Barnehager 2014, endelige tall [Kindergartens 2014, final figures], https://www.ssb.no/utdanning/statistikker/barnehager/aar-endelige/2015-05-04 (consulted 13 May 2016)

CPSIA information can be obtained at www.ICGtesting.com
Printed in the USA
LVOW09s0728021016

507014LV00011B/458/P